Android Tablets
Made Simple

Marziah Karch

Apress®

Android Tablets Made Simple

ISBN-13 (pbk): 978-1-4302-3671-9

ISBN-13 (electronic): 978-1-4302-3672-6

President and Publisher: Paul Manning
Lead Editors: Steve Anglin and James Markham
Technical Reviewer: Phil Nickinson
Editorial Board: Steve Anglin, Mark Beckner, Ewan Buckingham, Gary Cornell, Morgan Ertel, Jonathan Gennick, Jonathan Hassell, Robert Hutchinson, Michelle Lowman, James Markham, Matthew Moodie, Jeff Olson, Jeffrey Pepper, Douglas Pundick, Ben Renow-Clarke, Dominic Shakeshaft, Gwenan Spearing, Matt Wade, Tom Welsh
Coordinating Editor: Kelly Moritz
Copy Editor: Patrick Meader
Compositor: MacPS, LLC
Indexer: SPi Global
Artist: SPi Global
Cover Designer: Anna Ishchenko

Distributed to the book trade worldwide by Springer Science+Business Media, New York, 233 Spring Street, 6th Floor, New York, NY 10013. Phone 1-800-SPRINGER, fax (201) 348-4505, e-mail orders-ny@springer-sbm.com, or visit www.springeronline.com.

For information on translations, please e-mail rights@apress.com, or visit www.apress.com.

Apress and friends of ED books may be purchased in bulk for academic, corporate, or promotional use. eBook versions and licenses are also available for most titles. For more information, reference our Special Bulk Sales–eBook Licensing web page at www.apress.com/bulk-sales.

This book is dedicated to my husband, Harold, the best stay-at-home dad our kids could ever have; and to our kids, Pari and Kiyan. Their support makes it possible, and their praise makes it worthwhile. Yes, Harold, you can have a tablet now.

Contents at a Glance

Contents v

About the Author xiv

About the Technical Reviewer xv

Acknowledgments xvi

A Day in the Life of an Android Tablet xvii

Chapter 1: What Is Android: Choosing the Right Tablet 1

Chapter 2: Getting Started 15

Chapter 3: Typing, Copy, and Search 25

Chapter 4: Syncing with Your Google Account 39

Chapter 5: Syncing with Other Accounts 49

Chapter 6: Understanding Connection: Wi-Fi, 3G, and 4G 59

Chapter 7: Personalizing Your Home Screen 71

Chapter 8: Email on Tablets 81

Chapter 9: Managing Contacts 101

Chapter 10: Working with Calendars 111

Chapter 11: Using Maps 123

Chapter 12: Browsing the Web 141

Chapter 13: The Android Market 151

Chapter 14: Alternative App Markets 163

Chapter 15: Social Media 173

Chapter 16: Video and Voice Chat 189

Chapter 17: Reading E-books, Newspapers, and Magazines 201

Chapter 18: Taking Notes and Working with Documents 229

Chapter 19: Viewing Videos and Movies on Your Tablet 245

Chapter 20: Creating Photos, Videos, and Art 257

Chapter 21: Listening to Music 275

Chapter 22: Fun and Games 291

Chapter 23: The Clock, Calculator, and Other Utilities 307

Appendix A: Using Bluetooth for Keyboards and More 317

Appendix B: Advanced Troubleshooting 325

Index 339

Contents

Contents at a Glance iv

About the Author xiv

About the Technical Reviewer xv

Acknowledgments xvi

A Day in the Life of an Android Tablet xvii

■ **Chapter 1: What Is Android: Choosing the Right Tablet** 1

The History of Android 1

Android Honeycomb 2

    HTC and Sense 3

Other Uses for Android 3

    Android Readers 4

    Multimedia Players 4

    Netbooks 4

    Google TV 5

    Microwaves, Washing Machines, and Printers (Oh My!) 5

Choosing the Right Android Tablet 6

    Modified Honeycomb 6

    Deciphering Screen Size 7

    Pixel Resolution 8

Touchscreen Sensitivity 9

Screen Contrast 10

Cameras 10

Memory 11

Internal Storage 11

HDMI 12

USB 12

Accessories 12

Hacking a Nook 13

■ **Chapter 2: Getting Started** 15

Unlocking Your Tablet 15

A Typical Activation Sequence 16

Google Account 16

Activating Your Data Plan 17

The Basic Home Screen 17

Where Are the Buttons? 18

    The Action Bar and the System Bar 19

Recent Apps and Easy Multitasking 19

The Notification Panel 20

Basic Tablet Gestures 22

Long Pressing on the Home Screen 22

Chapter 3: Typing, Copy, and Search 25

The Virtual Keyboard 25

The Standard Keyboard Layout 26

    Displaying Capital Letters, Numbers, and Symbols 26

    Character Combinations and Long-Presses 27

Swype Typing 29

Word Suggestions 30

User Dictionary 31

Copy, Cut, and Paste 32

Input Settings 34

Voice Actions 35

Search 37

Chapter 4: Syncing with Your Google Account 39

Activating Your Google Account 40

Adding a Google Account 42

    Two Step Verification 44

Adding Another Google Account: the Short Way 44

Google Account Services 45

Getting Contacts from Your Old Planner to Google 47

    Fine Tuning Your Tablet Sync 48

Chapter 5: Syncing with Other Accounts 49

Adding an Account 49

Syncing with Exchange Email Accounts 51

    Security Warnings 52

Adding Other Email Accounts 53

Removing an Email Account 54

Data Syncing Settings 55

Alternative Syncing Apps 57

Chapter 6: Understanding Connection: Wi-Fi, 3G, and 4G 59

Does Your Tablet Have a Data Plan? 59

What Does 3G or 4G Mean? 60

CDMA and GSM 60

More on LTE and WiMAX 61

The Notifications Bar 61

    Wi-Fi 62

Setting up a Private Wi-Fi Connection 63

    Wi-Fi Security 64

    Bluetooth 65

    GPS 65

Creating a Hotspot 65
Troubleshooting Connections 67
    Roaming..67
    Managing Syncing 68
    Airplane Mode..69
VPN 69
    VNC 69

■Chapter 7: Personalizing Your Home Screen 71

Reviewing the Home Screen Interface...71
Exploring Widgets 72
    Adding Widgets...73
    REMOVING WIDGETS 75
    Moving and Resizing Widgets..76
App Icons 77
More...78
Wallpapers 78

■Chapter 8: Email on Tablets... 81

Understanding Gmail 81
    Gmail Inbox and Archive 82
    Priority Inbox..84
    Stars and Labels 85
    Creating and Deleting Labels...86
    Automatic Filters..86
    The General Settings Menu..87
    Adding Accounts to Gmail..88
    Forwarding and POP/IMAP...89
    Gmail Labs and Themes...90
    Web Gmail from Your Tablet 90
The Gmail App..90
Reading Gmail Messages...91
    Sending a Message..94
Receiving Messages with Attachments 94
Gmail App Settings 95
The Email App 96
Email and Gmail Action Bar Items...97
Email and Gmail Widgets 98

■Chapter 9: Managing Contacts 101

Tablets vs. Phones...101
The Contact App...102
Adding/ Editing a Contact 103
    Adding a Picture...104
    Adding Custom Fields 105
Filtering Contacts 105
Joining Accounts 107
Sharing Contacts..108
Importing and Exporting Contacts 109
Widgets 109

■ **Chapter 10: Working with Calendars**.. **111**

Google Calendar on the Web..111

Privacy Levels...112

Adding Calendars..113

Importing and Exporting Calendars 114

Syncing Calendars with Exchange..114

TouchDown...115

Google Calendar on Tablets 115

Adding Events...117

Adding Guests 118

Changing Your Calendar Settings 118

Widgets 120

Tasks 121

■ **Chapter 11: Using Maps** **123**

Understanding Google Maps...124

Find Your Location on the Map 126

    Getting Directions 126

Map Layers 129

    Traffic..129

    Satellite 130

    Google Labs Layers..130

Location Sharing with Latitude 131

Places Pages...133

    Google Places 134

    Starring Locations..135

    Google Street View...135

Email and Text Directions 137

Making Your Own Maps 137

Third-Party Navigation 137

Location-Sensing Social Media and Games..137

    Foursquare...138

    Gowalla 139

■ **Chapter 12: Browsing the Web** **141**

Chrome and the Android Browser..141

Android Browser Navigation 141

    Finding a Website 143

Bookmarking Pages...143

    Using Bookmarks and History..144

Syncing with Your Google Account 145

Setting Your Search Engine 147

Flash 147

Google Labs and Quick Controls 148

Desktop and Mobile Versions of Websites...148

Alternative Browsers 149

■ **Chapter 13: The Android Market** **151**

Introducing the Android Market...151

Paying for Apps...151

Installing Apps from Your Tablet...152
Paying for Apps..154
   Apps in Foreign Currencies..155
Uninstalling Apps..156
Getting a Refund...157
Updating Apps...158
Using the Android Market Website...160

■ Chapter 14: Alternative App Markets 163
Installing Apps from Unknown Sources..163
The Amazon Appstore..165
   My Apps..167
   Installing Apps from the Web...167
The Samsung App Store...168
Barnes & Noble Nook Apps...169
Handmark...169
GetJar..170
Uninstalling Apps..171

■ Chapter 15: Social Media 173
Facebook...173
   Creating Fan Pages..174
   Facebook Apps..175
Twitter and Microblogs...176
   The Mechanics and Culture of Twitter...177
   @Replies...177
   Direct Messages..177
   Retweets and Modified Tweets..177
   Hashtags...178
   URL Shorteners...178
   Picture Services...178
   Lists..178
Twitter Apps on Your Tablet...179
Choosing a Twitter App...179
Yammer...182
Salesforce...182
Google+...182
   Circles..183
   +1..183
   Stream...183
   Hangouts..183
   Sparks...183
   Huddles..184
   Photos...184
   The Google+ App...184
LinkedIn..185
Wordpress...186
Blogger..186
Tumblr...187

■ Chapter 16: Video and Voice Chat 189

Video and Voice Chat with Google Talk...189
    Setting Your Status Message...191
    Making a Video Call with Google Talk..192
    Making Voice Calls with Google Talk...192
Making Phone Calls with Skype...193
    Creating a Skype Account on Your Tablet..193
    Log into the Skype App...194
    Adding Contacts...194
    Making Calls with Skype on Your Tablet..195
    Receiving Calls with Skype on Your Tablet...196
    Chatting with Skype...196
    Adding Skype to Your Computer...197
Fring..197
Qik..198
OoVoo..198
Tango..198

■ Chapter 17: Reading E-books, Newspapers, and Magazines 201

Formats..201
Google Books...201
    Adjusting the Reading Options...203
    Reading Books Offline...204
    Buying or Downloading Google Books..204
    Google Books Website..207
The Kindle Reader..207
    Reading Kindle Books..208
    Looking up Words..209
    Saving Bookmarks and Taking Notes...209
    Adjusting Your Kindle Reading Options...211
    Purchasing Items for Kindle...211
    Buying Magazines or Newspapers..213
    Shelfari..214
    Sideloading Kindle Books..215
The Barnes & Noble Nook..216
    Reading Nook Books..218
    Saving Bookmarks, Taking Notes, and Researching Words.............................219
    LendMe Books..220
    Sideloading Nook Books..221
Kobo...221
    Reading Life..222
    Highlighting Text and Adding Notes..224
    Importing Books...225
Reading PDF Books..226
Converting Books from One Format to Another..226

■ Chapter 18: Taking Notes and Working with Documents 229

Google Docs..229
    Editing Spreadsheets..231

Editing Presentations 232
    Themes 234
    Downloading from Google Docs 234
Microsoft Live 235
Documents to Go...236
    Syncing Documents To Go 237
QuickOffice 238
    Editing Documents in QuickOffice 239
Printing Documents from Your Tablet 240
Sticky Notes 240
Evernote...241
    Evernote Premium 243

■ Chapter 19: Viewing Videos and Movies on Your Tablet 245

Adobe Flash 245
YouTube 245
Android Movie Rentals 246
    Rental Period 247
    Downloading (Pinning) Movies...248
Using Your Tablet to Display a Show on Your TV 249
Channel Apps 249
TWiT 250
iPlayer 251
Netflix 251
Amazon Videos 251
Watch Directly From the Web 253
Hulu+ 253
PlayOn..254
Using Your Tablet As the Remote 255

■ Chapter 20: Creating Photos, Videos, and Art 257

Tablet Differences 257
Taking Photos with the Camera App..257
    Special Features 260
    GPS 261
    Reviewing Pictures 261
    Deleting Photos 262
Shooting Video 262
    Time Lapse vs. Timers 264
The Gallery App 264
Sharing Photos and Videos 267
Third-Party Photo Apps 267
Editing Video 269
    Transitions 271
    Video Effects and Adjustments 271
    Adding Titles 272
    Uploading to YouTube 272
Using a Different Camera 272
Using Your Tablet for Art..273

Printing Photos...274

■ **Chapter 21: Listening to Music**.. **275**

Google Music...275

Getting Music to Google..275

Using Google Music on Your Tablet 277

Playing Songs on Google Music 279

Adding a Song to a Playlist 280

Instant Playlists..281

Listening Offline..282

Shopping for Music 283

Amazon MP3s and Cloud Player 283

Downloading Files..285

Purchasing Music from Amazon 285

Automatic Downloads 287

Pre-Installed Music Players 287

Pandora..288

Spotify..289

Finding Music When You Don't Know the Name...................................289

Beyond Listening 290

■ **Chapter 22: Fun and Games** **291**

Favorites on a Bigger Screen...291

Match-Three Games 292

Angry Birds 293

Arcade Classics...294

Tetris 294

Tower Defense...295

Board Games...296

Sports Games..297

Using Tablet Features 297

Mystery Adventure Games...299

MMOPRGs..300

Downloading Data..300

Pocket Legends 301

Dungeon Defenders 302

Virtual Simulations...303

Games for Children 304

■ **Chapter 23: The Clock, Calculator, and Other Utilities** **307**

The Clock 307

Repeating Alarms...310

Snoozing and Dismissing an Alarm 310

Extending the Clock 311

Alternate Alarms..312

The Calculator..312

ES File Explorer..313

The Grocery List...315

■ **Chapter 24: Using Bluetooth for Keyboards and More** **317**

Turning on Bluetooth 317

Bluetooth Profiles...318

Bluetooth and Pairing 319

Pairing with Keyboards and Headsets 322

Using a Keyboard 322

   Remote Control 323

Transferring Files 323

Unpairing Bluetooth Devices 324

▨ Appendix A: Advanced Troubleshooting 325

Steps for Troubleshooting...325

   Soft Resets 325

Factory Data Resets 326

Rooting Your Tablet...327

Tablet Development 327

▨ Appendix B: App Guide for Developers 329

Typing, Copy, and Search 329

Syncing Your Tablet With Google...329

Understanding Connection 330

Icons and Widgets, and Tabs 330

Email and Instant Messaging...330

Working With Calendars 331

Using Maps 331

Browsing the Web..331

Social Media 331

Video Conferencing..332

Reading E-books, Newspapers, and Magazines..333

Taking Notes and Working With Documents...334

Viewing Videos and Movies 334

Creating Photos, Videos, and Art on Android 335

Listening to Music..336

Games on Tablets 336

The Clock, Calculator, and Other Utilities 337

Index 339

About the Author

Marziah Karch enjoys the challenge of explaining complex technology to beginning audiences. She is an education technologist for Johnson County Community College in the Kansas City metro area with over ten years of experience. She holds an MS in instructional design and has occasionally taught credit courses in interactive media.

Marziah also contributes to New York Times-owned About.com and has been the site's Guide to Google since 2006. Her first book was *Android for Work: Productivity for Professionals* (Apress, 2010). When she's not feeding her geek side with new gadgets or writing about technology, Marziah enjoys life in Lawrence, Kansas with her husband, Harold, and two children.

About the Technical Reviewer

 **Phil Nickelson** spent more than 11 years as a copy editor, page designer, and news editor at a daily newspaper in Florida before taking the reins of Android Central in December, 2009. Phil's current weapon of choice: An HTC ThunderBolt, Samsung Infuse, or whatever he happens to be reviewing that week.

When he's not playing with phones, Phil enjoys hot baths and long walks on the beach. He lives in Florida with his wife, two daughters, and a 75-pound foxhound.

Acknowledgments

I'd like to thank my editors Steve, Kelly, Pat, James, and all the other staff at Apress that contributed to making this book a success. I'd also like to thank Phil for his technical review expertise.

A special thanks to Samsung for the use of a Galaxy Tab 10.1. Thanks also go to the friendly staff at the Best Buy store in Lawrence, Kansas for putting up with my constant questions and visits.

Portions of this book contain pictures that are modifications based on work created and shared by Google, and used according to terms described in the Creative Commons 3.0 Attribution License.

A Day in the Life of an Android Tablet

6:00 am	My tablet alarm goes off. It automatically rings a little earlier on Wednesdays, because I get to work a little earlier. I notice there's a chance of rain, so I pack my umbrella.	Chapter 23
6:50 am	I head into work and listen to some tunes on Google Music as I drive.	Chapter 21
8:30 am	I've got an early meeting, so I grab my tablet and a Bluetooth keyboard to take a few notes with **Evernote**.	Chapter 3, 18 and 24
8:45 am	I notice I've got an email message, so I check to see if it's something I need to read right away or reply to later.	Chapter 8
10:00 am	I've got an appointment across town. I've never been there, so I use **Google Maps** and my tablet's GPS to find the quickest spot for the traffic conditions.	Chapter 11
10:30 am	My clients arrive, so I give my presentation on my tablet using the **PowerPoint** file I saved in my **Dropbox** folder.	Chapter 18
12:00 am	My meeting went well, so I spend some of my lunch hour decompressing. I plug in my headphones and listen to my favorite **Pandora** station while reading a Kindle book I purchased last week.	Chapter 17 and 21
1:00 pm	I start working on my next presentation. This time, I take some photos and make a video slide show for YouTube.	Chapters 19 and 21
2:00 pm	I get a quick video call from a colleague in New York. The front-facing camera is great for video chats.	Chapter 16
4:00 pm	I check the **Calendar** app to make sure I've met all my work obligations, and then head home to my family.	Chapter 10
5:30 pm	I look up a chicken recipe on the Internet and take my tablet with me to the kitchen to try it out.	Chapter 12
6:00 pm	While I'm in the kitchen cooking, I sneak in a quick TV show on **Netflix.**	Chapter 19
7:00 pm	The kids borrow the tablet to play a few rounds of **Angry Birds** before bed.	Chapter 22
10:00 pm	I check on my family and friends on **Facebook**, and then I put my tablet on its charging cradle, knowing it will wake me up again in the morning.	Chapter 15

Chapter 1

What Is Android: Choosing the Right Tablet

Android followed the iPhone to the market, yet it has surged in popularity. Android is already found on phones by virtually every phone manufacturer, and it is available on every major US wireless company, plus most of the regionals. It's flexible, fun, and boasts thousands of apps. It doesn't hurt that Google released the OS for free.

In this chapter, you'll learn about the history of the Android OS. You'll also learn how Android has evolved beyond the phone and into tablets. In the next chapter, you'll learn how to pick the right tablet for you.

The History of Android

Back in 2005, two years before Apple would revolutionize the phone world with the iPhone, Google bought a small, two-year-old company founded by Andy Rubin. Rubin was best known at the time for starting Danger, Inc., which created the T-Mobile–branded Sidekick phones. Rubin's new company, Android, also included Richard Minor from Orange (a UK phone company), Chris White from WebTV, and Andy McFadden from WebTV and Moxi. Originally, Rubin approached Google for possible startup money, but Google instead ended up acquiring Android and the talented team behind it.

What was so different about Android? Previous phone operating systems were either made by the device manufacturer or licensed to them for a fee. Rubin's idea was to give away the operating system and find some other way to make money. Since Google gives away most of its Web products for free and makes money from advertising, the idea resonated with Google.

On November 5, 2007, Google announced the Android OS and the Open Handset Alliance, a group of companies that would help develop it. Open Handset Alliance members include phone carriers, software developers, device manufacturers, and component makers.

Android has a very different philosophy compared to Apple and the iPhone. Anyone can use Android in devices for free, anyone can modify Android, and anyone can develop apps for it without the complicated pre-approval process required of iPhone apps.

Google also seeded the Android app market by holding developer contests with cash prizes. So, by the time the first Android phone arrived in stores, there was a selection of apps already available for download. The picture on the right shows the G1, the 2008 model that became the first Android phone to hit the market.

Today, Android has moved beyond the phone. It's powering e-book readers, photo frames, Google TV, netbooks, and even car stereos. Its low cost and easy customization lend it to all sorts of applications for portable devices.

The most important of these Android devices for this book is, of course, the Android tablet. You might wonder why it took so long for Android tablets to hit the market, especially after Apple introduced the iPad. There were Android tablets available, but they required modified versions of Android; and, with the exception of the Samsung Galaxy Tab, they never had much of a market. Why? Google was counting on Honeycomb.

Android Honeycomb

Android operating system releases are all given dessert code names. The names are also in alphabetical order, so you can tell which release is more recent. A and B are reserved names, so the Android versions released to the public are Android 1.0 (no code name), Cupcake (1.5), Donut (1.6), Éclair (2.0 and 2.1), Froyo (2.2), Gingerbread (2.3), and Honeycomb (3.0 and 3.1). The next release is Ice Cream Sandwich, which was introduced in October 2011.

Android Honeycomb is the most significant release for tablet users because it's the only release Google explicitly intended for use on tablets, and it has full access to the Android Market. I'll discuss the Android Market in more depth in Chapter 13. "The Android Market." Ice Cream Sandwich was mainly intended to bring the Honeycomb tablet features to phone users.

That isn't to say that there weren't devices that tried to hit the market before Honeycomb. ViewSonic had the G-tablet. Samsung released the Galaxy Tab, and Archos introduced a whole line of Android tablets in different sizes. At the time of writing, there are plans to release at least one more pre-Honeycomb device, the HTC Flyer, although it will eventually upgrade to Honeycomb.

The problem is that pre-Honeycomb tablets don't scale well: apps and widgets are simply larger instead of really taking advantage of the space available, they often require a lot of OS tweaking to work, and third-party apps don't always behave well. The scalability problem hasn't been entirely resolved in non-tablet apps, but it has improved.

HTC and Sense

Manufacturers are free to tweak Android any way they see fit; and in the mobile world, that's meant a lot of new user interfaces.

HTC makes a variety of Android phones, and it plans on releasing the Flyer at about the time this book will go to press. One of the advertised features of the Flyer is that it will use a new version of the HTC Sense UI (User interface).

Sense UI is based around widgets. Widgets are small, always-on applications that run on your phone or tablet home screen for specific purposes, like showing weather information or posting Twitter updates. This is similar to Windows Gadgets on desktop computers. You can learn more about widgets in Chapter 6: "Icons, Widgets, and Tabs."

When Android 1.6 was only offering three screens for customization, Sense offered seven. The screens centered on common activities, such as work and social media, and HTC created several custom widgets to make using phone activities easier. Sense also ties some information together, such as combining phone contact information and Facebook.

Other Uses for Android

One of the more interesting uses for Android has been in devices that aren't phones. Android powers e-book readers and netbooks (and it could even power your microwave). Google also introduced the Android-based Google TV, which is being upgraded to run Honeycomb.

Android Readers

The Barnes and Noble Nook Color Reader may not look like an Android device, but it is. The Nook's version of Android has been heavily modified, although there's a small hacker community dedicated to restoring such devices to a more standard version of Android. Other e-readers that use Android include the Springboard Alex, enTourage eDGe, and Velocity Cruz. Amazon.com offers the Android-powered Kindle Fire tablet.

You might wonder what the difference is between a reader and a tablet. The Nook even runs apps, so the difference seems to mainly be the spelling. However, most devices that advertise themselves as readers are centered on reading. They're often tied to a specific bookstore and are less powerful. Some of them also have a screen designed to be less responsive to touch, so that you won't accidentally lose your place in a book. The Kindle Fire is the big exception to this rule. It packs as much processing power as larger tablets.

Multimedia Players

Samsung publicly introduced its Galaxy Player line in 2011. Devices in this line are essentially Galaxy phones without the phone. They're also a bit unique in their ability to run apps. At the time of writing, Galaxy Player devices are the only non-phones running Gingerbread to get Google's blessing to use the Android Market (although HTC is also introducing a tablet that runs Gingerbread and uses the Sense UI).

Other companies have introduced multimedia players that range from pocket sized to 10-inch tablet sized, although none of them have made a huge market splash.

Netbooks

The 2010 Consumer Electronics Show was full of companies hoping to sell netbooks and trying to use the free Android OS to give themselves a competitive edge for pricing. By the time 2011 had rolled around, most companies had given up on Android as a netbook OS. However, the ASUS EeePad Transformer may reverse that trend, depending on whether you consider it to be a netbook or a tablet with a keyboard.

> **CAUTION:** I'll warn you against using Android as a netbook OS. At the time of publication, Android doesn't run well on systems without touchscreens, and such devices don't work as well as a netbook running an OS designed for full-sized computers, such as Ubuntu Linux or Microsoft Windows. Google is developing the Chrome OS for netbook users.

Google TV

Google introduced a platform for integrating TV and Internet programming called Google TV. The "remote" uses a keyboard instead of just a series of buttons, and it includes Google's Chrome Web browser.

This is part of a new generation of TVs that are Internet-connected and run apps. Rather than passively accepting programming, you can use connected TVs to find streaming programs, check the weather, browse the Web, listen to music, or update your Facebook status.

The Google TV platform runs on a modified version of Android, and Google plans on introducing an app market for the platform and upgrading Google TV to run Android 3.1 by the time this book goes to press.. Sony, Logitech, Samsung, and other companies introduced Google TV devices, although they've yet to take off with consumers either.

Microwaves, Washing Machines, and Printers (Oh My!)

Touch Revolution makes an Android-powered touch interface for other companies called the NIM1000. Touch Revolution is an *original design manufacturer (ODM)*, which means it creates products for other companies to brand as their own. You'll never see Touch Revolution on the interface, but a representative told me that its technology was being used to create Android-powered interfaces for medical devices and the computers on the back of airline seats. The picture on the right shows an Android-powered microwave the company used for a demonstration in 2010. Parrot used Android to power ASTEROID, an automobile car stereo system. It also used Android in high-end digital photo frames.

Companies picked Android because it's easily customizable and free. Touch Revolution also felt Android was better designed than Windows CE. To prove the versatility of its design, Touch Revolution demonstrated an Android-powered washing machine, microwave, printer, and enterprise phone set. That doesn't mean anyone will *actually* use Android to determine the length of the spin cycle. In fact, in 2011 the major manufacturers were skipping the Android and programming "smart" appliances using their own proprietary systems. However, people are still likely to use Android interfaces on devices that have nothing in common with phones.

Google introduced the **Android @ Home** project in 2011. This is Google's framework for creating smart appliances that communicate using Android. Who knows? Your next refrigerator may very well send your Android tablet an email to let you know you should buy more milk. Speaking of tablets, if you don't own one already, the next section will help you find the perfect Android tablet.

Choosing the Right Android Tablet

As mentioned earlier, the first version of Android that Google intended for tablet use is version 3.0, code-named *Honeycomb*. Honeycomb is designed around larger screen sizes and allows apps to do things like offer expandable menus. As an incentive for tablet makers to adopt Honeycomb, Google restricted access to the Android Market to phones only. (The UK version of the Galaxy Tab can make phone calls, which is likely how Samsung got around the restriction.) Google also later made exceptions for the Samsung Galaxy Player, which is a phone-sized media player, and the HTC Flyer, which is also known in the US as the EVO View 4G.

That doesn't mean there aren't a few tablets out there that run on previous versions of Android. The original Samsung Galaxy Tab, some Archos tablets, and the HTC Flyer are all tablets that run on Android 2.2 or earlier.

The problem is that these previous versions of Android require a lot of modification by the device manufacturers. Google won't certify all of them to use the Android Market, so some of them need an alternative app market. That cuts down on the number of available apps. Many also have modified user interfaces, and that may mean apps need to be customized, which further erodes the number of available apps.

Android is free and open-source, but Honeycomb has some hefty minimum hardware requirements. Many tablets that don't support Honeycomb may simply be incapable of the upgrade.

Modified Honeycomb

There are a few tablets that are capable of running Honeycomb, but will sport a modified user interface. This will likely include the HTC EVO 4G. It's not available at the time of writing, but HTC has announced that the device will upgrade from Gingerbread to run a version of Honeycomb modified to look more like HTC Sense phones. The Notion Ink Adam runs a modified version of Android called Eden. The Samsung Galaxy Tab 10.1

shipped with Honeycomb and offer an upgrade to a modified interface. The Kindle Fire uses a heavily modified interface that isn't recognizable as Android.

It's difficult to purchase an Android phone without some sort of modified interface, and device makers think it distinguishes their brand for consumers. The problem is that a modified interface also slows down upgrades and makes developers work harder to tweak apps for different versions of Android. The good news for now is that there are plenty of Android Honeycomb tablets that offer a "pure Google" experience, and Google is making it easier to write apps that handle different versions of Android.

Deciphering Screen Size

You'll likely see screen size listed in one of two ways: a single measurement in inches, such as "10 inches," or a measure of pixel resolution, such as "1280 x 720." It's important to understand both of these measurements and what they mean.

The first measurement of screen size in inches refers to the diagonal measurement of a screen. This is the same way TV and computer monitors are usually measured; and while it gives you an idea of the size, this measurement can seem misleading when you view two screens with identical diagonal measurements, but different aspect ratios.

> **NOTE:** Some people find that screens with 16:9 aspect ratios seem smaller than screens with 4:3 ratios, even if their diagonal measurements are the same.

Figure 1–1 illustrates how diagonal measurements can distort the true size of a screen. Most screens for phones measure between three and five inches, while most tablet screens measure between seven and twelve inches. Laptops measure between ten and seventeen inches, with ten inches considered "netbook" sized and seventeen inches considered pretty large.

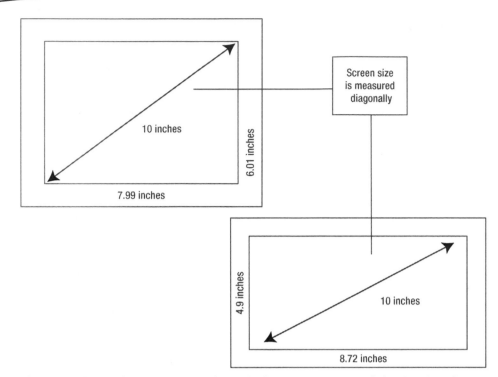

Figure 1–1. *Screen sizes are measured diagonally. One screen's aspect ratio is 4:3, and one is 16:9*

Pixel Resolution

The other measure of screen size is the pixel resolution of the screen. You could have a twenty-inch screen on your tablet (that's huge), but it won't provide a great experience if it still has the resolution of a standard-definition TV.

Pixel resolution is the total number of pixels a screen displays, and usually that number is given as a simple measurement of the pixels in the width and height of a display, such as 640x480. The smaller your screen, the fewer pixels it needs to create a satisfying picture. However, even small screens benefit from higher resolution displays. Text is easier to read in eBooks, and movies and pictures look much sharper with those extra pixels.

Android doesn't assume all screens have the same size, aspect ratio, or resolution, so there's a lot of room for variety. Here are a few common standards to give you a point of reference:

- **320 x 240:** This is a common smartphone resolution, called *HVGA* (for *half* VGA, though it's more correctly called *QVGA* for *quarter* VGA). You'll find this on many older or low-end Android smartphones.

- **640 x 480:** This standard is known as *VGA (Video Graphics Array)*, and it was originally a standard for computer monitors, though it's now considered very low quality. This size is close to the same size as standard definition TV broadcasts. (Technically TV video is 720 x 480 or 720 x 540, but the pixels on analog TVs were not square shaped like those on computer and tablet displays.)

- **800 x 480:** *WVGA (Wide VGA)* is a common phone resolution that is giving way to *qHD*.

- **800 x 600:** This is called *SVGA* for *Super* VGA. It's another computer standard that has gone out of fashion with higher resolution displays.

- **960 x 540:** This is a standard for some displays because it's half the pixels in either direction of an HD display. It's a *quarter of the resolution* of HD because you'd have to put four of these displays together to have the same resolution as a 1080 HDTV display. For this reason, it's also known as *qHD*.

- **1280 x 720:** This is one common standard for HDTVs. The other, higher standard is 1920 x 1080. In both cases, HDTV usually talks about the second number, 720 or 1080, when measuring resolution.

- **1024 x 786:** This is a computer standard known as *XGA* for *Extended Graphics Array*.

- **1440 x 960:** This is the widescreen version of *XGA* known as *WXGA*.

- **2560 x 2048:** This is *QSXGA* for *Quad Super Extended Graphics Array*, and it's like the Cadillac of current standard computer screen resolutions. No tablets are shipping with anywhere near this resolution at the time of writing, although I'm sure some eventually will.

Touchscreen Sensitivity

Before you buy a tablet, you should play with one in the store and check to see how sensitive the screen is to your touch. You may find that some screens are really sensitive, and some require a stylus or fingernail to react to your touch.

There are two basic technologies used for most tablets, **resistive** and **capacitive** touchscreens. In general, resistive touchscreens are more accurate, but usually require a stylus or fingernail and a small amount of physical pressure. Capacitive touchscreens respond very well to bare fingers, a metallic stylus, or any other conductive object, but they can't be used with non-conductive gloves.

The rationale for using a resistive touchscreen in Android is in devices that are intended primarily as e-book readers. The less responsive screen makes it harder to accidentally turn pages while reading. If you're looking for an all-purpose tablet, your best bet is to stick with capacitive touchscreens.

Screen Contrast

You may not plan on taking your tablet out into bright sunlight and curling up with a good e-book in a lawn chair or hammock; but even if you stay indoors, you'll still likely run into glare from windows, which can render a low-contrast display totally unreadable.

When you buy a traditional e-reader like the Amazon Kindle, it has an amazing high contrast display using a technology called *E Ink*. The problem is that E Ink doesn't do well with color, has a slow refresh rate, and isn't backlit–so it's pretty limited.

Pixel Qi (pronounced "Pixel Chee") is a company that makes a special form of LCD screen that can display either with or without a backlight. This not only saves battery life, but it means you can still check your email or read a map in direct sunlight.

At the time of writing, there are only a few Android tablets that offer screens by Pixel Qi, but that may change in the future. Screens by Pixel Qi add to the price, but they may be worth it. The Kindle Fire does not offer Pixel Qi screen, which may be one of the reasons the battery life is only advertised as eight hours.

Cameras

If you want to take pictures or hold video chats, you'll want a camera (or two) on the tablet. We'll discuss the specifics of cameras in a later chapter, but here are a few things to examine as you make purchasing choices.

Most tablets have one camera, but some have two or even three. The camera on the back of the tablet is for taking pictures, and the camera on the front is for video chat. In some cases, there might be two cameras on the back to take 3D photos and video images.

Be sure to look at the camera pixel resolution. Most cameras list their resolution in units of *megapixels*. A megapixel is a unit of one million pixels.

> **NOTE:** A general rule of thumb is that the more megapixels, the better the camera, though this is not always true. If your camera has lousy optics, each extra megapixel could just represent one million more blurry pixels. Test the quality of pictures in the store before you buy instead of relying on the stats on the side of the box.

In general, you'll want to look at tablets with at least 5 megapixel cameras on the back. If you want 3D pictures or video, look for a tablet with two cameras. It's much harder to fake 3D after you've already taken a picture, so it's important to get a tablet that offers the feature out of the box.

The front camera can be smaller since you're only using it for video chat. In this case, .3 to 1.5 megapixel cameras will do just fine. The back camera(s) should have a flash. Some tablets may even have a single camera that you swivel around from front to back, in which case you should look for a 5 megapixel camera.

You should also check out the quality of video capture. Most tablets with 5 megapixel cameras are capable of high-definition video capture, even if the tablet isn't capable of playing the video back at full resolution.

If photos are totally unimportant, you might be able to find a lower cost option with a poorer quality camera; however, you should look for tablets that have some sort of camera, even if you don't think you'll need one. You may want to try an augmented reality app or take a quick picture to use for contact icons, and you can't add a camera later.

Memory

RAM is the working memory for your tablet. It works the same on tablets as it does on other computers, by temporarily storing working files to speed processing along. It's also used to run the OS on your device. When your tablet has plenty of RAM, it runs faster and can handle multitasking and larger apps. When your tablet has less RAM, it slows down because the slower hard drive storage has to store these working files. In some cases, there might not be enough RAM to properly run Android.

The Motorola Xoom has 1 GB of RAM. That's a great minimum starting point for tablets running Android Honeycomb, and it's currently all that's available on the market. Remember that Google wrote Honeycomb with Xoom hardware in hand, so be very cautious when looking at any tablet with hardware specs below that of the Xoom.

Internal Storage

In addition to RAM, your tablet will have internal storage space and possibly removable storage space. Internal storage allows you to install apps and store files, and removable storage allows you to expand this capacity. On computers, this internal storage was traditionally through a hard disk, but most tablets use a *solid-state drive* (*SSD*), like USB thumb-drives. Solid-state drives don't need to spin, so they're instantly available when you turn on your device.

Looking at the Xoom as a starting point, the minimum internal space you'd want to see is 16 gigabytes of space. A tablet with less space will work; however, if you use your tablet heavily, eventually you'll fill up the drive with books, pictures, apps, and files.

In addition, SD storage is a way to add capacity for your tablet if you find you're filling up all the space. Not all tablets offer SD storage, so you'll have to check to see if it's offered for the tablet you'd like to purchase. Motorola rushed the Xoom to market without SD storage, but started offering free upgrades in late September of 2011.

> **CAUTION:** You can make up for a lack of internal storage by buying a larger SD card, but not all apps can be installed on SD cards. You may still run into storage problems even with the extra removable space.

HDMI

Do you want to use your tablet to project movies, slideshows, or presentations? If so, then you should look for a tablet with HDMI out. *HDMI* stands for *High Definition Multimedia Interface*, and it's the cable used by most modern HDTVs and many computer monitors and projectors to stream pictures and sound. Some tablets and phones with HDMI output are even Dolby-certified to stream in 5.1 and 7.1 surround sound. That makes your tablet a portable piece of home theater equipment.

The HDMI output is different from the USB output, which brings us to the next item.

USB

The USB connection in most tablets can be used to sync with a computer for transferring files and photos. You can also use your tablet with the **doubleTwist** app to transfer your music from your iTunes library, although you may want to skip the USB connection and store your iTunes library in the cloud with Google Music. I'll discuss this in more detail in Chapter 21**:** "Listening to Music."

Nearly every tablet will have a USB connection. But when you shop for tablets, you may want to make sure it's a standard connection, so you can use third party cords and other accessories.

You'll also want to check to see if you can use the USB port to charge the tablet. In many cases, such as the Motorola Xoom, the answer is going to be "no." The Galaxy Tab 10.1 does offer this feature. Third-party USB battery backups are useless for any device that can't charge via USB.

Accessories

Some accessories, like microphone headsets and Bluetooth headsets, are pretty universal (if your tablet has Bluetooth). Others, like charging docks, are specific to your device. Take a look at the available accessories for any tablet you're eyeing, just to make sure it offers at least a keyboard, case, and charging dock. You may not think you need a keyboard, but you may change your mind later, and it's nice to know you still have options.

Hacking a Nook

If you're OK with a tablet that doesn't run Android Honeycomb, still has a few quirks, but only costs half the price of many fancier tablets, you could try hacking a Barns and Noble Nook Color e-reader.

This isn't an option for the Android newbie or anyone who worries about volding his warranty. However, the Nook has developed an active hacking community. The Nook runs an Android variation and can even run Nook-specific apps, but it doesn't have access to the Google Android market. By using a process called "rooting," you can change the Nook operating system and use the Nook as a more standard Android tablet. I've heard that Honeycomb runs pretty slowly on Nooks, so earlier versions of Android are better.

If you're up for the challenge, visit nookdevs.com/Portal:NookColor for more information. The Kindle Fire will likely also develop an enthusiastic hacker following, but the tablet is being released at about the same time as this book.

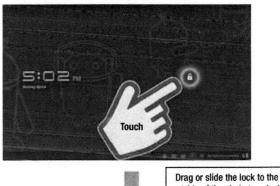

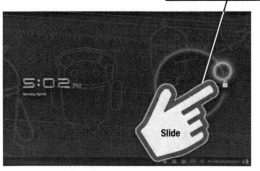

Chapter 2

Getting Started

This chapter is here to help you once you've gone from eyeing a tablet to actually buying one. There are quite a few Android tablets available, so we'll stick to those running Android 3.0 Honeycomb and above, unless otherwise noted. Your screens may not look exactly the same as those shown here, but they should look very similar.

Unlocking Your Tablet

Touch

Drag or slide the lock to the outside of the circle to unlock the screen.

Slide

Different tablets may have slight variations for how you unlock them, but they generally start out with an easy dragging unlock gesture.

The example on the left comes from the Xoom. Simply touch the **Lock** icon and a circle will appear. Drag the lock out of the circle by swiping your finger and you'll unlock the screen.

This isn't your only option for a screen lock, but this is the default. You can use passwords, patterns, and in Android 4.0 (Ice Cream Sandwich), you can use facial recognition.

A Typical Activation Sequence

Not all tablets will have the same activation sequence, but the sequence will usually be similar. Here's how a Xoom with a Verizon Wireless data plan activates:

1. **Choose a Language:** The default is English.

2. **Activate Verizon Wireless:** Activate your tablet on Verizon. Wi-Fi-only customers will be prompted to enter information about their Wi-Fi access point instead.

3. **Use Google Location Service:** Do you want Google to detect your location for things like Google Maps directions and search results? The default is yes.

4. **Sign in with Your Google Account:** If you have a Gmail or another Google account, enter it here.

5. **Restore and Back up Your Data:** If you've entered a Google Account in the previous screen, you can choose to have your data restored and backed up. If you own another Android device, it will even start downloading compatible apps you use on other devices.

Google Account

Technically, you don't need a Google Account to use an Android tablet. However, it's in your best interests to create one, anyway. Google Accounts are free and allow you to sync your Google data between your tablet and any other computer you use with your Google Account.

When you start your Android tablet for the first time, you'll be asked to enter information for your Google Account or create a new one. You may skip this step if you wish and sync your Google Account information later.

You can read more about the benefits of syncing with a Google Account in Chapter 4: "Syncing Your Tablet with Google."

Activating Your Data Plan

Some tablets are sold with cellular data access, and some can only be used with Wi-Fi networks. You can learn more about data in Chapter 6: "Understanding Connection: Wi-Fi, 3G, and 4G."

If you've purchased a data plan for your tablet, you'll need to activate it. Your carrier or the store where you purchased your device should give you the specifics on how this is done. For some tablets, this will involve installing a SIM card that identifies the device on the network (AT&T and T-Mobile devices); other tablets will have this information built into the device (Verizon and Sprint). Your tablet will take a few moments to connect to your network of choice and authenticate.

If you've purchased a tablet that has cellular data capability, but you have not purchased a data plan, then you can skip this step and use the tablet in Wi-Fi only mode until you choose to purchase a data plan.

The Basic Home Screen

Once you've completed your tablet's setup, you'll finally see the **Home** screen. This looks pretty similar to the **Home** screen of an iPad, and some of it functions the same way. If you swipe your finger from side to side, you can switch through the various pages of your **Home** screen. You'll also notice small app icons that you can tap to launch the corresponding apps. You can find any installed apps you don't see by tapping on the **App Tray** launcher on the upper-right corner of the screen.

There are also a few items that you won't find on iPad, such as the larger items called *widgets*. This new **Home** screen may be a bit intimidating at first, but as you get used to the terrain, you'll find it's very easy to use. Figure 2–1 goes over some of the basic features.

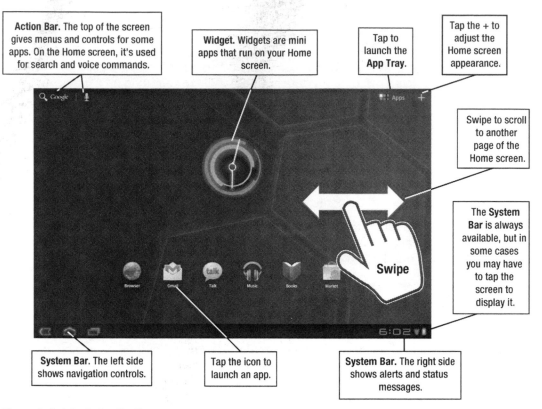

Action Bar. The top of the screen gives menus and controls for some apps. On the Home screen, it's used for search and voice commands.

Widget. Widgets are mini apps that run on your Home screen.

Tap to launch the **App Tray.**

Tap the + to adjust the Home screen appearance.

Swipe to scroll to another page of the Home screen.

The **System Bar** is always available, but in some cases you may have to tap the screen to display it.

System Bar. The left side shows navigation controls.

Tap the icon to launch an app.

System Bar. The right side shows alerts and status messages.

Figure 2–1. *Introducing the Home screen*

Where Are the Buttons?

Once you've completed activation and the initial setup for your Android tablet, you may notice that Android tablets usually have fewer buttons than their phone counterparts. In fact, the Motorola Xoom and most other Honeycomb and Ice Cream Sandwich tablets only have physical power and volume buttons. All other buttons are created through the software.

There's a good reason for that. You can tilt an Android screen up or down in any orientation you'd like, and the position of your navigation controls will still be on the bottom left of your screen.

> **CAUTION:** There is an exception to your button location. Some apps lock the screen in a certain orientation, such as **Portrait** or **Landscape** mode only. In the case of a locked screen, your buttons will also be locked with the orientation of the app.

The Action Bar and the System Bar

Android tablets have two main areas of control: the **Action** and **System** bars. The **Action** bar is an optional place for app-specific menus and options. It's on the top of the screen, as shown in Figure 2-1; and what you see could vary from complex menus to nothing at all, depending on what the app developer decided to do.

The **System** bar, on the other hand, is not optional. It's available in every app on Android Honeycomb tablets. In some cases, such as e-book readers and movie players, the app developer might want to hide the **System** bar; however, tapping the screen will bring it back.

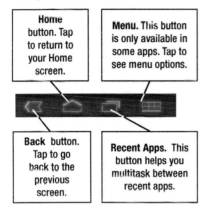

Home button. Tap to return to your Home screen.

Menu. This button is only available in some apps. Tap to see menu options.

Back button. Tap to go back to the previous screen.

Recent Apps. This button helps you multitask between recent apps.

The **System** bar is divided into two basic areas: navigation controls are on the left; and system controls, alerts, and notices are on the right.

The figure to the left shows the navigation controls. Three of them—**Back**, **Home**, and **Recent Apps**—are always available. The **Menu** button is sometimes available, depending on the app. For Honeycomb-optimized apps, menu functions are on the **Action** bar.

If you use an Android phone, you may recognize this as being very similar to the navigation controls used on the physical buttons for most phones. The notable exception is the **Recent Apps** button.

Recent Apps and Easy Multitasking

The **Recent Apps** button is Google's answer to easy multitasking on a tablet. Tablet screens are pretty small relative to most notebooks, so it's hard to have more than one window open at once. That doesn't mean you don't want more than one app to run at a time, and it doesn't mean you don't want to bounce from app to app occasionally.

For instance, assume you're writing an email to your boss. You'll want to quickly check your calendar to make sure your schedule is clear, and then verify some research on the Web. You can check the dates and then bounce back to your open email letter by using the **Recent Apps** button. Follow these steps to do so:

1. Tap the **Recent Apps** button from any app or the **Home** screen.

2. You'll see preview windows of your five to seven most recently launched apps as they appeared when you exited them. Tap any preview window to return to that app.

> **TIP:** Tilt your screen to **Portrait** mode to see more app previews.

Tap **Recent Apps** and then tap an app preview to return to that app.

The Notification Panel

Now that you've explored the left side of the **System** bar, it's time to look at the right side. Figure 2–2 shows the **Notification** panel and the quick settings area. You'll see system notifications, such as time, battery status, and data signal strength.

You'll also see alerts and status messages from different apps. For instance, you may see a notice that you've got a new email message, an alert that someone has commented on your Facebook post, or a message that there's an update available for **Angry Birds**.

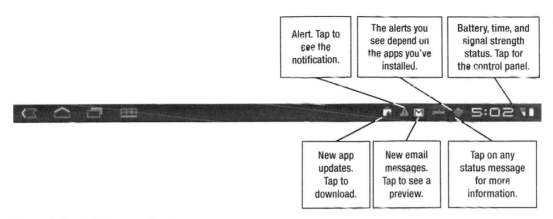

Figure 2–2. *The Notification Panel*

When you get a new notice, tap that icon to see a preview and then tap it again to launch the app. If you want to see all your notices at once, tap the **Clock** icon. This expands the **Notification** panel, as shown in Figure 2–3.

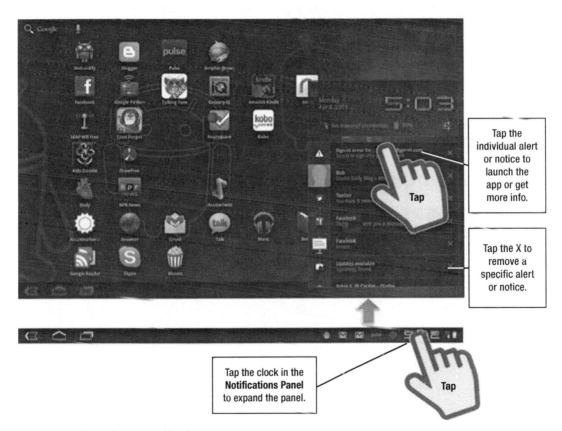

Figure 2–3. *Expanding the Notification panel*

Once you've expanded the panel, you can view all the previews of your email messages, Facebook alerts, and status messages. Click the message to launch the associated app or click the **X** icon to the right of the notification to remove it from your list.

Notifications generally remain until you click them or use the X to remove them, so don't worry if you don't have time to read that email right this second.

Basic Tablet Gestures

As you explore your tablet, there are a few basic finger gestures that will help you on your way. Some gestures use one finger, and some use two. Most of the following gestures should be familiar if you've used an Android or similar smartphone in the past:

- **Tapping:** Tapping is exactly how it sounds. Press lightly on the screen in a single spot for a short amount of time.

- **Long-press:** Instead of tapping, hold your finger in place on the screen for a few seconds until something happens.

- **Swiping or dragging:** Take one finger, press on the screen, and move it along the screen without losing contact.

- **Pinching:** Bring two fingers together in a pinching motion. This is generally used to zoom out from a screen and make everything appear smaller.

- **Expanding:** This is the opposite of pinching. Take those two fingers and move them apart. This is generally used to expand something and make it bigger.

Long Pressing on the Home Screen

If you long-press on the **Home** screen, you can change its appearance. You can do the same thing by tapping the **Plus** sign (**+**) on the upper-right corner of the **Home** screen.

This is covered in Chapter 7 "Icons, Widgets, and Tabs"; however, it bears mentioning now because the first time you accidentally launch this screen, you may not realize what just happened. You'll see something that resembles Figure 2–4.

Figure 2–4. *The 3D Customization Panel*

Should you unintentionally open the **Customization** panel, just touch any panel of the **Home** screen, and you'll return to Home sweet Home.

Now that your tablet is activated and you've learned to navigate it, it's time to talk about typing and text.

Chapter 3

Typing, Copy, and Search

One of the great things about owning a tablet is that you're not constrained to typing on a tiny thumb keyboard, as is the case when you are on a phone. As it turns out, you're not even constrained to typing at all. In this chapter, you'll explore how to handle text by typing. You'll also look at the copy and paste and auto-correction features, as well as explore some alternate methods of entry, including voice dictation and the **Swype** app.

The Virtual Keyboard

The keyboard on Android tablets appears when you tap anywhere with a text entry blank or when you open an app requiring text input. It's a virtual keyboard that appears on screen. Some tablets offer optional physical keyboards, but you still have the option of using the virtual keyboard whenever it's more convenient.

You can use the virtual keyboard from either **Landscape** or **Portrait** orientation. You have more space to type in **Landscape** mode and more room to see the screen in **Portrait** mode. Some people find themselves more successful at typing on the virtual keyboard in **Landscape** mode by using all ten fingers than they do with a physical keyboard. However, if you're a touch-typist, this may not be ideal. You don't get the same feedback from a smooth glass surface as you do from physical keys.

Smaller tablets, such as the Nook Color or original Galaxy Tab, are a bit too small for comfortable typing, so they work better as large thumb keyboards. On some tablets, such as the Galaxy Tab, you also have the option of using **Swype**, a text entry system designed originally for phones.

NOTE: The virtual keyboard generally doesn't appear when you've got your tablet connected to a Bluetooth keyboard. This gives you more room on the screen as you type.

You can use the softkey shortcut in the **System** bar to temporarily disable this feature or simply turn off your physical keyboard if you'd like to use the virtual keyboard instead.

The Standard Keyboard Layout

On tablets using Honeycomb, the standard keyboard layout looks something like Figure 3–1. Some keys may vary slightly, depending on the context of the text field. For instance, the **Emoticon** combination key may become a **.com** key when you open an email app.

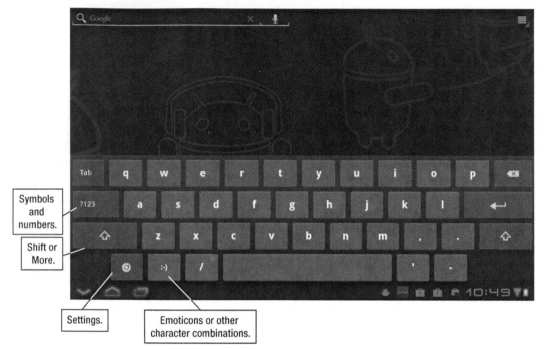

Figure 3–1. *The standard keyboard layout in Honeycomb*

NOTE: The keyboard layout in Gingerbread and earlier versions of Android was slightly different. The **Delete** button was on the lower right of the keyboard, and the **Emoticon** icon appeared on the bottom-right row. Modified Android tablets may also have modified keyboard layouts.

Displaying Capital Letters, Numbers, and Symbols

To make more room for keys and allow for faster typing, the virtual keyboard hides a few of the less-used characters. On physical keyboards, you often hold two keys at once, such as the **Shift** and **B** keys to form a capital B; however, this is a bit trickier on tablets. On Honeycomb, you can also tap keys sequentially instead.

Some sequential combinations are where you'd expect to find them, such as the **Shift** key, which is tapped for capital letters. Tap once for a single letter. Tap a second time for caps lock, and then tap again to resume lowercase letters. The **123?** key shows numbers and symbols, and tapping the **More** key reveals even more symbols. Figure 3–2 shows the keyboard combinations for Honeycomb.

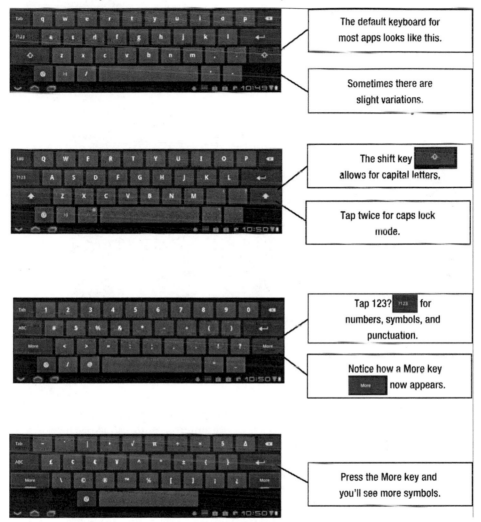

The default keyboard for most apps looks like this.

Sometimes there are slight variations.

The shift key allows for capital letters.

Tap twice for caps lock mode.

Tap 123? for numbers, symbols, and punctuation.

Notice how a More key now appears.

Press the More key and you'll see more symbols.

Figure 3–2. *Entering special characters in Honeycomb*

Character Combinations and Long-Presses

You may notice the key to the left of the **Slash** key types more than one character at a time. It can also change, depending on where you're typing. When you type email addresses, it may become a **.com** key; however, when you type within the body of that email message, it may transform into a **:-)** or **Emoticon** key.

That's very convenient if you're writing to a .com address; however, what if you're writing to a .net address, and you want to type a sad face in your message instead of a smiley? If you press and hold (also known as a *long-press*), you'll see more key combinations for different emoticons or first-level domains. Figure 3–3 illustrates some of these combinations. Simply long-press and then slide your finger to the appropriate choice.

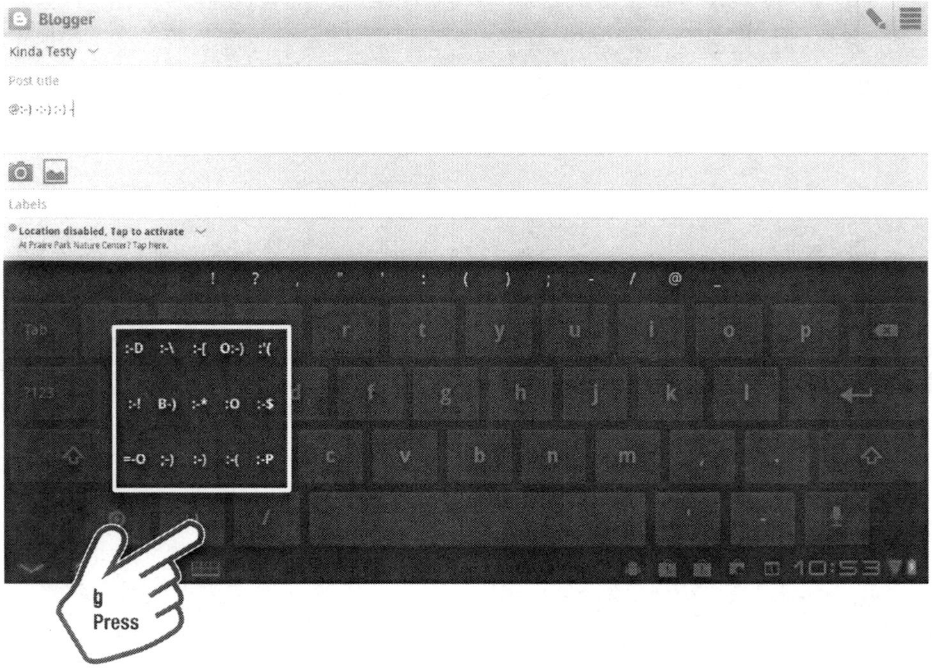

Figure 3–3. *Long-pressing an emoticon reveals more options*

But wait, there's more! What if you want to type a *ü* or make a proper *é* with an accent above it? Long-press on the vowels, and you'll see options for common foreign characters. A few consonants also have extra options, such as the *ñ* from the **n** key and the *ç* from the **c** key.

You might also notice that some keys have another character on the upper left. Rather than pressing a **Shift** key to reach them, you can just long-press the character itself. The **Slash** key (/) becomes an **At Sign** key (@), and the **Comma** key (,) becomes an **Exclamation Point** key (!). Once you get used to this system, it's easy to type what you need.

Swype Typing

Some tablets, such as the Samsung Galaxy Tab, ship with the **Swype** app pre-installed. **Swype** is also available as a separate app download for some tablet and phone users (the version shown on the right); and by the time this book is published, it's likely to be available for tablets running Honeycomb.

When using **Swype**, you don't peck each letter out one at a time; instead, you slide your fingers along the virtual keys. For instance, the word "wish" would be typed this way:

1. Press down on the first letter of the word, the **w** key.

2. Keep your finger pressed down and slide between the **i**, **s**, and **h** keys.

3. Pick your finger up at the end of the word, or the **h** key.

Swype will guess what you were sliding your fingers to type; and if it doesn't have a clear guess, it will make suggestions.

You don't need to do anything to choose the first suggestion.

You can also tap instead of sliding when using **Swype**—just as you would with the standard virtual keyboard—and **Swype** will still make suggestions as if you slid your fingers between letters.

Just as with other Android virtual keyboards, the long-press substitutes for the **Shift** key.

> **TIP:** You don't need to type spaces when using **Swype**; just lift your finger between words, and the space will be automatically added.

If you find that you're lost using **Swype**, you can find a built-in tips and tutorial module. Just long-press the **Swype** button on the lower-right corner to access this tutorial. You can press the **Back Arrow** or **Forward Arrow** to navigate through the tips or tutorial, and you press the **Red X** icon on the upper-right corner to end the tutorial.

Word Suggestions

Both **Swype** and standard Android keyboards will offer suggestions as you type in order to speed up your word entry. In **Swype**, the suggestions appear in the form of a word choice window; and in the Android virtual keyboard, suggestions appear just above the keyboard, as shown in Figure 3–4. Tap the correct word suggestion to select it, and Android will type it on the screen for you. Next, just move on to the next word.

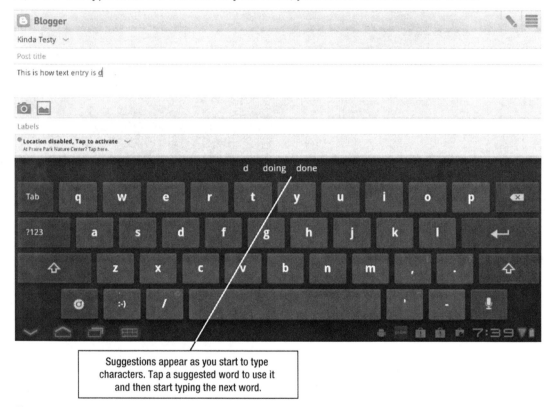

Suggestions appear as you start to type characters. Tap a suggested word to use it and then start typing the next word.

Figure 3–4. *Honeycomb word suggestions appear above the keyboard*

If the first suggestion in **Swype** is the correct word, you don't need to specifically select it. Instead, simply pick up your finger and move to the next word. The standard Honeycomb virtual keyboard is similar, except that the suggestions are listed alphabetically. If the underlined word suggestion is the correct choice, you don't need to select it—simply tap the **Spacebar** key and start typing the next word.

NOTE: You can turn off suggestions or make them invisible, so that your typing is auto-corrected as you go. If you're not seeing any suggestions as you type, you can change your settings to get them back. See the "Input Settings" section later in this chapter for more information on how to change this setting.

User Dictionary

Android tablets come with a built-in dictionary. It's used to make suggestions and correct typos as you type, but it doesn't know about every word you use.

One of the first things I like to do with a new device is add "Marziah" to the user dictionary, so my name doesn't get autocorrected to *March*, *Maryland*, or *Maria*; and so I don't have to type the entire thing out in order to write it. Maybe you also have an unusual name, or you use an acronym at work that throws off the word suggestions. Follow these steps to add a word to the user dictionary in Honeycomb, as shown in Figure 3–5:

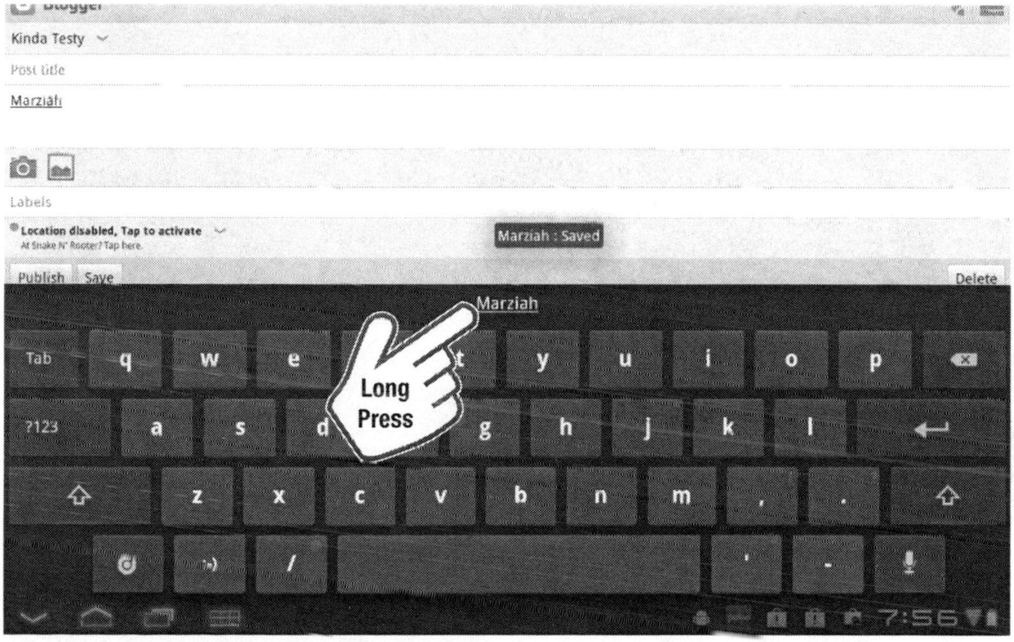

Figure 3–5. *Adding words to the user dictionary*

1. Type out the word on your tablet, with no spaces.

2. The word suggestions above the keyboard should include the word you've just typed. Long-press on the word in the suggestions area.

3. You should see a message saying that the word was "saved." This means it was added to the user dictionary.

> **TIP:** If you ever want to check the user dictionary, whether to verify that you've added a word or to remove any words that you've accidentally added, go to **Settings ➤ Language and Input ➤ User dictionary**. You can't add words from this menu, but you can remove undesired words by tapping on the **Red X** icon to the right of the word.

Copy, Cut, and Paste

Long Press within the text entry area until the **Text selection** menu appears at the top of the screen.

Now that you're reasonably fast at typing and have a user dictionary full of words, it's time to save even more data entry time. You can copy and paste between documents or even between apps.

The key to doing any copy and pasting in Honeycomb is simply to long-press in a text entry area. This will invoke the green **Text selection** menu on the top of the screen, as shown on left.

You'll also see an insertion point or two selection points, depending on whether you've already copied some text.

Once you've invoked the **Text selection** menu, you need to either select some text or select an insertion point to paste some text. Figure 3–6 illustrates the concept.

Follow these steps to copy and paste some text in Honeycomb:

1. Long-press in a text entry area until you see the **Text selection** menu.

2. Slide the start and end points around the word or words you wish to copy. The text you've selected will be highlighted in green.

3. Tap **Cut** if you want to copy and remove the text from the current location; tap **Copy** if you just want to copy it.

4. Navigate to the place where you want to insert your text. It can be in the same document, in another document, or even in another app.

5. Long-press to invoke the text entry area.

6. Because you have an item in your clipboard, you'll see an insertion point by default and a **Paste** button will appear above the insertion point. Tap It and your text will be pasted into the selected insertion point.

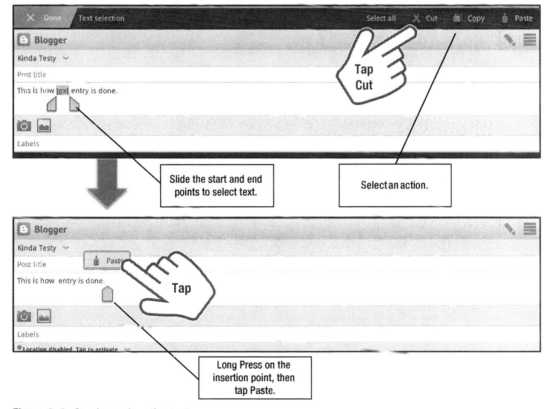

Figure 3–6. *Copying and pasting text*

Input Settings

There's one key left to discuss: the **Keyboard Settings** button. That's the odd looking key near

the bottom left of the virtual keyboard. ▨ Tap this button once, and you'll see a small screen that allows you to choose between **Android keyboard settings** and **Input Languages**. If you're always typing in English, there's no need to worry about the language; however, if you're using more than one language or more than one keyboard, you can use this option to switch to an international keyboard on the fly.

> ▦ Input options
>
> Input languages
>
> Android keyboard settings
>
> Cancel

If you long-press the **Keyboard Settings** key, it will skip the small dialog box and assume you want to go directly to **Android keyboard settings**.

The **Android keyboard settings** options include one that lets you dictate whether touching keys makes a sound. This might be handy if you're using all ten fingers, but it might be annoying if you're taking notes during a business meeting. You can also change your preferences for auto-correction, auto-capitalization, and whether you can see suggestions.

Follow these steps to turn on visible suggestions:

1. Tap any text entry area to pull up the Android keyboard.

2. Long-press the **Keyboard Settings** button.

3. Tap the option labeled **Show correction suggestions**.

4. Your three choices are **Always show**, **Show on portrait mode**, and **Always hide**. Tap **Always show** or **Show on portrait mode**, depending on your preference.

5. You'll automatically return to the keyboard settings area.

The auto-correction option allows you to decide how aggressively you want your words to be auto-corrected. You can turn it off if you find it causing more errors than it fixes, or you can set it at **aggressive** if you find it really helpful. In most cases, the **moderate** setting should be fine.

Voice Actions

OK, you know your way around the keyboard. But wouldn't it be faster if your tablet could just take dictation? It can. There's a small caveat, however. Voice command isn't perfect, so you'll still end up having to type every once in a while to correct a few mistakes. That said, it's still pretty good.

If you want to use your voice instead of your keyboard, tap the **Microphone** button on the keyboard.

You should see a screen resembling the one on the right that prompts you to **Speak now.** Speak a short phrase into your tablet's microphone or a microphone-enabled headset. Your words will be interpreted by Google's voice recognition technology, and your tablet will attempt to type what you've just said.

You may need to clean up anything that was misunderstood by using the keyboard.

Now you can take this feature to the next level. Tap the **Microphone** key on the **Google Search** widget on the top left of your **Home** screen. By default, the words you say here will lead to a Google search; however, some words will trigger a different response. These are called *Voice Actions*. The words in bold in the examples that follow indicate Voice Actions.

Say "**Navigate to** Washington, D.C" and you'll see something similar to the image on the left, which will pull up Google Maps and give you navigation directions to Washington, D.C.

Now try saying, "**Send email to** [someone on your contact list]." You can even get more specific and include a subject and then body message; however, it's usually easier to wait for Gmail to launch and then dictate the message.

Next, send a note to yourself by saying, "**Note to self:** Buy more raisins at grocery store."

Or, you could play music by saying, "**Listen to** Moonlight Sonata."

Google is adding more Voice Actions all the time, and these commands usually involve easy-to-guess natural language. So if you think a term should be a Voice Action, try saying it.

Search

It just wouldn't be a Google-designed OS if it didn't search. You can use the **Browser** app to search the Web using Google. However, there's another way to do it.

Honeycomb tablets by default have a **Google Search** widget on the upper-left corner of the **Home** screen. You can use this to search the Web or search through your contacts, calendar entries, apps, and more.

As you start typing, your tablet will make suggestions from all the stored content on your device. The image on the right shows the possibilities for just "an." Notice how many of those suggestions are from books stored in the Kindle Reader and how many of them are apps.

Tap a word suggestion from the column on the left or tap an app or document suggestion on the right to launch it. Tap the item (with the **Star** icon) on the top of that list to do a quick Web search.

> **NOTE:** Some tablets may have Bing or other search engines installed by default. You can usually override this by downloading the **Google Search** app, but you can't delete the **Bing** app.

Chapter 4

Syncing with Your Google Account

In order to use an Android tablet, you really should have a Google Account. A Google Account is the username and password you use for most Google services, including Gmail. Fire and Nook tablets are exceptions to this rule and don't use Google Accounts.They use Barnes & Noble or Amazon accounts instead.

You *can* use your tablet without a Google Account, but you'll miss out on some of the best cloud-based features of Android. You can still check your work email and use non-Google accounts on your Android tablet, so you don't need to give those up in order to get a Google Account. When you activate a new Android tablet, setting up a Google Account is one of the first things you'll do, as described in Chapter 2: "Getting Started."

Your Google Account is your default contact list, email, and calendar on your tablet. You can add other services, like Twitter, Facebook, and Exchange email; however, by default all the new contacts you create sync with Google.

One of the driving forces behind Google and Android is the concept of *cloud computing*. What this means is that, rather than rely on a single computer, nearly everything at Google is driven by a bank of servers on the Internet—*in the cloud*.

When you send Gmail messages, make Google Calendar entries, or add contacts to your Google Contact list, that information is available on your tablet, your Android phone, and on any computer you connect to the Internet with, as long as you sync it with Google.

Activating Your Google Account

You have three basic choices when selecting a Google account to use, as shown in Figure 4–1. You can use a Google Account you've already created, you can create one when you first activate your new tablet, or you can skip that process and add a Google Account later. Once you've activated your tablet, you can also go back and add or create multiple Google Accounts; so if you have one email for home and another for work, it's no problem.

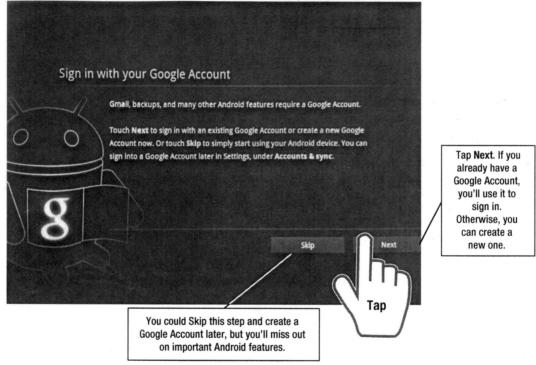

Figure 4–1. *Register for a Google Account when you register your tablet*

When you first activate your tablet, you'll face two more choices that will affect how your tablet works with your Google Account. The first choice, shown in Figure 4–2, is whether to allow Google to back up and restore data using the information from your Google Account.

What does this mean? If you've logged into Google and stored contacts, sent Gmail messages, or created events in Google Calendar, you'll get that information on your phone. However, the real magic happens if you own an Android phone or another tablet. In that case, restoring from your Google Account means that your tablet will start downloading copies of the compatible apps you've installed on your other device.

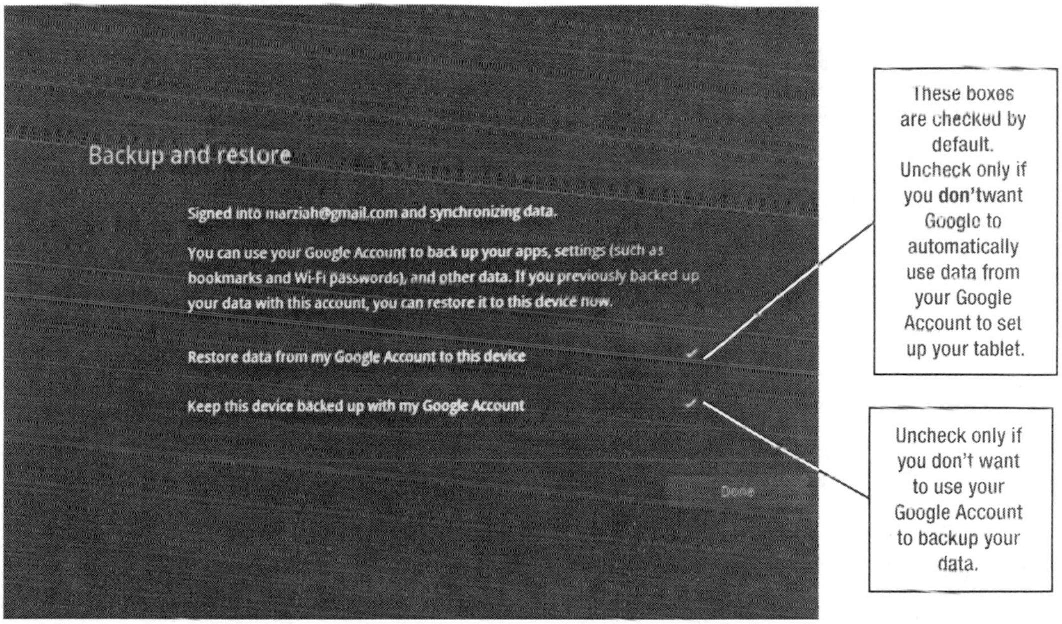

Backup and restore

Signed into marziah@gmail.com and synchronizing data.

You can use your Google Account to back up your apps, settings (such as bookmarks and Wi-Fi passwords), and other data. If you previously backed up your data with this account, you can restore it to this device now.

Restore data from my Google Account to this device

Keep this device backed up with my Google Account

These boxes are checked by default. Uncheck only if you **don't** want Google to automatically use data from your Google Account to set up your tablet.

Uncheck only if you don't want to use your Google Account to backup your data.

Figure 4-2. *Back up and restore settings*

The second choice is whether to allow Google to use your device to track your location. The iPhone 4 ran into trouble for tracking a user's location without asking and storing it from the time of the phone's activation. Android devices track locations, too, but they ask permission, as shown in Figure 4-3.

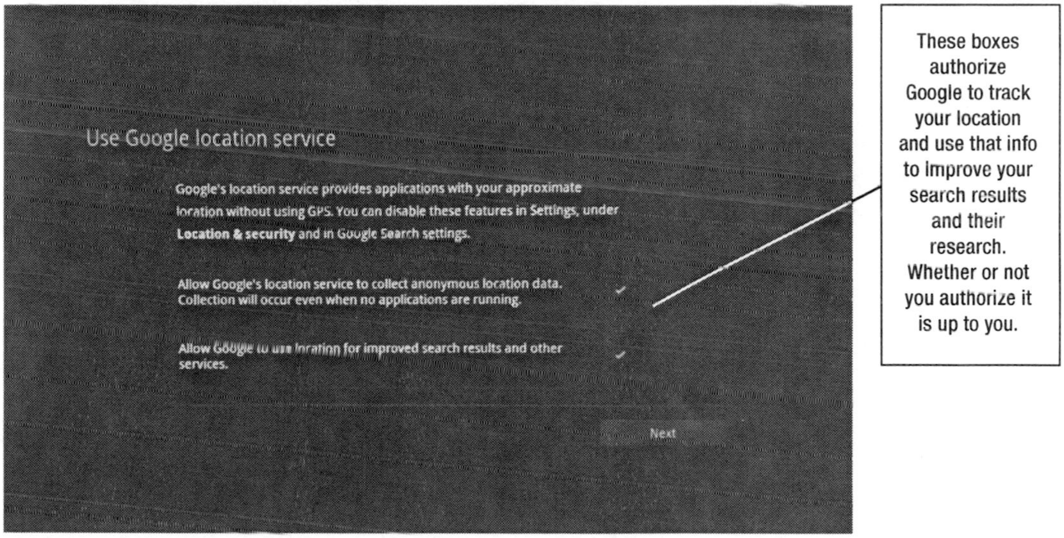

Use Google location service

Google's location service provides applications with your approximate location without using GPS. You can disable these features in Settings, under **Location & security** and in Google Search settings.

Allow Google's location service to collect anonymous location data. Collection will occur even when no applications are running.

Allow Google to use location for improved search results and other services.

These boxes authorize Google to track your location and use that info to improve your search results and their research. Whether or not you authorize it is up to you.

Figure 4-3. *Granting permission to use location services*

By default, both options are checked; however, you can disable one or the other if you're uncomfortable. The first option is probably the most lenient in terms of privacy: "Allow Google's location service to collect anonymous location data. Collection will occur even when no applications are running." It all comes down to whether you trust Google to use your location data wisely.

The second option is whether to allow Google to use your location to improve search results. This means that, when you search for a product or location, Google can tell you if it's nearby.

Adding a Google Account

Once you've set up your tablet, how do you add another Google Account? Figure 4–4 shows the steps required to add a Google Account on Honeycomb tablets.

Follow these steps to add a Google Account:

1. Tap the **Notification** bar on the bottom right of the **Home** screen.

2. Tap the **Settings** button, which will bring up the quick **Settings** menu.

3. Tap the **Settings** button again to bring up the full **Settings** menu.

4. Tap **Accounts & Sync.**

5. Tap the **Add account** button in the upper-right corner of the screen.

6. You'll see a screen asking what type of account you'd like to add. In this case, choose **Google.**

7. From here, you can either enter your existing Google Account information or create a new account. If your desired username isn't available, Google will suggest something similar that is.

CAUTION: Keep in mind that bad guys can use Google to find obvious answers about you, so avoid questions like your city of birth or high school. You could also make up an answer to these questions that you'll remember, but strangers can't research.

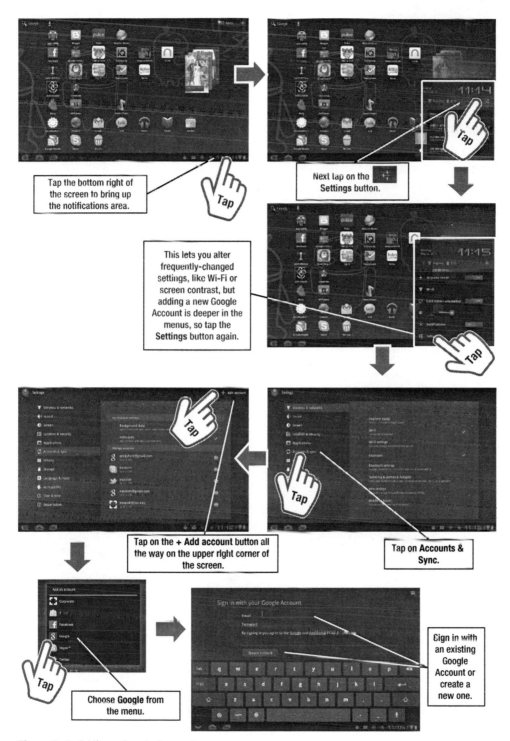

Tap the bottom right of the screen to bring up the notifications area.

Next tap on the Settings button.

This lets you alter frequently-changed settings, like Wi-Fi or screen contrast, but adding a new Google Account is deeper in the menus, so tap the **Settings** button again.

Tap on the **+ Add account** button all the way on the upper right corner of the screen.

Tap on **Accounts & Sync.**

Choose **Google** from the menu.

Sign in with an existing Google Account or create a new one.

Figure 4–4. *Adding a Google Account*

Two Step Verification

One option for setting up a new Google Account is to use *two-step verification*. This is a process where Google sends you a verification code by text message. You'll have to do this once every 30 days. It's more secure because it requires that you have access to your phone, as well as your username and password. You can download the Google Authenticator from the Android Market here: `http://goo.gl/XNup1`.

It's more secure, but as with many security measures, it's also less convenient. It's your choice whether to use it.

Adding Another Google Account: the Short Way

I showed you the long method for adding accounts, and that will work with all sorts of accounts, including Twitter, Facebook, and Exchange. Follow these steps to add a shortcut for Gmail accounts (see Figure 4–5):

1. Launch **Gmail** by clicking its app icon.

2. Tap the **Menu** button in the upper-right corner and select **Settings.**

3. Tap **Add account** in the upper-right corner.

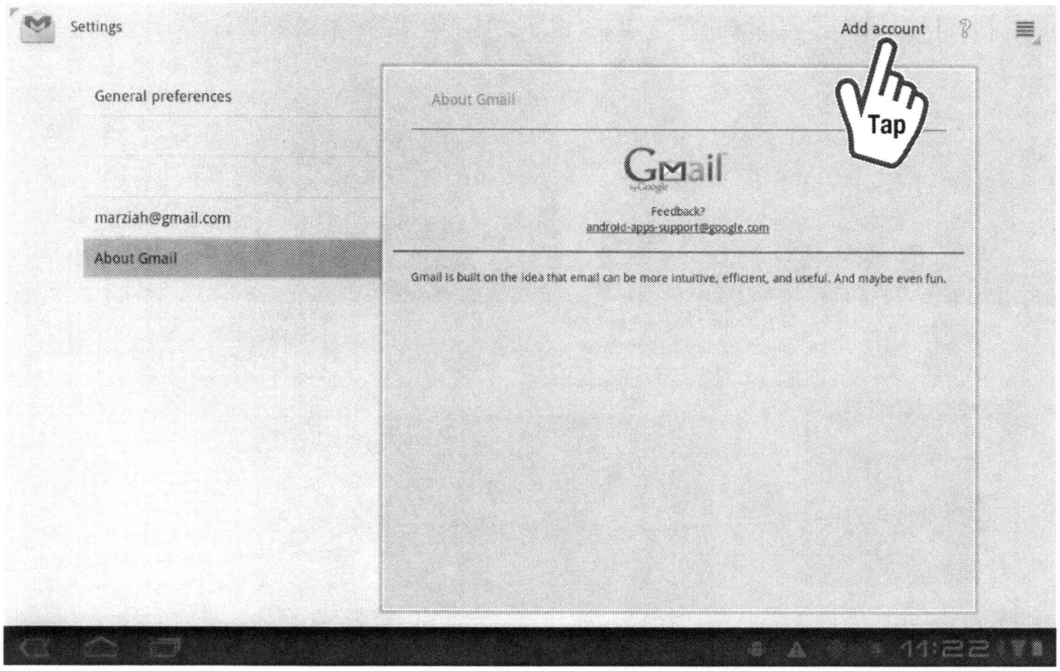

Figure 4–5. *Adding another Gmail account*

Google Account Services

Your Google Account is good for more than just Gmail, and you can fine-tune the services you use with each account.

If you purchase apps in the Android Market, you'll use your Google Account and **Google Checkout** to complete the transaction. The default email account on your tablet Is Gmail, and the default calendar is Google Calendar.

Here are a few of the Google services you'll get to know as you use your tablet:

Gmail: Gmail is a free Web-based email service, arguably the best free email service out there. I'll go over Gmail in more detail in a later chapter.

Google Voice: Google Voice is a service that allows you to use a single phone number to forward your calls, create a visual voicemail message with speech-to-text, and make low cost international long distance calls. It's not officially available on tablets as an app; however, you can use the service on the Web to check your messages.

Google Calendar: Google Calendar works a bit differently from Outlook's calendar. You have standard features like events and invitations, but Google Calendar is meant to be even more collaborative. You manage Google Calendar by adding multiple *calendars* and sharing them with others. For instance, you can have a calendar you allow colleagues to see but not edit, a calendar team members can all edit, and another calendar of fully public events.

Google Maps: You're probably already familiar with this mapping service. Google Maps is the engine behind most of your phone's geographically sensitive apps. Not only can Google Maps give you driving directions, but it can provide you with walking and public transport directions. This is invaluable when you're on the road.

Google Checkout: Google Checkout is a tool for buyers and merchants to complete credit card transactions without revealing the credit card info to the merchant. It's a competitor to PayPal. You'll need to set up an account with credit card information if you want to purchase apps from the Android Market.

Picasa: Picasa Web Albums is Google's answer to Flickr. If you want to upload pictures from your phone to the Web, this is the default location for sharing on most tablets. You may want to set up your account with albums and public or private sharing permissions if you need to share photos as part of your job. It's more efficient to upload photos to Picasa than it is to send them as email attachments, though you can do both. Picasa also has a desktop program you can use for syncing and editing photos.

Picnik: Picnik is an online photo-editing suite. You can use either the free version or pay for extra features with the premium edition ($25 per year). It can take photos directly from Picasa Web Albums, Flickr, or Photobucket. Once you've finished editing a picture, you can save it back to your online photo album.

There's no Android app for Picnik yet, but it runs on Honeycomb tablets in the Web browser, and it seems ready-made for tablet users who want to paint with their fingertips.

Blogger: Blogger is Google's blogging service. You can create ad-free blogs on Blogger for no charge. And there's even a specialized app for tablets, which means you can tap out blog posts with pictures and video from a single device.

Google Books: **Google Books** is Google's e-book reading app and website. You're not limited to **Google Books**, but the app is installed by default on standard Honeycomb tablets, and the **Google eBook Market** icon is prominently featured on your tablet.

 **YouTube:** If you have any reason to take quick videos with your tablet, set up a YouTube account with your preferred username beforehand. You can upload videos directly instead of offloading them to your desktop computer first. You can also use a YouTube account to comment, rate, and add videos to playlists.

Getting Contacts from Your Old Planner to Google

If you're switching from your laptop to a tablet, you'll need to get your data transferred. The secret is to use Google wherever possible. If you sync the data with Google, you can get it on your tablet.

> **NOTE**: If you can get the data to Google Contacts at www.google.com/contacts, it will appear on your phone. You can go through your phone and add contacts directly.

Follow these steps to sync your data from Outlook or the Apple Address Book:

1. Export your contacts as a CSV or vCard file.

2. Use the import link in the upper-right corner of **Google Contacts**, as shown in Figure 4–6.

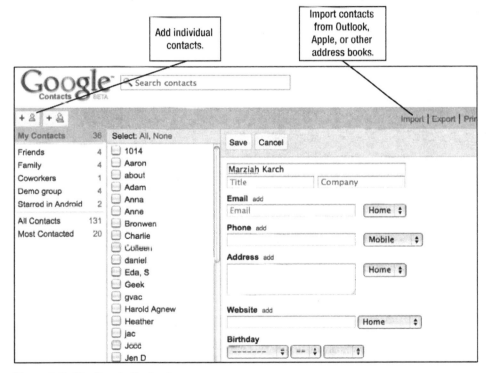

Figure 4–6. *The Google Contacts app*

Fine Tuning Your Tablet Sync

When you add Google Accounts, you choose how much information you want to sync, as shown in Figure 4–7. You may not want to check your work mail on your tablet; or you may want to read your email, but ignore the contact list. It's your choice.

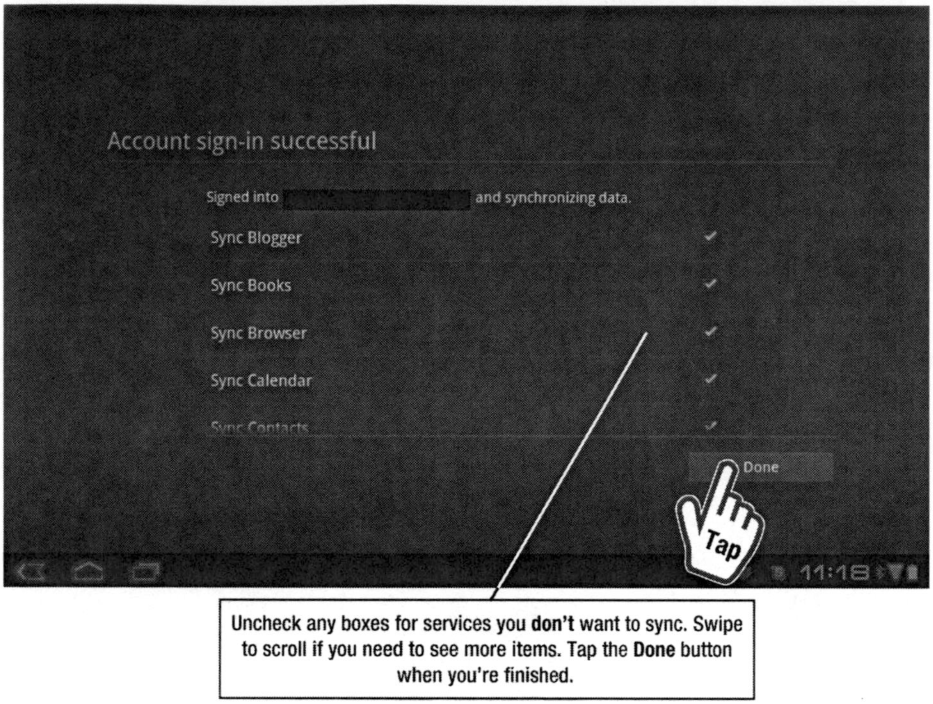

Uncheck any boxes for services you **don't** want to sync. Swipe to scroll if you need to see more items. Tap the **Done** button when you're finished.

Figure 4–7. *Choosing syncing services with Google Accounts*

You'll be asked to verify your syncing options whenever you add or create a Google Account, but you can also go through and change them at any time. Follow these steps to change your settings for a given account:

1. Tap the **Notification** bar in the bottom-right corner of the **Home** screen.

2. Tap **Settings** twice, just as you do to add an account.

3. Navigate to **Accounts & Sync** in the **Settings** menu.

4. Click the account you'd like to modify.

Now that you've set up your Google Accounts, it's time to explore other types of accounts in the next chapter.

Chapter 5

Syncing with Other Accounts

In Chapter 4, you learned how to sync with your Google Account. In this chapter, I'll cover syncing with other accounts. Gmail is fantastic, but there's a good chance that your work email uses Exchange. In this chapter, I won't go into the details for using your tablet's email or social networking apps; instead, I'll discuss how you can sync your tablet with Exchange email and other non-Google accounts.

Adding an Account

You can add Exchange, Twitter, Skype, POP3 email, and many other account types like Hotmail and Yahoo! using the same process described in Chapter 4. The process for adding accounts is very similar. The only significant difference is what account information you need to provide. Follow these steps to get to the **Accounts & Sync** area of your tablet preferences and add an account (see Figure 5–1):

1. Tap the **Notification** bar on the bottom right of the **Home** screen.

2. Tap the **Settings** button, which will bring up the quick settings.

3. Tap the **Settings** button again to bring up the full settings menu.

4. Tap **Accounts & Sync.**

5. Tap the **Add account** button on the upper-right corner of the screen.

6. You'll see a screen asking what type of account you'd like to add. You may see different choices, depending on the type of tablet you own and the apps you have installed. For instance, if you have the **Skype** app installed, you'll see the option to add a Skype account.

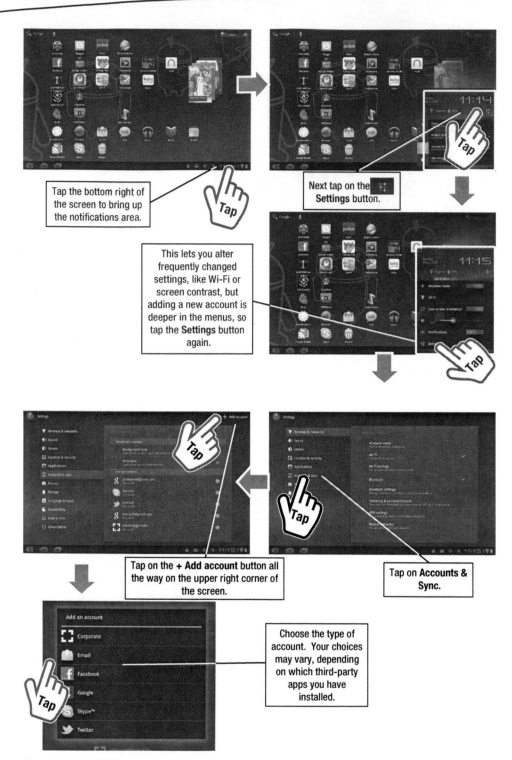

Tap the bottom right of the screen to bring up the notifications area.

Next tap on the Settings button.

This lets you alter frequently changed settings, like Wi-Fi or screen contrast, but adding a new account is deeper in the menus, so tap the **Settings** button again.

Tap on the **+ Add account** button all the way on the upper right corner of the screen.

Tap on **Accounts & Sync.**

Choose the type of account. Your choices may vary, depending on which third-party apps you have installed.

Figure 5–1. *Adding an account*

Syncing with Exchange Email Accounts

If your workplace uses **Google Apps for Business**, you can add your business email just like any other Google Account.

However, many work email accounts are hosted on Microsoft Exchange. Android Honeycomb tablets are capable of syncing with Exchange accounts and can handle corporate provisioning and other security measures, as long as your workplace allows you to log in with Android devices.

To add an Exchange email account, go through the steps described in Figure 5–1 to add an account, and then select either **Email** or **Corporate**, if available. The only difference when you add a corporate account from a Honeycomb tablet is that you need to bypass the screen asking you what type of account you're adding (see Figure 5–2).

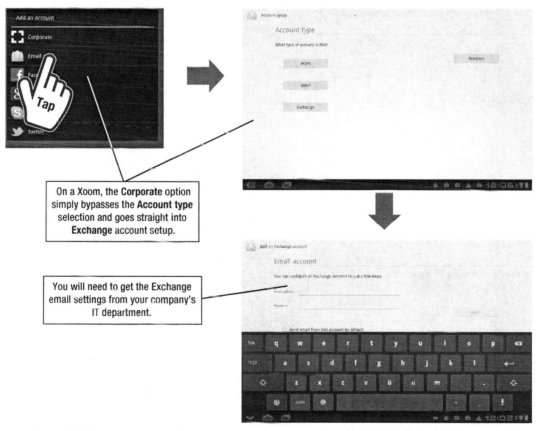

On a Xoom, the **Corporate** option simply bypasses the **Account type** selection and goes straight into **Exchange** account setup.

You will need to get the Exchange email settings from your company's IT department.

Figure 5–2. *Adding a corporate email account*

You can also get to this screen through the **Email** app. The first time you launch the **Email** app, it will prompt you to set up an email account (assuming you haven't already added one). Otherwise, you can use the same steps covered for adding Gmail in Chapter 4 to set up an Exchange account:

1. Launch the **Email** app by clicking its app icon.

2. Tap the **Menu** button on the upper-right corner and select **Settings.**

3. Tap **Add account** on the upper-right corner.

4. Finally, enter the settings for your Exchange account, as specified by your employer.

Security Warnings

During the process of setting up your corporate email account, you may see some security warnings (see Figure 5–3).

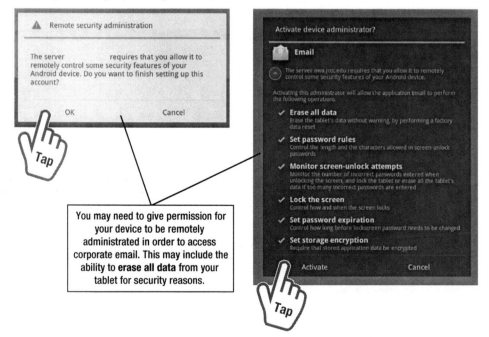

You may need to give permission for your device to be remotely administrated in order to access corporate email. This may include the ability to **erase all data** from your tablet for security reasons.

Figure 5–3. *Giving permission to allow device administration*

In order to use corporate email on mobile devices—including tablets—many companies require that you adhere to and accept certain security measures. These measures can include specified password lengths, encrypted storage, screen locks, and even remote data wipes. You'll be warned that remote administrators can wipe all the data from your tablet, essentially performing a *factory data reset* and returning the tablet to the same state it was in when you first purchased it.

Don't panic. These security measures are in place in case your tablet is stolen, so valuable company emails are not stolen with it. Even if the worst happens and your tablet is reset, you won't lose everything. Your email, calendar, contact, and purchased app records are stored *in the cloud* (on the Internet). Pictures and movies you've synced with Picasa or uploaded to photo sharing sites will still be available, although you'll lose any pictures that were stored only on your tablet. The only data that will be gone for good is data that was only stored on the device itself and not in the cloud.

Once you accept the security settings, you'll see a message confirming that you've set up your account. Press the **Next** button, and you can start reading your email.

> Account setup
>
> ### Your account is set up, and email is on its way!
>
> Give this account a name (optional)
>
> _____
>
> Next

Adding Other Email Accounts

You can use the **Email** app to add an Exchange account, but you can also add POP and IMAP email accounts. Typically, the latter email account types are ones that your Internet service provider issues (i.e., they are personal, not corporate email accounts).

To choose an email account type other than Exchange, select the appropriate account type and enter the settings from your service provider.

Removing an Email Account

If you leave your job, you'll want to remove your Exchange email account; this enables you to avoid the whole remote data wiping scenario:

1. Launch the **Email** program by clicking its app icon.

2. Tap the **Menu** button on the upper-right corner and select **Settings.**

3. Scroll down by swiping your finger and tapping **Remove account.**

You can also use the preceding approach to remove other email accounts when you no longer need them (Figure 5–4 shows the **Remove account** button).

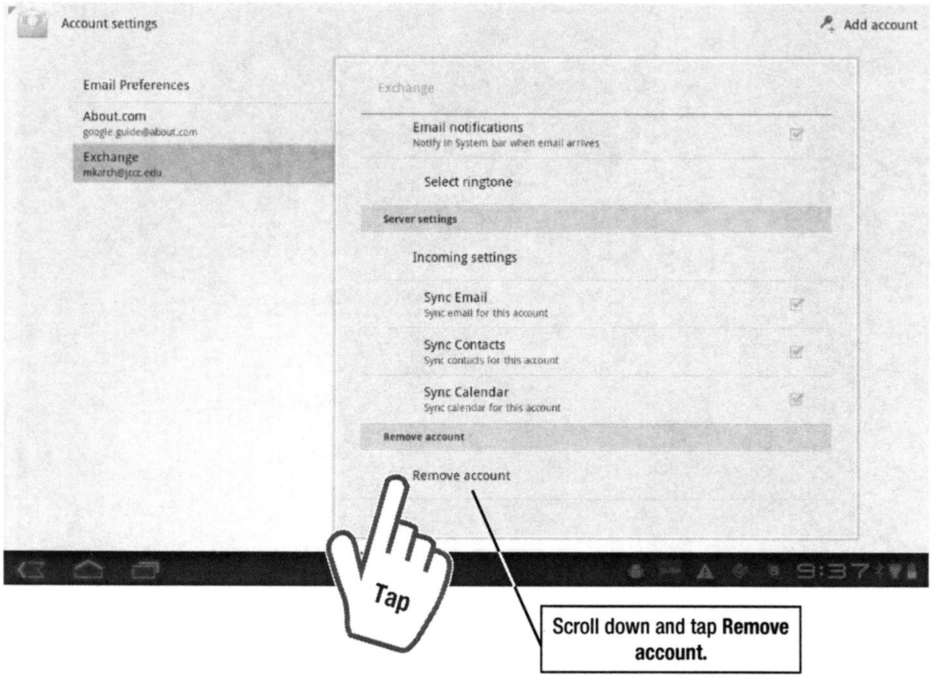

Figure 5–4. *Removing an email account*

Data Syncing Settings

When you add an account—whether it's Twitter, Facebook, Exchange, or Gmail—you'll have a few choices to make about what data syncs with your tablet and how often. Follow these steps to get to **Accounts & Sync**; this feature enables you to adjust your syncing options:

1. Tap the **Notification bar** on the bottom right of the **Home** screen.

2. Tap the **Settings** button, which will bring up the quick settings.

3. Tap the **Settings** button again to bring up the full settings menu.

4. Tap **Accounts & Sync.**

The first two choices are under **General sync settings**, and they're both enabled by default: **Background data** and **Auto-sync**.

The **Background data** option determines whether your applications can sync in the background while you're using other apps or even when you're not using the tablet at all. If you disable this feature, some apps will still sync in the background, but most will not. Disabling this option will save battery life, but it will also make it take longer to use some apps because they'll have to sync data as soon as you launch them.

The second choice, **Auto-sync**, allows apps to fetch data on the schedule that the app developer has determined. Disabling this option means that you'll have to manually request a data sync by tapping the **Sync refresh** button next to the account.

> **NOTE:** General settings apply to all accounts.

If you want to change the sync settings for a specific app, tap the name of that app under **Manage accounts**, as shown in Figure 5–5.

Tap to manage the syncing options on an account.

Figure 5–5. *Managing your syncing options*

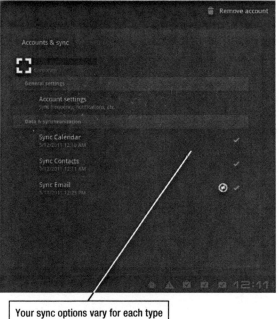

Your sync options vary for each type of account. Tap the checkboxes to enable or disable syncing.

What you see will depend on the type of account you've selected. The only syncing option for a Skype account is whether it syncs your contacts. Exchange accounts, as shown on the left, can sync Email, Calendar, and Contact information. You can individually enable or disable the sync options one-by-one. If you're using a different method to sync your calendar with Google Calendar, you may want to disable calendar sync, for instance.

You may see the option on the upper right to **Remove account**. While that option works fine for most accounts, *do not use it to remove Exchange accounts*.

Using this option doesn't cleanly remove an Exchange email account. Removing an Exchange account from the **Email** app itself (as shown earlier) is the best way to go.

Alternative Syncing Apps

You may have noticed that, while your calendar and contact info can sync with an Exchange account, your notes and tasks cannot.

Third-party apps, like **Nitrodesk TouchDown** and **CompanionLink DejaOffice**, can extend your tablet's syncing power. Both apps are commercially sold through the Android Market and other app stores.

TouchDown offers Exchange task syncing, in addition to the other standard options offered in Android 2.2 and later.

DejaOffice is a great choice for Galaxy Tab owners. It enables you to sync various items with Exchange, including tasks and notes. You can also change the display to represent the Getting Things Done or Franklin Covey task organization systems.

Chapter 6

Understanding Connection: Wi-Fi, 3G, and 4G

One of the best features of an Android tablet is its ability to connect to the Internet. Going online doesn't just mean using the built-in Web browser. When you use many apps, add contacts, save your email, and do a wide variety of other activities on your tablet, you're going to use data.

All tablets being sold at the time of writing are capable of Wi-Fi connections. Some tablets are also capable of using mobile data, just like a smartphone. Of those mobile-capable tablets, some use 3G, some are capable of 4G, but none of them work across *all* 3G and 4G networks.

In this chapter, we'll explain how to get online with your tablet. We'll also go over the different ways tablets can access data, as well as how to get connected without draining your battery.

Does Your Tablet Have a Data Plan?

Many Android tablets are sold as Wi-Fi only devices. On these devices, you use whatever Wi-Fi network you use for your laptops; and when you're out of Wi-Fi range, you can't connect to the Internet. Even tablets that are sold with 3G or 4G data access can be used with Wi-Fi networks. In fact, if you don't purchase separate data access from a cell phone service provider, that's your only option.

Some tablets, such as the T-Mobile G-Slate, allow you to buy short-term, pre-paid data plans just as you would on a 3G iPad. Others, such as the Motorola Xoom (at the time of writing), either don't offer pre-paid monthly service or make it prohibitively expensive. So far, all the tablets with 3G/4G data plans have a contract option that gives you a discount on the purchase price of the device, while also locking you into a monthly data contract for two years—mirroring the model used for most cell phones.

> **NOTE**: If your tablet didn't come with at least 3G access, you *can't* add it later. The Motorola Xoom shipped with 3G-only access, but users can upgrade the connection to 4G. However, most tablets cannot be upgraded in this way.

What Does 3G or 4G Mean?

Back when "mobile" meant your very expensive phone fit inside a giant briefcase, the cell phone technology used an analog signal to carry your voice to and from the cell tower. That analog signal was retroactively named *1G*, or first generation.

The next stop along the way was *2G*, which uses a digital signal instead of an analog signal. It also allows you to send data instead of just voice. 2G networks are still in use today, especially in rural areas, although cell carriers have worked hard to upgrade 2G towers to *3G*, or third generation. 3G technologies are significantly faster than 2G ones, but they're still slower than a strong Wi-Fi connection.

The next generation, *4G,* promises ultrafast speeds and improved technology. 4G networks are still in the process of being rolled out. And at this point, no carrier has completely upgraded its networks. There are three competing technologies—*LTE*, *HSPA+*, and *WiMAX* (all of which are marketed as 4G)—but all of these are actually transitional steps toward *LTE-Advanced* and *WiMAX 2* networks. At this point, it looks like LTE Advanced will be the stronger technology, and even companies invested in WiMAX may move towards LTE Advanced instead.

Your speed will depend on the type of network you're using, how close you are to the tower, and how many other users are on the network. However, 4G is capable of speeds several times faster than 3G networks, and LTE Advanced could rival the speeds found on fiber optic networks. You'll also get faster speeds when you're standing still than you will when you're on the road because the cell towers won't have to negotiate passing your connection from one tower to the next.

CDMA and GSM

One of the reasons cell phones are so complicated in the U.S. is because competing technologies are used to deliver 2G and 3G signals. Verizon Wireless and Sprint use *CDMA* networks, while AT&T and T-Mobile (which are in acquisition negotiations at the time of writing) use *GSM*. Regional carriers vary, but many of them use CDMA.

There's no huge advantage or disadvantage between the two approaches. The speed is similar for both technologies. Aside from their incompatibility with each other, you'll notice a few other differences:

- GSM carriers use SIM cards. These are tiny cards that carry your identifying information for the network. If you switch devices, you just put your old SIM in your new device.

- CDMA carriers don't use SIM cards for their network. Your device is tracked internally, but that also means you'll never lose a SIM card.

- GSM is the more common standard in the rest of the world. Not all phones or tablets can travel internationally, but there's a better chance yours can if it uses a GSM signal.

More on LTE and WiMAX

LTE Advanced, which stands for *Long Term EvolutionAdvanced*, is the standard most carriers are moving toward. Aside from the speed benefits, one advantage of this approach is that mobile devices will all share a common standard that is backwards compatible. This makes it more likely mobile devices will be able to play nicely with each other and roam between former CDMA and GSM networks with ease.

The US is still years away from this happening, but this is why phone companies get excited about the possibilities of LTE Advanced.

WiMAX (*Worldwide Interoperability for Microwave Access)* is often called "Wi-Fi on steroids" because WiMAX can send a strong signal over long distances. To clarify, it's *like* Wi-Fi, but it isn't Wi-Fi. You can't connect to a WiMAX network without a WiMAX capable tablet, phone, or modem.

Sprint and Google are both investors in Clearwire, a company that markets WiMAX access to cities; however, even Clearwire has been exploring LTE, and many analysts think WiMAX will eventually be replaced with LTE Advanced.

If your tablet didn't come with the capability to use 4G, you may be able to buy a portable WiMAX or LTE hotspot.

The Notifications Bar

The **Notifications** bar on the bottom of your screen shows the status of your connection. There will be some variation in what you see, depending on what type of data connection you have and what version of Android your tablet uses. Figure 6–1 shows some sample notifications.

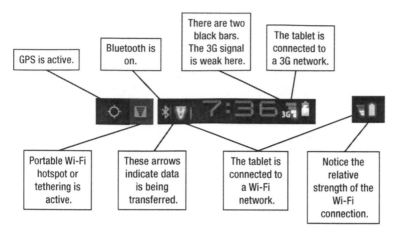

Figure 6–1. *Sample status bar notifications*

Wi-Fi

Wi-Fi signals are fast, easy, and avoid the data limit fees charged by some carriers.

Some book stores, fast food chains, and restaurants offer free Wi-Fi access to anyone within range of the signal. Connecting is easy. Your tablet will notify you that a network is available.

Tapping the **Notifications** bar on the bottom-right corner provides some quick options to start using the Internet (see Figure 6–2).

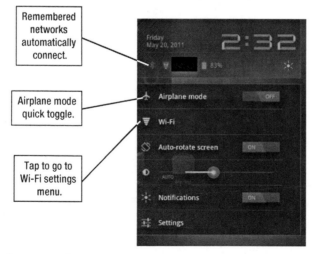

Figure 6–2. *Connecting to Wi-Fi*

> **NOTE:** On a lot of these "open" networks, you still have to open your Web browser and consent to the terms and conditions for the network. If your device says you're connected, but your apps give you connection errors, you can try launching the Web browser and connecting first.

Setting up a Private Wi-Fi Connection

You may want to set up a private network such as your home or workplace Wi-Fi. You can set up your network on a Honeycomb tablet by following these steps:

1. Tap the **Notifications** bar to make it expand.

2. Tap the Wi-Fi option.

3. This will bring up the **Wi-Fi settings** in the **Wireless & networks** settings menu. You'll see a history of every network you've connected to and all publicly broadcast networks that are in range. You can tap an in-range network and just enter the password (see Figure 6–3).

4. If you're adding a network that does not have a publicly broadcast SSID, you can add it by scrolling to the bottom of the history and tapping **Add Wi-Fi network.**

> **CAUTION:** If you're hoping to use an enterprise network that uses LEAP (a CISCO Wi-Fi protocol), you should be aware that Android doesn't fully support that standard, yet. However, you may have luck with a third-party app like **Full WiFi** or **Advanced LEAP**.

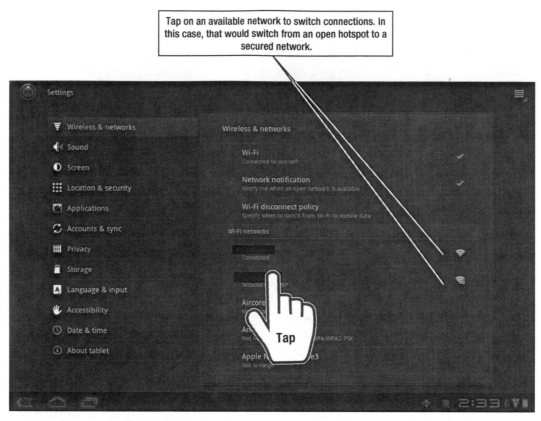

Figure 6–3. *Switching to a secure network*

Wi-Fi Security

A big consideration with Wi-Fi is security. If you're using an encrypted connection, this isn't as much of a problem. However, those convenient, open Wi-Fi access points at the coffee shop may in theory expose your tablet to unwanted eavesdropping through an exploit called the *man-in-the-middle attack*.

Wi-Fi security usually involves some sort of password protection to access the network. An older, less secure security method is WEP, while a more secure method is WPA or WPA2. Most personal networks, like your router at home, can be set to use WPA2-PSK (Pre-Shared Key). This is a fancy way of saying that you have to type in a password or passphrase to get access to the network.

> **CAUTION:** WEP is the oldest standard, but it's also the easiest to crack.

Businesses that want to sell or restrict access to their network use a form of WPA-enterprise. This type of connection usually requires you to log in when you open your first Web page, and it compares your username with a list of authorized users. In some cases, you don't actually have to log in, but you do have to click something to agree to the location's terms of service. This is also part of WPA security.

If you aren't required to log into anything, you don't at least need to click **OK** to agree to the access rules, and you don't need a password to get onto the network—chances are that you're using an open Wi-Fi access point. A skilled hacker may be able to intercept your signal.

Bluetooth

Bluetooth is a very short range technology meant as more of a wire replacement than a way to get onto the Internet. Bluetooth can be used to communicate with a wireless headset or keyboard; and in some cases, you can use Bluetooth to create a modem from your tablet to another device, like a laptop. However, you can't use Bluetooth to get to the Internet by itself.

GPS

GPS stands for *Global Positioning System*. It's one of the few acronyms in this chapter worth spelling out because the long name explains what it does. GPS triangulates your position through satellite signals. This isn't the only way your phone can tell where you are, but it's the most common method.

Whenever you use maps or tag your photos by location, the GPS signal is most often used. Android can also supplement this with the location of nearby cell towers and the location of any Wi-Fi networks you're using. However, plenty of apps require a GPS signal to tell you what movies are showing nearby or the location of the nearest Thai restaurant.

GPS activity is represented by what looks like a target symbol on the bottom of the screen (see Figure 6–1). Whenever you're using an app that senses your location (e.g., **Google Maps** or **Yelp**), you'll see the **GPS** symbol. As noted previously, there's also some variation in the **GPS** symbol used on different devices and versions of Android, so yours may look more like a satellite.

Creating a Hotspot

Mobile hotspot access is an add-on service for some tablets and phones. If you pay for such access (and sometimes even if you don't pay for it), then you can share your data connection between your tablet and your laptop or other devices. You can also *tether* devices together using a USB cable or your Bluetooth connection.

If you've got an Android phone, you can do the same in reverse and share your phone's data signal with your tablet, which creates a portable hotspot. The act of doing so is called *tethering*.

To turn on tethering, go to **Settings: Wireless & networks** and tap **Portable Wi-Fi hotspot** (see Figure 6–4). You'll immediately see a notice that tethering is on, and you can tap the notice to configure your hotspot. It's a good idea to do so.

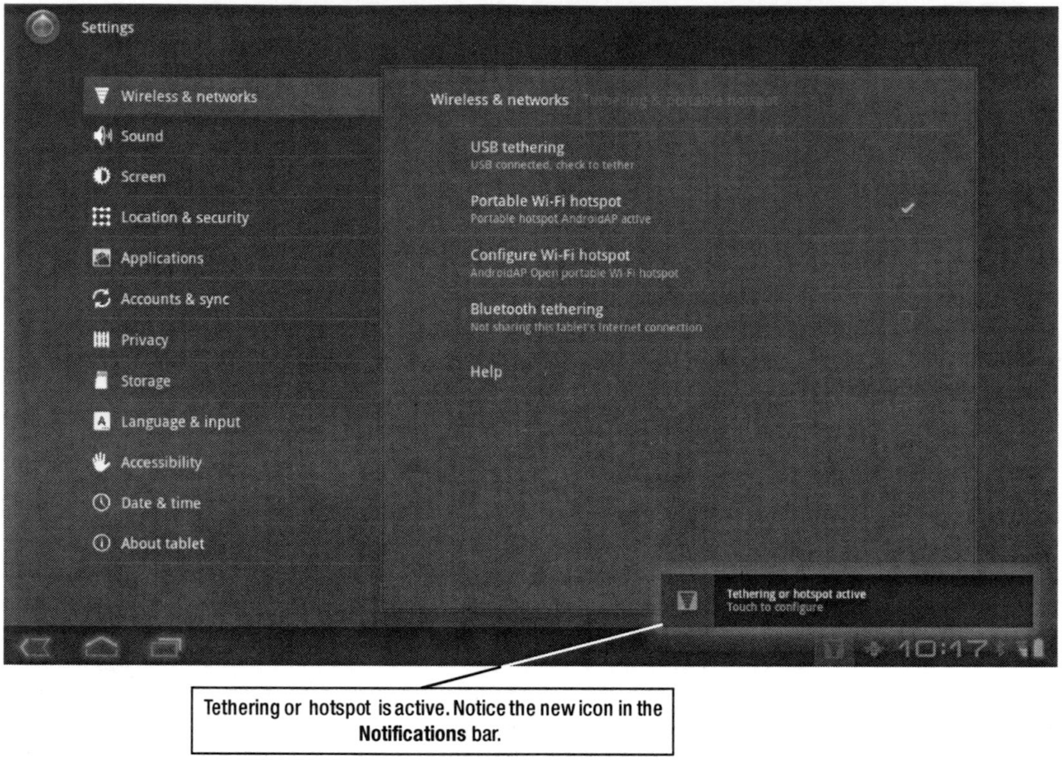

Tethering or hotspot is active. Notice the new icon in the **Notifications** bar.

Figure 6–4. *Creating a hotspot*

By default, your access point will be called *AndroidAP*, and the security will be open. If you feel like sharing your hotspot and data access with anyone and everyone who happens to be in range, have at it! However, in most cases, you'll want to make your access point a closed network.

Your best bet is to select **WPA2-PSK** and then specify a password, as shown in Figure 6–4. If you're having trouble typing a password out on the keyboard, check the box labeled **Show password**. This only makes the password visible on your tablet, and you can uncheck the option when you're done to avoid inadvertently revealing it to anyone else (see Figure 6–5).

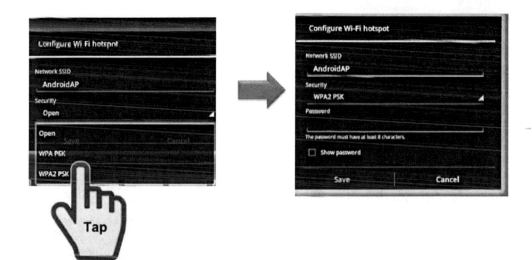

Figure 6–5. *Giving your hotspot a password*

You can connect your laptop or other device to this hotspot just as you would to any other Wi-Fi network. You can even connect more than one device, such as sharing your connection with a friend. However, the more devices you connect, the slower the speed.

TIP: Creating a Wi-Fi hotspot uses a lot of battery juice, so be sure to turn off your connection when you're done with it.

Troubleshooting Connections

The **Notifications** bar will indicate which types of signals you're using and the relative strengths of those signals, as shown in Figure 6–1. It will also show **Up-and-Down** arrows that indicate an active data transfer.

If you're having trouble, first check to make sure that you have an adequate signal and are using the network you intended to use. If you're using Wi-Fi, make sure you are correctly signed into the network. Sometimes that means opening your Web browser and tapping a checkbox to indicate that you consent to your hotspot's user agreement.

Roaming

When you wander outside the range of cell towers that belong to your carrier, you start roaming. You may be billed for roaming fees if roaming is not covered by your service plan.

By default, roaming should be set to **Off**; however, it might not hurt to double-check this setting. Follow these steps to turn off data roaming on your Honeycomb tablet and avoid roaming charges:

1. Tap **Settings** in the **Notifications** bar.

2. Tap **Settings** again.

3. Tap **Wireless & networks.**

4. Tap **Mobile networks** (see Figure 6–6.)

5. Deselect **Data roaming** if it's selected.

Figure 6–6. *Data roaming*

Managing Syncing

In addition to turning connections on and off, you can save power by controlling which accounts sync data and how often. Chapters 4 and 5 cover setting up Google and other accounts. In order to save batteries and data, turn off **Auto sync** and **Background sync** in the **Accounts & sync** area of the **Settings** menu.

Airplane Mode

If you're on an airplane, on a cruise ship, or in an area you know is roaming (or if you just want to shut off data for some reason), you may want to put your tablet into **Airplane** mode. **Airplane** mode means you will not get any connection at all, whether data, cell, or GPS.

Airplane mode is an easy two taps from the **Home** screen, as shown in Figure 6–2. Simply tap the **Notifications** bar and then tap the **Airplane** mode toggle.

VPN

VPN, or *Virtual Private Networks*, allows you to log into your workplace intranet and enjoy the security of your corporate firewall without having to be hardwired into the network. Some places require this in order to access Exchange email or view sensitive corporate files.

VPN is natively supported on your Android Honeycomb tablet, but this feature won't necessarily work with every VPN setup.

Follow these steps to log into VPN:

1. Go to the **Home** screen and then tap the **Settings** button.

2. Go to the **Settings: Wireless & network** settings.

3. Next, select **VPN settings**. If you've already configured a VPN, it will be available here.

4. Otherwise, you need to tap **add a VPN**.

You'll need to obtain the specific format and settings for your workplace. These settings include PPTP, L2TP, L2TP/IPSec with pre-shared key (PSK), and L2TP/IPSec CRT (certificate-based). If your workplace doesn't support one of these protocols, you'll need to work with your company's IT staff to see if there's any other way to log in securely.

VNC

VNC is a way to share screens remotely and control one device from another, even if that device runs on a different platform. If you leave your office or home computer on at all times and your office allows it, you can use VNC to check documents, email, or execute work tasks from wherever you are. VNC can be used with Macs, Windows, and Linux computers.

For VNC to be used securely, it should also be paired with VPN. There are several VNC clients available for Android. Check the specific client to make sure it is compatible with tablets.

Chapter 7

Personalizing Your Home Screen

There's a lot you can do with a tablet without leaving the **Home** screen. In Chapter 2: "Getting Started," you learned a little about the Android tablet's **Home** screen. In this chapter, you'll learn how to personalize the **Home** screen with interactive widgets, app icons, and live wallpapers.

> **NOTE:** This book focuses on Honeycomb features. If your tablet runs an earlier version of Android, your options might not look the same. You can still add app icons and widgets and change your wallpapers, but you won't be able to do so with Honeycomb's *holographic* interface.

Reviewing the Home Screen Interface

In Chapter 2, I introduced the Home screen interface (you can see its basic elements in Figure 7–1). You swipe your finger along the screen to navigate between the pages of the **Home** screens. The top portion is the **Action** bar, which can contain menu items. On the upper right, you'll find the **Apps** button for browsing through all your available apps. Next to that button, you'll find the + icon, which you can use for many **Home** screen adjustments, including adding widgets, app icons, and shortcuts. You can also use this icon to change your wallpaper.

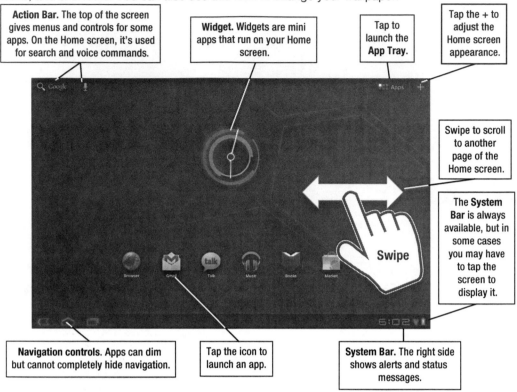

Action Bar. The top of the screen gives menus and controls for some apps. On the Home screen, it's used for search and voice commands.

Widget. Widgets are mini apps that run on your Home screen.

Tap to launch the **App Tray.**

Tap the + to adjust the Home screen appearance.

Swipe to scroll to another page of the Home screen.

The **System Bar** is always available, but in some cases you may have to tap the screen to display it.

Navigation controls. Apps can dim but cannot completely hide navigation.

Tap the icon to launch an app.

System Bar. The right side shows alerts and status messages.

Figure 7–1. *Elements on the **Home** screen*

Exploring Widgets

Widgets are small, continually running app windows. Widgets from different developers can check your mail, display your calendar, show your music selection, check off your grocery list, display pictures, and notify you of new Twitter posts. They can have transparent backgrounds, and some are designed to have different windows stacked on each other that you can swipe to rearrange. Often, tapping a widget launches the full app.

Figure 7–2 shows some of the widgets available by default in Honeycomb. You can download many more widgets, and many developers package widget views with their apps.

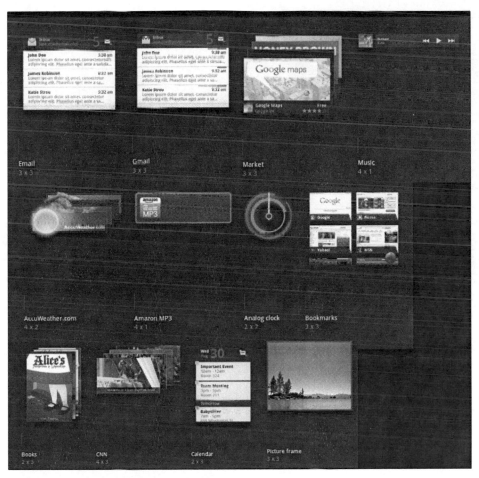

Figure 7–2. *The default Honeycomb widgets*

Adding Widgets

Follow these steps to add widgets to your **Home** screen:

1. Press the + symbol on the upper-right corner of the screen or press your finger down on an empty section of the screen. You'll see something resembling Figure 7 3. This is Honeycomb's *holographic* interface for adding **Home** screen elements.

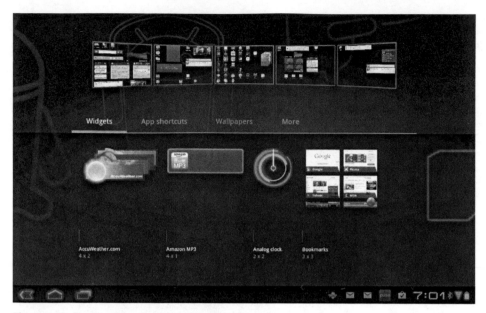

Figure 7–3. *The Home screen customization interface*

2. By default, **Widgets** should be selected; but if it isn't, tap the **Widgets** selection on the left-middle section of the screen.

3. The next step is to swipe your finger along the bottom half of the screen to find the widget you want to add.

4. Once you find it, just press and drag the widget to the screen where it should go, as shown in Figure 7–4.

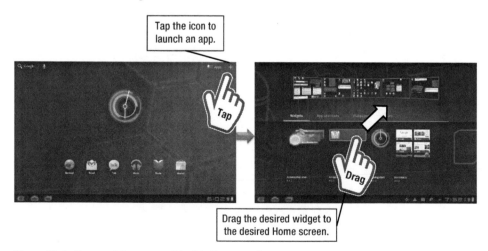

Figure 7–4. *Drag and drop your widget to the correct screen*

5. Once your finger is over the correct screen, you can lift your finger, and the widget will be added.

> **NOTE:** Widget sizes are listed on the bottom of each widget in the interface with numbers like "4x2" or "3x3." The number refers to how many app icons would fit in the same space. Thus, 4x2 is four app icons wide by two app icons high.

REMOVING WIDGETS

What if you want to get rid of a widget? You can remove widgets even more easily than you can add them. Follow these steps to do so:

1. Long press the widget until the screen changes. One thing you may notice is that + symbol on the upper-right corner is now a **Trash Can** icon.

2. With your finger still pressing down, drag the widget to the **Trash Can** icon on the upper-right corner of the screen, as shown in Figure 7–5.

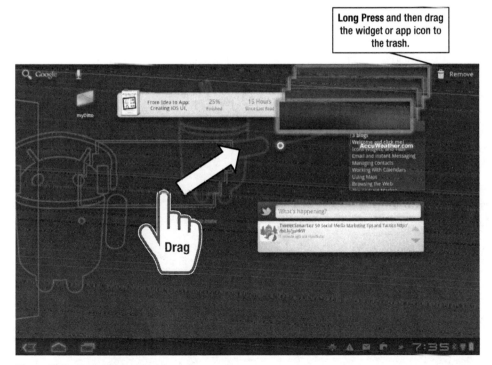

Figure 7–5. *Removing a widget*

Removing a widget does not uninstall it from the tablet. It merely removes it from display on your **Home** screen. You can add a widget again anytime you choose.

Moving and Resizing Widgets

Now that you've added and removed widgets, it's time to rearrange and resize them. This process is pretty similar to removing them. All widgets can be repositioned, as long as there's available space on the **Home** screen:

1. Long press the widget until the screen appearance changes. You'll see a light blue grid form.

2. Drag the widget to the new location.

3. Lift your finger.

Resizing widgets uses a similar process, but there's a caveat: not all widgets can be resized. Resizing widgets is a feature of Android 3.1, and widgets must be specifically programmed to take advantage of it. Follow these steps to resize a widget:

1. Long press the widget until the screen appearance changes. If you see a light blue outline around the widget with diamond control points, you can resize it (see Figure 7–6).

2. Drag the widget by the diamonds to resize it either smaller or larger in a given direction. Not all widgets are resizable in both directions; and in some cases, you may not have enough room to make the widget larger.

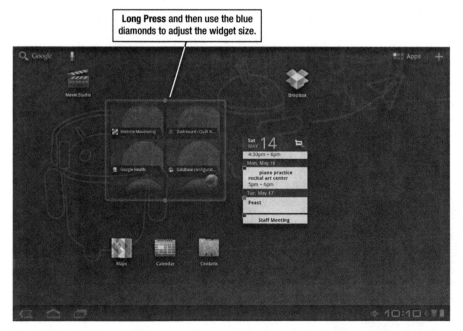

Figure 7–6. *Resizing widgets*

TIP: When you're dragging an app to a **Home** screen, you can keep your finger pressed down on that screen, and it will magnify, letting you place your widget exactly where you want it to go.

App Icons

App icons or app shortcuts are simple buttons that launch an app. You can find all of them by tapping the **App Launcher** button on the right side of the **Action** bar. However, there are probably apps you use more often and want to add to your **Home** screen. Sometimes apps automatically place an app icon on your **Home** screen when you download them, and you may want to remove a few to save screen real estate.

The good news is this: the fact that that you can now add, remove, and reposition widgets means you can do exactly the same thing with app icons. The process is almost exactly the same.

When you add app icons, you'll select the **App shortcuts** choice in the **Home** screen customization interface, as shown in Figure 7–7. App icons are not resizable; every one of them has a size of 1x1.

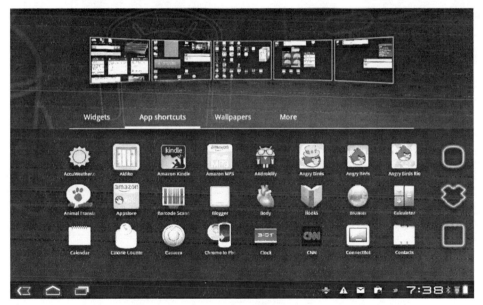

Figure 7–7. *App shortcuts in the customization interface*

More

The right-most choice in the customization interface is ambiguously labeled **more** (see Figure 7–8). This is the place where you'll find special app shortcuts that aren't quite app icons and aren't quite widgets. These are more like bookmarks to specific points in apps, and **Bookmark** is even an option!

Figure 7–8. *The More menu*

Your choice will depend on the apps you have installed, but you can use this menu to create quick shortcuts to things like Gmail messages with specific tags, music playlists, contacts, or frequently changed system settings.

Drag and drop these shortcuts from the customization interface the same way you would app icons. As soon as you release your finger, you'll be asked to specify the tag, list, blog, or bookmark for your shortcut. Your choices will depend on the type of shortcut.

Wallpapers

The final element to explore in the **Home** screen customization interface is wallpapers. Wallpapers change the background on your **Home** screens. Wallpapers change every screen; there's no way to change one screen and leave the other four untouched.

When you launch the **Home** screen customization interface and select the **Wallpapers** option (see Figure 7–8), you'll see three basic choices for the types of wallpapers you can add.

Chapter 8

Email on Tablets

Android tablets add a new ease to keeping up with your email. The relatively large screen makes it easy to see what you're doing, and the Honeycomb interface makes it easy to see and respond to your messages.

Some tablets may package additional software, but in general your email is handled by two apps:

- Gmail
- Email

Between those two apps, you can read Microsoft Exchange, POP3, Gmail, and IMAP accounts. You can also use Android's **Browser** app to check web-based email accounts, and you can download third-party apps that support other types of email accounts. Refer to Chapter 4: "Syncing with Google Accounts" to see how to add Gmail accounts to your Android tablet and Chapter 5: "Syncing with Other Accounts" for instructions on adding Exchange, IMAP, and POP3 email accounts.

Honeycomb tablets also come with interactive widgets for both the **Email** and **Gmail** apps, so you can check your message summaries at a glance before launching the full app. Chapter 7: "Widgets and the Home Screens" explains how to add and resize the **Email** and **Gmail** widgets.

Understanding Gmail

Gmail is a Google product. It's used for Google's corporate email system, and it's very well supported on Android. Anyone can create a personal Gmail account for free at http://mail.google.com, and enterprise customers can use Gmail to power their corporate email accounts through a product suite called **Google Apps**.

In order to understand the **Gmail** app on your tablet, it's helpful to understand how Gmail works on the Web. Remember, you can always use the web version of Gmail on your tablet because your tablet has a built-in **Browser** app.

Gmail is arguably the best free email service available. There's no automatic tagline at the end of your messages advertising the fact that you're using a free email service, and you don't have to pay extra in order to use a desktop or mobile app to access your email. The spam filtering is above average, and you get plenty of storage space.

> **NOTE:** Although it's not a faux pas to use a Gmail address for professional correspondence, you can use Google Apps to send and receive Gmail through custom business URLs. If you own a small- to medium-sized business, you can take advantage of Google's services from either the limited free *standard* account or the $50 per-user/per-year *premium* account. If you qualify for the free standard version, you can even set up Google Apps as a free email service for a domain name you already own. For more information, visit the Google Apps site at www.google.com/a.

Gmail Inbox and Archive

Rather than folders, the Gmail service uses labels. I'll cover folders in more depth in the next section; however, let's just say that for most purposes, there are only three places for email you want to keep: the *Inbox*, the *Priority Inbox*, and the *Archive*.

And there are two places for email you don't want to keep: the *Trash* and *Spam*. Generally, you'll want to mark spam messages as such before deleting them because this helps train the spam filters to recognize unwanted messages.

If you don't ever want read a message again, by all means delete it. Email sent to the Trash is permanently deleted after thirty days. However, messages you might need later should be *archived*. To archive a message using Gmail's web interface, select the **Checkbox** icon next to the message, and then press the **Archive** button. It's on left side of the buttons above the Inbox, as shown in Figure 8–1.

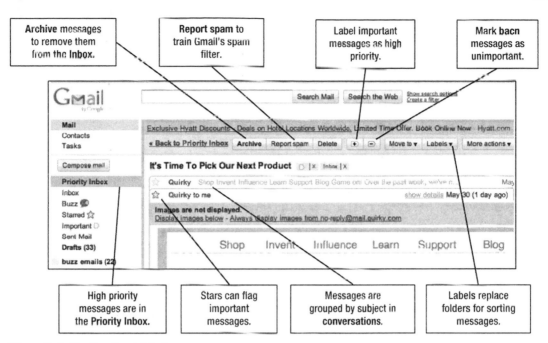

Figure 8–1. *The Gmail web interface*

When you archive a message, it no longer shows up in the Inbox (you've removed the **Inbox** label). You can still find the message by using the **All Mail** label or by using Gmail's **Search** box. For messages of low importance, you may even want to set up a filter that archives the messages immediately, so they never clog your inbox. I'll explain filters later in this chapter in the "Automatic Labels" section.

NOTE: Gmail messages are grouped into conversations. Rather than showing each message in the order they arrived, conversations are clusters of messages to and from a person or group. The messages are stacked together, so you can view the conversation in context. They also appear in reverse chronological order in the Inbox, according to the last message received. Any actions you apply to one message in the conversation will apply to all of them. If you want to view or act on the messages individually, just click the Expand all link to the right of the message.

If you keep seeing a super long conversation that you'd rather ignore, use the **mute** option to archive the current and future messages in that conversation. The messages will still be available and marked as unread; they just won't appear in the Inbox.

Priority Inbox

Google has an optional but useful feature called the *Priority Inbox.* This is one way to help sort your important email from what some call *bacn.* Bacn (pronounced like bacon) messages are those newsletters, alerts, and coupons that you did at some point sign up to receive, and you probably do want to read—just not right now. They're not really spam, but they're not really important. They're bacn.

The Priority Inbox flags important, unread messages and displays them at the top of your Gmail Inbox in the web interface. You can train Gmail to better recognize which messages are important and which are not by flagging them  , and you can customize the Priority Inbox to also separate items with specific labels, as shown earlier in Figure 8–1.

If you're not seeing a Priority Inbox, you'll need to enable the feature by following these steps:

1. Using the web interface, go to **Mail settings**. You access this from the **Gear** button on the upper-right corner of your Gmail window. You'll need to click the **Gear** icon and then click **Mail settings**.

2. Click the **Priority Inbox** tab, as shown in figure 8–2.

3. Toggle the option labeled **Show Priority Inbox.**

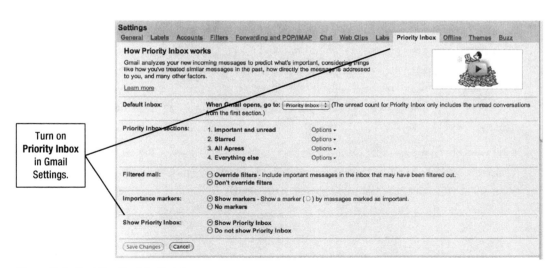

Turn on Priority Inbox in Gmail Settings.

Figure 8–2. *Enabling the Priority Inbox*

You'll also notice that there is a list of **Priority Inbox sections**. Gmail lets you specify the sorts of messages you want to prioritize. You can have up to four sections, including all starred messages, all important and unread messages, and everything else. In this case, I've added an Apress section.

The Priority Inbox is a useful way to sort email. Behind the scenes, this is really just a new way to display a label or star.

Stars and Labels

Many email accounts work by allowing you to place email messages in folders. Gmail would prefer you use labels. What is the difference? A single piece of email can only exist in a single folder. You'd have to copy an email message for it to be both in the "work" and "tax related" folders, but the same email can have multiple labels.

Use labels to organize your messages by topic. You can click one of the labels on the left side of the screen (as shown in Figure 8–1) in order to view only messages with that particular label, including messages that have been archived.

Gmail automatically creates the following labels:

- Inbox

- Buzz

- Starred

- Chats

- Sent Mail

- Drafts

- All Mail

- Spam

- Trash

You can create other labels as needed. I sometimes set up temporary labels for upcoming conferences or events, and then remove or hide the labels after the conference.

You'll notice that **Starred** is also a label. Click the **Empty Star** icon ☆ to the left of a message in order to *star* it or give it the **Starred** label. That highlights the message with

a **Yellow Star** icon ⭐. Since you can apply more than one label to an item, adding both a star and a different label could emphasize urgent messages or highlight items that need a response or required action. Adding a star also automatically adds your message to the **Starred** items section of your Priority Inbox.

Creating and Deleting Labels

You can create labels in many ways using Gmail's web interface. Follow these steps to do so:

1. Click the **Labels** button at the top of your Inbox.

2. Click **Manage labels** from the dropdown menu, as shown on the right.

3. You now are in the **Label settings** area. You can enter new labels by typing into the box labeled **Create a new label**.

You can also get to this menu by clicking **Settings** on the upper-right side of the screen and then clicking **Labels**. Another method is to click **More** on the bottom of your list of labels on the right side of the screen, and then click **Manage labels**.

> **TIP:** You're limited to 40 characters in a label, but it would be wise to keep it even shorter. Long labels mean less space for your message previews.

You can edit a label by clicking the label's name in the **Label** settings and then typing in the new name. You can show or hide labels by clicking the link to the right of the labels, and you can delete them using the same procedure.

> **NOTE:** Deleting a label does not delete the message/s associated with that label.

Automatic Filters

Automatic filters are probably one of the most powerful tools in any email program. When combined with labels, filters enable you to accomplish quite a lot in Gmail. Follow these steps to adjust or apply automatic filters in Gmail:

1. Click the **Checkbox** icon next to one or more messages.

2. Click the **More actions** button.

3. Select **Filter messages like these**.

4. Gmail will try to guess the criteria you're using, such as messages from a certain sender or messages containing a particular subject line. If the guess is wrong, you can change the criteria. Once you've got the correct criteria, click the **Next Step** button.

5. Now choose an action. Your choices include **archive** (the **Skip the Inbox** option), **star**, **mark as read**, **apply a label**, **forward it**, **delete it**, or **never flag it as spam**. If you're using Priority Inbox, this is a choice as well. You can select more than one action for an item, such as **star** and **never flag it as spam**.

6. Next, create the filter. You can also select the checkbox to apply that filter to any previous messages that matched your criteria.

I use filters to automatically prioritize messages from business contacts with stars and subject labels. I also limit clutter by archiving distracting mailing lists and other back items I may want to read later, as well as notifications from Facebook and Twitter. I also make sure important senders never have their messages marked as spam.

NOTE: You can create an easy filter for a group or project by creating a custom email address. Your Gmail address supports adding words to your address by adding them on with a **Plus (+)** sign. For instance, you can have everyone involved with a project send messages to *YourUserName+YourProject*@gmail.com. Next, add a filter for messages sent to that specific address, and then apply the desired label.

The General Settings Menu

We've already explored filters and labels. There are many other options on the **Settings** menu worth mentioning. To adjust settings, click the **Gear** icon on the upper-right corner of the screen and then click **Mail settings**.

The first tab, **General**, offers some general settings. There are a lot of options here, and they change as Google adds more Gmail features.

You can create text signatures and set automatic vacation replies through the appropriate boxes here. Be aware that any signatures you create on the web interface will *not* translate to your tablet's **Gmail** app. You have to set those up separately.

If you change anything here, be sure to press the **Save changes** button before moving on.

Adding Accounts to Gmail

You can add additional email accounts through Gmail and check and respond to them from the same inbox as your Gmail account. These accounts must be standard POP3 accounts, but that includes most web-based email and email accounts offered through Internet service providers (ISPs). However, that generally does *not* include Exchange accounts.

The settings for managing other accounts via Gmail are shown in Figure 8–3. Follow these steps to add an email account to your web-based Gmail account:

1. Log into Gmail on the Web.

2. Click the **Gear** icon on the upper-right corner of the screen and then click **Mail settings**.

3. Click **Accounts and Import**.

4. Click **Add POP3 email account**.

5. Enter your email address and password, as well as any specific settings provided by your ISP.

6. Decide how you handle messages on the old account. Do you delete them as they're imported or are they left on the server?

7. Decide if you'd like to add a custom label (by default your email address will be the label) and if you'd like to automatically archive new messages.

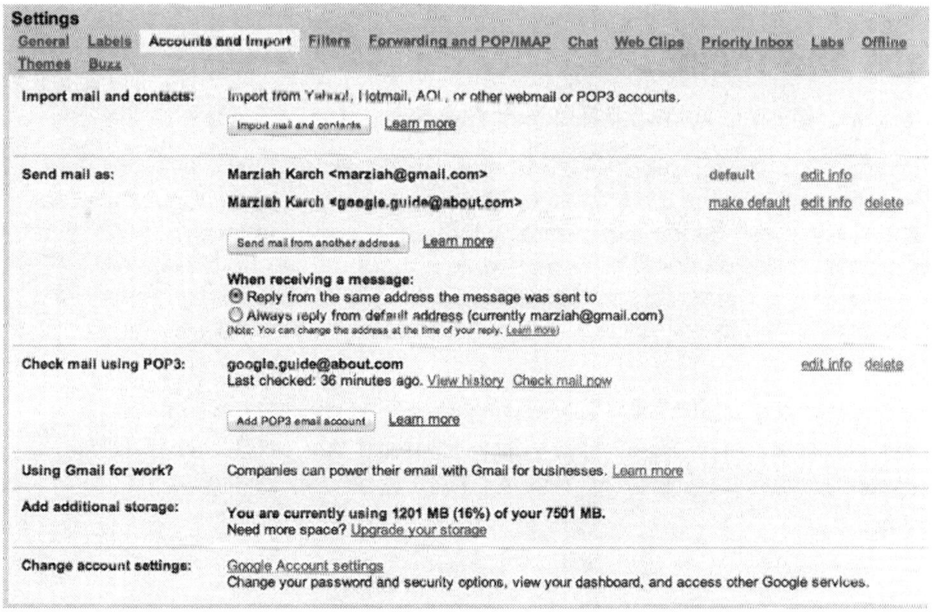

Figure 8–3. *Adding email accounts to a single Gmail*

If you add accounts, you'll want to decide if you should respond from the address that received the email or always use your default email address. I find it less confusing to respond with the same account that originated the email, but you may want to train people to just use your Gmail account. Your default address is the address you'll use to compose new messages.

You can add POP3 email accounts directly to your **Email** app on your tablet. It's a matter of how you want to manage your email. Adding email accounts via the web interface ties them to your Gmail account.

Forwarding and POP/IMAP

You can automatically forward a copy of each mail message to a different account and either keep, archive, or delete the original message. This applies to *all* messages to that account, but you can forward selectively by creating a filter.

To access email on your Android phone, you'll want to enable *IMAP* (Internet Message Access Protocol). This is the mail protocol that allows your account to sync with your phone. You can also enable *POP* (Post Office Protocol) if you wish, but this isn't necessary for Android access.

Gmail Labs and Themes

Labs and **Themes** are options in your **Mail settings** menu that only apply to the web-based version of Gmail. **Gmail Labs** 🧪 allows you to add experimental features that may or may not make it into the main release. **Themes** allow you to customize the look-and-feel of your Gmail web-based experience, while **offline access** lets you read and compose Gmail messages on some browsers while not connected to the Internet. Messages sync once your Internet connection is resumed. Feel free to experiment and explore, but be aware that these settings do *not* necessarily transfer to your tablet.

> **NOTE:** One interesting Labs tool is called **Super stars**. This add-on allows you to have multiple stars and star-like icons appear instead of just a single yellow star. When this feature is enabled, you can rapidly click a star to toggle to different icons. This way, you can prioritize even within **Starred** items.

Web Gmail from Your Tablet

When you use your **Browser** app on your tablet, by default you'll see a mobile version of Gmail that is trimmed down and simpler to use on mobile devices. However, your tablet is capable of viewing the full version, too. Follow these steps to view the full version of Gmail's web interface on your tablet:

1. Launch the **Browser** app and go to `http://mail.google.com`.

2. When you are logged in, scroll to the very bottom of the screen. You'll see that you're viewing Gmail in: **Mobile** mode.

3. Click the link next to that indicator that says **Desktop**.

The Gmail App

There are two basic ways to access Gmail from your tablet. You can either use the **Gmail** app , or you can use Android's **Browser** app to access Gmail from the Web.

The **Gmail** app on Android tablets uses *push email*. That means that you don't need to keep checking for new email. Your email is always on and always ready to receive new messages. This is just like keeping your desktop email client on in the background when you use your laptop. It's the big advantage of Android's **Gmail** app over your tablet's **Browser** app, though the **Browser** app is useful when you need to tweak settings.

> **NOTE:** There are generally several ways to do anything in the **Gmail** app. Use whichever methods you prefer.

When new messages arrive, by default you'll see a notice in the **Notifications** bar. You can tap a notification that appears to view the message in the **Gmail** app, or you can tap the **Notifications** bar to see a preview of the message, as shown in Figure 8–4. Notice that Gmail messages have an envelope with an "M" on it, while regular mail has a more traditional envelope.

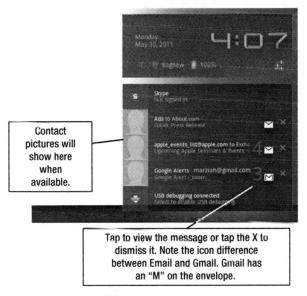

Contact pictures will show here when available.

Tap to view the message or tap the X to dismiss it. Note the icon difference between Email and Gmail. Gmail has an "M" on the envelope.

Figure 8–4. *The Notifications bar*

Reading Gmail Messages

If you've read Gmail on your phone, reading it on a Honeycomb tablet is a treat. There's finally enough room to really browse through your messages. When you launch the **Gmail** app by clicking the **Gmail** app icon or clicking an email alert, you'll see something resembling Figure 8–5.

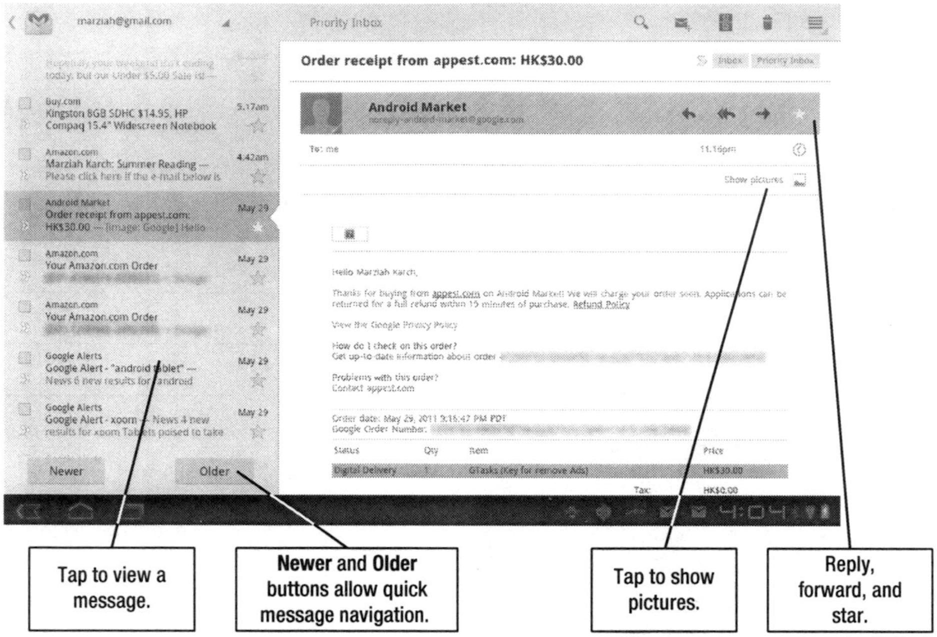

Figure 8–5. *Viewing a Gmail message*

Notice that your email message appears on the right. The controls to reply to the message or forward it are located above the message itself. The column to the left is designed to allow you to easily navigate to new messages, and the **Newer** and **Older** buttons can be used by the thumb of the hand you're using to hold the tablet.

The **Action** bar at the top of the screen shows menu options. If you tap the **Gmail** icon on the upper-left corner (where the arrow points to the left), you'll see something resembling Figure 8–6.

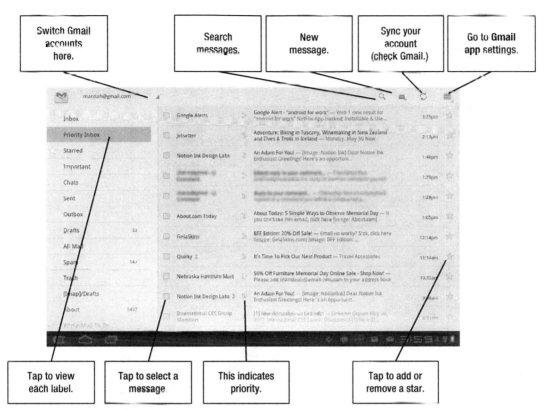

Figure 8–6. *Navigating Gmail labels*

This view allows you to navigate within different labels, including the Priority Inbox, if enabled. Now that you understand how Gmail's web interface works, this should look familiar, even though the interface has changed for the tablet.

> **NOTE:** You can tap and drag or just hold down your finger and drag messages to labels or to the Trash.

The **Action** bar options in the upper right include **search**, **new message**, **sync accounts**, and **the Gmail settings menu**.

> **NOTE:** Gmail messages are grouped into conversations, rather than strictly chronologically. Messages with the same subject header are grouped together, which makes it easier to track a conversation that spans several messages.

Sending a Message

You can send a message by replying to an existing message or by tapping the **New message** button (see Figure 8–6). Once you tap the **New message** button, you'll see the **Compose** area, as shown in Figure 8–7.

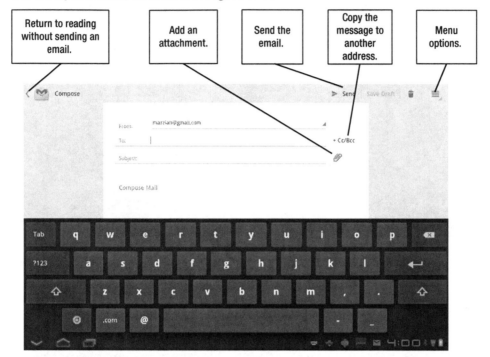

Figure 8–7. *Composing a message*

Tap in the **To:**, **Subject:**, or **Compose Mail** fields to start typing in those areas. As you type your addressee in the **To:** field, you'll notice that Android will start to autocomplete the address.

You'll also notice that you can tap the **Paperclip** icon to add an attachment from your tablet to your message. When you tap that icon, just browse to the location of your attachment to add it.

Receiving Messages with Attachments

If you receive a message with an attachment, you'll see a **Paperclip** icon, the name of the attached file, and two buttons to either **View** or **Save** the file. If you choose to **Save** the file, it will be downloaded to your tablet (or your tablet's SD card, if you have one) in a file named download. You can browse to it using an app like **ES File Explorer**. If you press the **View** button, you may need to specify which app you want to use to view it (see Figure 8–8).

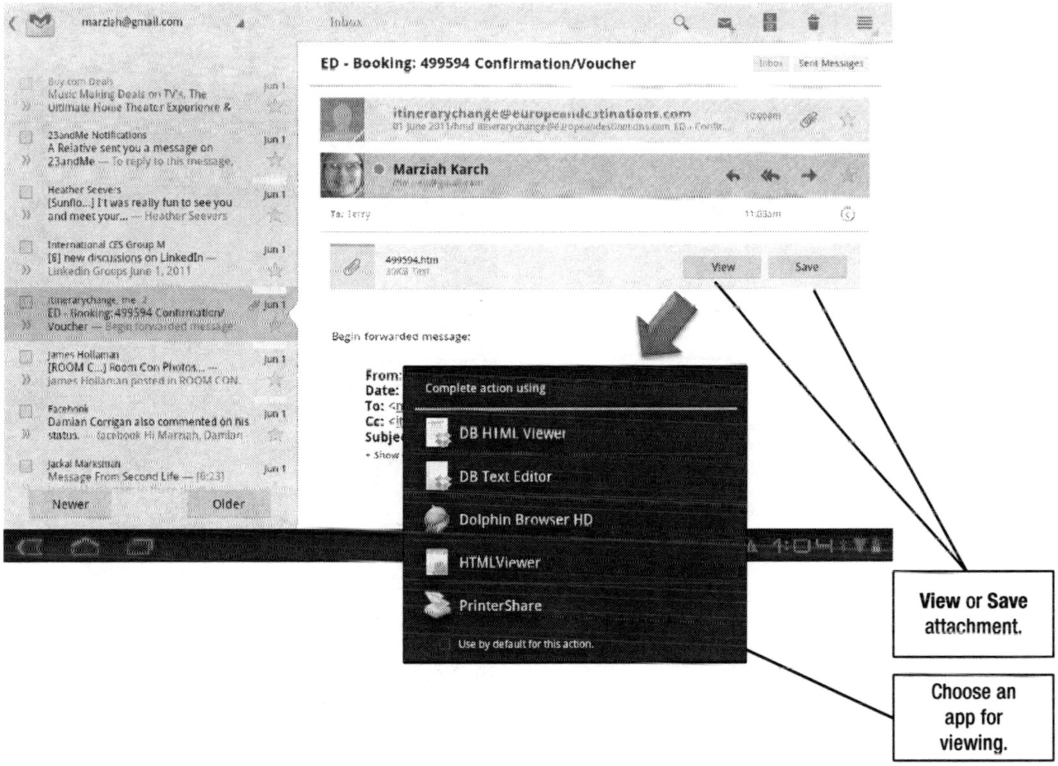

Figure 8–8. *Viewing an attached file*

Gmail App Settings

Once you've mastered reading and composing messages, it's time to move on to the **Settings** menu. This is where you can do things like set alerts and change your signature. Tap the **Menu** button on the upper-right corner of the **Action** bar and select **Settings**. If you're syncing with more than one Gmail account, select the one you wish to modify by tapping it (see Figure 8–9).

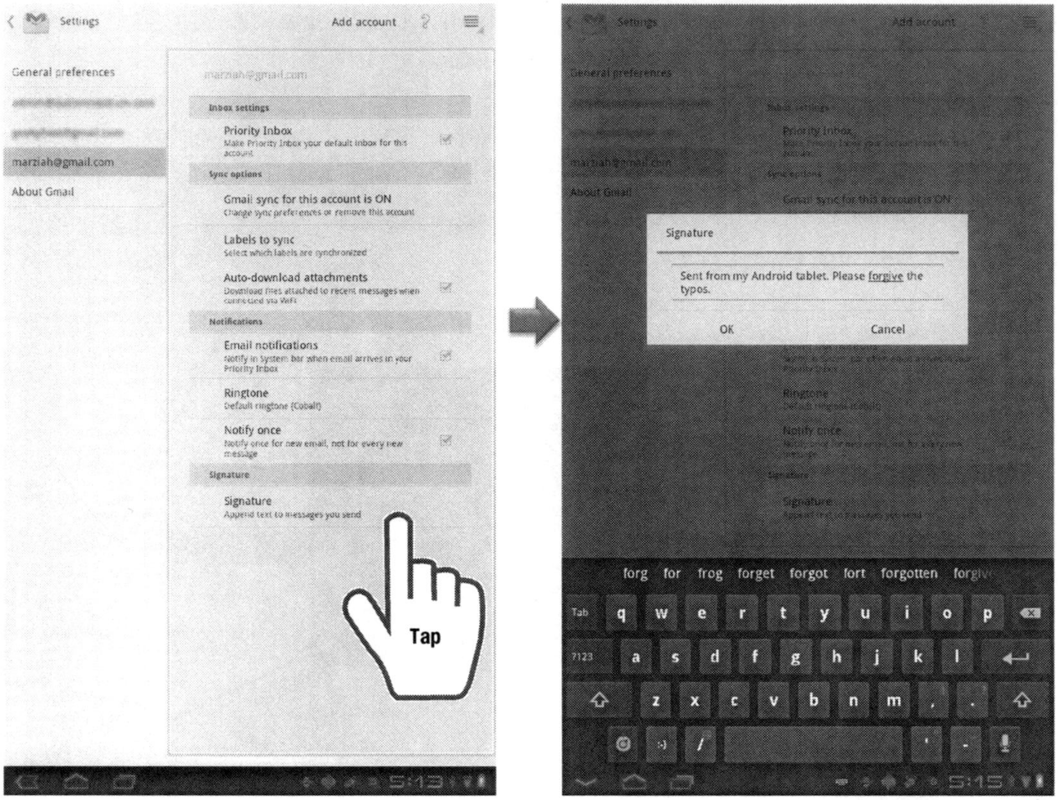

Figure 8–9. *The Settings menu*

One of the first things I like to do is tap the **Signature** setting and change the *signature file*. This must be a text message, not an image.

Remember: The signature you create here will *only* display in messages you send from your tablet. That means you can tell people you're tapping out your message on a tablet, either for bragging rights or to have typos overlooked.

Another important setting is **Ringtone.** Even though this is a tablet, not a phone, it's still called a ringtone. This just refers to the audio sound that plays when you receive a new message. I set mine to **Silent.**

The Email App

As explained earlier, Gmail and regular email are handled by two different apps. However, the **Email** app does not require a huge learning curve. The process of reading, replying, and composing messages is virtually identical in the two apps; if you know how to use one app, you'll be perfectly comfortable using the other.

There are a few differences if you're using an Exchange account. For instance, your Microsoft Exchange server supports folders, not labels. Likewise, you'll see differences when you use a POP or IMAP account.

Rather than displaying labels on the left menu, as the **Gmail** app does, the **Email** app shows the more specific folders for your Exchange account, as shown in Figure 8–10.

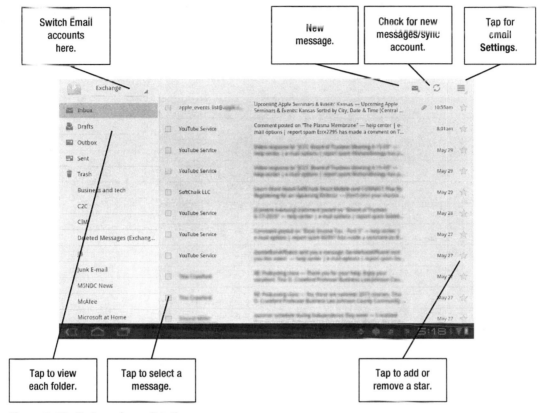

Figure 8–10. *Exchange's email options*

You can see another important difference is the Combined Inbox. In the **Email** app, you can click the account name on the upper-left corner to switch accounts, just as you can with Gmail. One of the options is for a **Combined** view. The **Combined** view simply shows all your unread email messages (other than Gmail) in a single inbox.

Email and Gmail Action Bar Items

Not only do the **Email** and **Gmail** apps have a similar interface for reading and replying to messages, they have similar approaches to the **Action** bar. When you select a message in either the **Gmail** or **Email** apps by tapping on the **Checkbox** icon next to it (see Figures 8–6 or 8–10), you'll see a difference in the **Action** bar (see Figure 8–11). The **Email** app is shown on the top, and the **Gmail** app is shown on the bottom. They're both very similar, but **Gmail** offers an additional archive option, while **Email** allows you to move messages instead of changing labels.

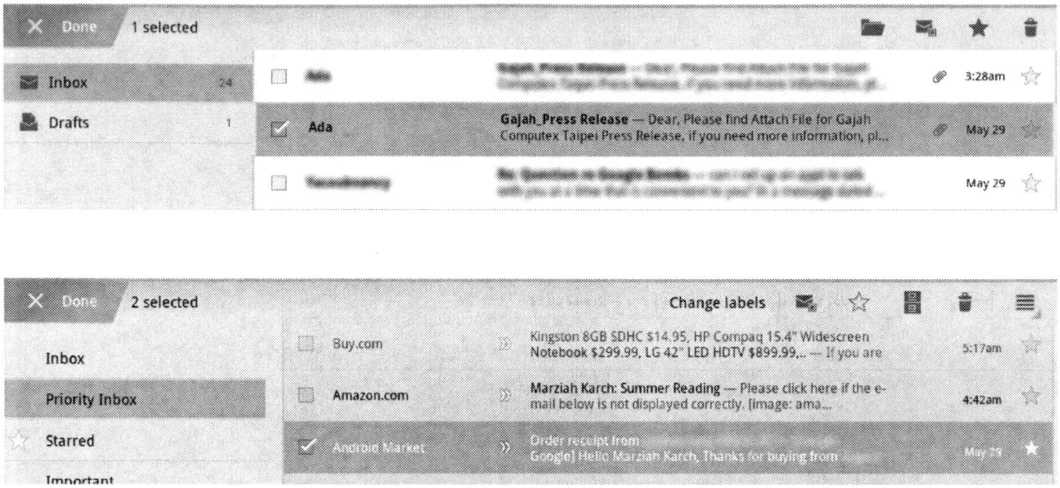

Figure 8–11. *The Action bar options for the Email and Gmail apps*

> **NOTE:** Moving to folders is not supported for POP3 accounts. You'll still see the button in the **Email** app, but you'll get an error message warning you that it doesn't work when you try to use it.

Email and Gmail Widgets

You can take advantage of the built-in **Email** and **Gmail** widgets shown in Figure 8–12 to glance through summaries of your new email messages without launching the apps themselves. These are also resizable apps, as explained in Chapter 7: "Icons and Widgets."

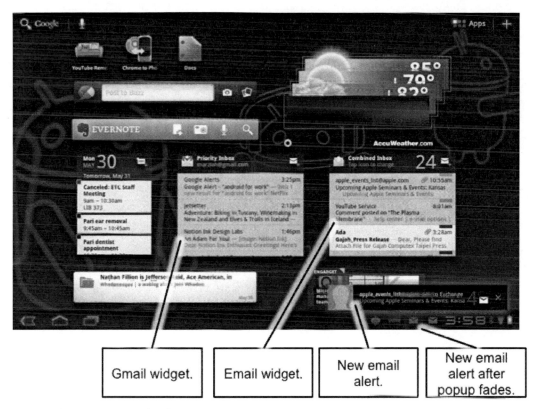

Figure 8–12. *The Email and Gmail widgets*

You'll notice that the **Gmail** and **Email** widgets can be set to display specific inboxes, and the **Email** widget can use either one inbox or the Combined Inbox. This is a great way to set up a view of all your different email accounts at once in small windows on your **Home** screen.

Chapter 9

Managing Contacts

This chapter assumes you've set up your Google, Exchange, and other email accounts. This is important because you won't have many contacts to manage if you're not syncing with any accounts. You may have even set up your Twitter, Facebook, and Skype accounts, but it's OK if you haven't.

All of the aforementioned account types make a handy virtual Rolodex of all your contacts. You can add contacts from your tablet, your phone, and the Web; and they'll all be available in the **Contacts** app on your tablet. You use the same basic steps to manage to manage your contacts, regardless of account type.

Tablets vs. Phones

On previous versions of Android, contacts were rolled into the **Dialer** app, which managed contacts and calling. There are a few Android tablets that are also phones, like the Dell Streak and the UK version of the original 7-inch Galaxy Tab. All of them currently run previous versions of Android, although the interface has been modified. The U.S. version of the original Galaxy Tab does not make phone calls.

You can use *VoIP* (Voice over Internet Protocol) tools like Skype to make voice calls to other users and even make voice calls to outside phone numbers (with a paid subscription). There's more on Skype in Chapter 16: "Video Conferencing and Skype." However, the general rule of thumb is that your Android tablet doesn't make traditional phone calls.

The Contact App

You can access your contacts by tapping the **Contacts** app.

The interface is similar to that of the **Email** and **Gmail** apps. You've got a list of contacts on the left that you can scroll through by dragging your finger. On the right, you can see the details for the currently selected contact.

Along the top of the screen, there are buttons to filter, search, add, and edit contacts. Figure 9–1 shows the basic layout.

Figure 9–1. *The layout of the Contacts app*

When you view a contact, you'll notice that there are symbols along the right. Those symbols let you make instant contact by whatever method you have listed for your contact. You can potentially email, instant message, Skype, video chat, and Tweet with a contact. If you list an address, you can find the location on Google Maps. You may see an instant messaging or Twitter status displayed underneath the contact's name. You may even have more options, depending on the apps you have installed on your tablet.

However, even if you have a phone number listed, you can't call a contact unless your tablet supports voice calls.

Adding/ Editing a Contact

Follow these steps to add or edit a contact:

1. To add a new contact, tap the **New** button on the upper-right corner of the screen, as shown in Figure 9-1.

2. Choose an account to use for this contact (if you have more than one). Once you do that, you'll see a screen resembling Figure 9-2.

The blank form pre-populates with a standard template, but you can customize this template with as little or as much information as you wish. If you want to edit a contact instead of adding a new one, tap the **Pencil** button instead of the **New** button, as shown in Figure 9-1.

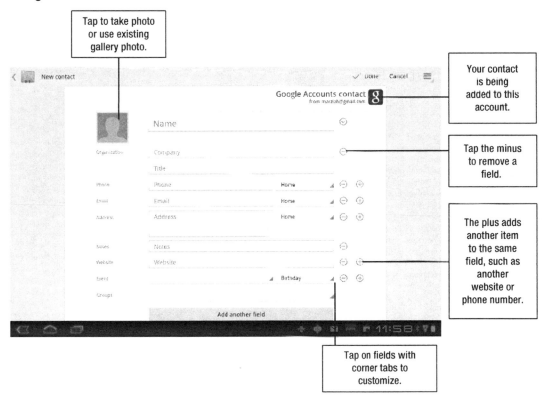

Figure 9–2. *Adding a new contact*

Several areas have what looks like a corner tab. This type of tab indicates that you can tap to customize the label for that item, such as the label next to the **Phone** field. Tap to change **Home** to **Work** or **Mobile**. Tap to the right of the **Name** field to split it into the following: **first**, **last**, **middle**, **prefix**, and **suffix**.

The last field listed is **Groups**. This field can be used to organize your contacts by categories, such as **Work**, **Friends**, and **Family**. If your desired group doesn't exist, you can click the bottom choice to create a new group. You can also add a single contact to more than one group.

> **NOTE:** Once you're done entering information for your contact, be sure to tap the **Done** button on the **Action** bar.

Adding a Picture

You can also add a photo to your contact to make it easier to recognize him. Tap the gray silhouette outline or the existing photo. You can choose either to take a photo using your tablet's camera or to use an existing photo from you tablet's gallery.

Adding Custom Fields

The default template may not have all the fields you'd like. To add another field, just tap the **Add another field** button near the bottom of the screen, as shown in Figure 9–3.

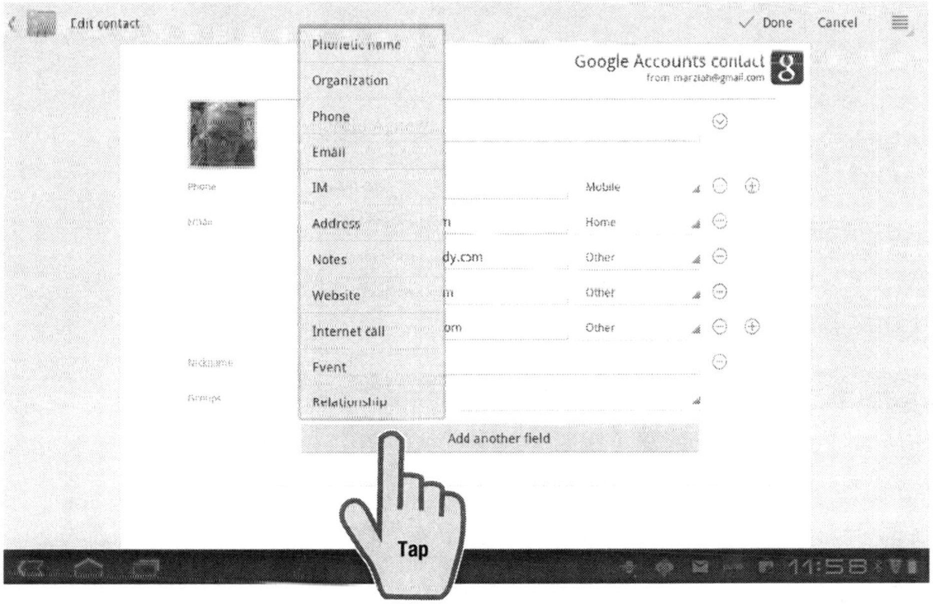

Figure 9–3. *Adding another field*

You can add a huge variety of fields, including your relationship to the contact, her website, and a phonetic name pronunciation guide (it's *Mar-Zee-uh*). The **Notes** field can work as a catch-all for any field that may be missing.

Filtering Contacts

If you've got a lot of contacts, you'll want some easy ways to sort through them. For example, you can use the search feature to locate a contact. However, sometimes you might not remember the name of someone, or you might actually be looking for a group of people. That's where filters come in.

When you're looking at your contact list, there's an **Action** bar item on the upper left 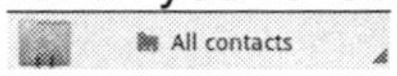 that lets you choose which contacts to view. The default is **All contacts**, but you can tap to choose only to display the contacts from a specific account or a specific group within an account. For instance, Figure 9–4 lists only the Twitter accounts.

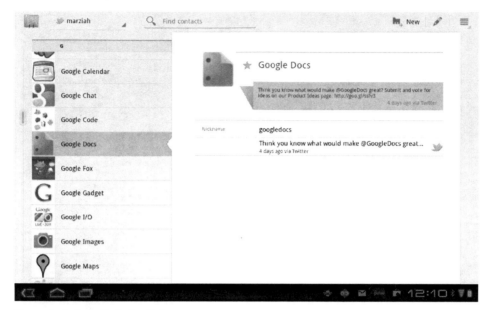

Figure 9–4. *Only displaying Twitter accounts*

If you want to take it a step further, you can create a custom view of specific groups within your contacts, such as **Friends** and **Family**, but not **Coworkers** (see Figure 9–5).

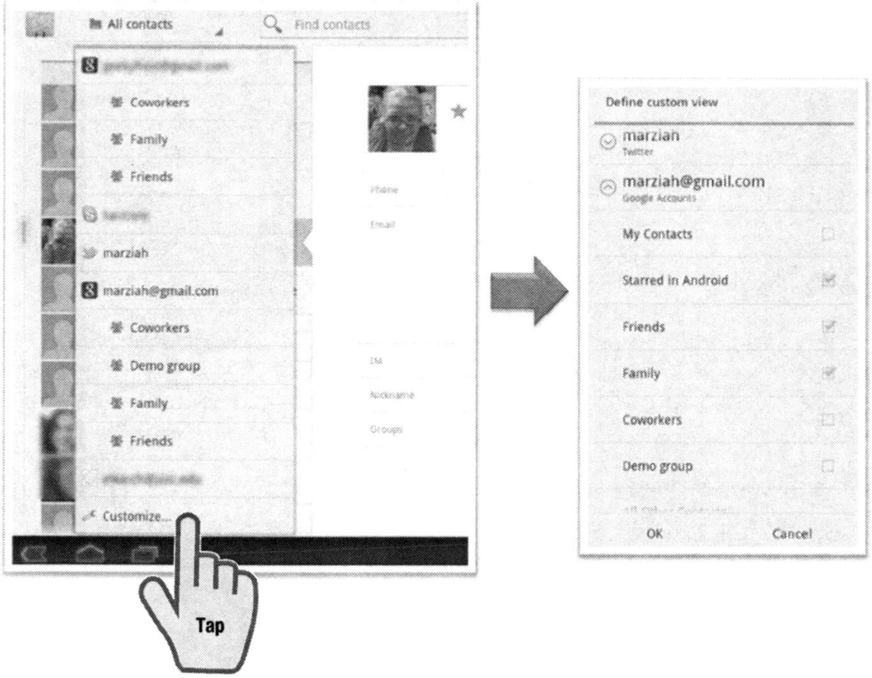

Figure 9–5. *Customized filtering of contacts*

Joining Accounts

As you go through your contacts list, you may notice that you have lots of duplicate contacts. That's because your contacts are pooling from any account you've authorized for account syncing on your tablet. You may have separate Twitter, Skype, Exchange, and Gmail listings for the same person.

The solution is to join those accounts. This action just groups them together in the **Contacts** app, and you can separate the accounts later if you desire.

Follow these steps to join an account:

1. Tap the **Pencil** icon to start editing the desired contact.

2. Tap the **Options** button on the upper-right corner of the screen.

3. Select **Join**.

4. Choose which contacts you'd like to merge, as shown in Figure 9–6.

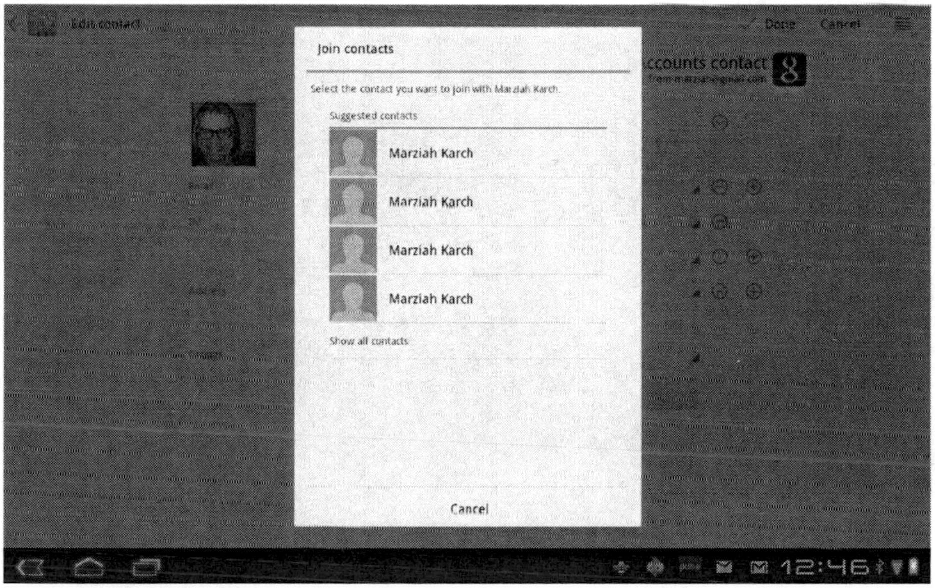

Figure 9–6. *Joining contacts*

You'll automatically see any contacts with the same name; but in case you've got multiple contacts with different names, such as maiden names or company names, just tap **Show all contacts** to find them.

Contacts that are joined will say so on the upper-right corner of the display, rather than show a specific account. All available fields for that account will be displayed.

Sharing Contacts

You can share your contacts in an impressive variety of ways, depending on the apps you have installed on your tablet. Follow these steps to share a contact:

1. While viewing a contact, press the **Options** button on the upper-right corner of the **Action** menu.

2. Press **Share contact**.

3. Choose your method of sharing.

Pick **Email** or **Gmail** to send your contact as an attachment. If you have the app installed, **Evernote** will create a new note. Bluetooth attempts to send the info to a Bluetooth-capable device.

The **Share via barcode** option makes a *QR Code* (a square barcode easily scanned by mobile phones) that you can hold up and allow someone else to scan with his phone.

NOTE: If you add yourself as a contact, you can use sharing to send someone your address instead of using business cards.

Importing and Exporting Contacts

You may have noticed that one of the options right above **Share contact** is **Import/Export**. You can use this option to import contacts from an SD card or export them to your tablet's card for later reference.

The format the **Contacts** app uses is .vcf (or vCards). This is a standard format for virtual business cards.

Import/Export contacts

Import from storage

Export to storage

Share visible contacts

Cancel

Confirm export

Are you sure you want to export your contact list to "/mnt/sdcard/00001.vcf"?

OK   Cancel

Widgets

You can add a **Contacts** app widget to your **Home** screen. This is a shortcut for one contact that you may frequently email or instant message. Tap the contact on the widget, and you've got easy access to your available contact methods.

Chapter 10

Working with Calendars

In this chapter, you'll learn how to use calendars. On default Android Honeycomb tablets, Google Calendar is the primary calendar tool. You'll learn how to use the **Calendar** app on your tablet, even with Microsoft Exchange accounts. I'll also discuss alternatives.

Google Calendar on the Web

Google Calendar is a full-featured, web-based calendar app. You can use it to manage personal, shared, and public events, and Android tablets make your calendars easy to see and read.

You only need a Google Account to register for Google Calendar; and since you probably already have such an account to use Gmail on your tablet, you're all set. If you're using a laptop or desktop computer, you can visit Google Calendar on the Web at http://calendar.google.com.

Figure 10–1 shows the basic web-based Google Calendar layout.

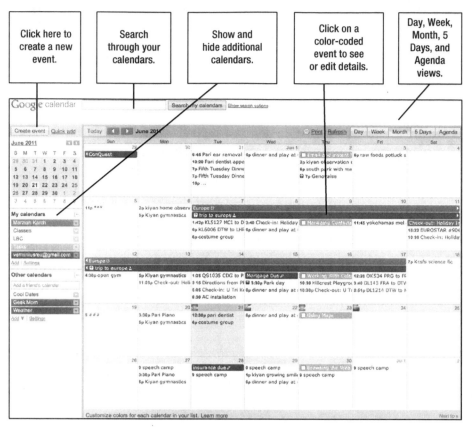

Figure 10–1. *Google Calendar on the Web*

The basic calendar layout is meant for Web browsers on computers, which generally have larger monitors than tablets or phones, so there's a lot of densely displayed information. Rather than dragging and zooming, you navigate the online calendar mainly through mouse clicks or track pad taps.

You have five views: **Day, Week, Month, 5 Days** (to look at your work week), and **Agenda**. There's also a **Print** view for people who would like a printed copy. In addition to creating events by using the **Create event** button, you can click the **Quick add** button and make a new event using natural language, such as "Dinner at Jason's on Tuesday at six." I'm pointing out these features now because not all of them are available on your tablet's **Calendar** app. However, you can always use your tablet's Web browser to view your Google Calendar if you need a missing feature.

Privacy Levels

Google Calendar displays a series of calendars, all of them color-coded and stacked together. This allows you to view or hide calendars as needed. It also allows you to set different default permissions for each calendar. That means you can decide whether a calendar is totally public (e.g., sales and promotions at a local business or events for a club or conference); shared with a few individuals (e.g., a family calendar or workplace collaboration); displays only busy or available information (e.g., client meeting requests); or is visible only to you.

All of those options actually stem from two choices: public or private. Within public entries, you have completely public calendars where all events are visible to everyone, indicating when you are busy or available. Within private calendars, you may choose to share select events or availability with other individuals. You may override these settings when you enter new events.

> **NOTE:** You can create a calendar with one default behavior and change the permissions on an individual item. However, I'd caution you against that (other than inviting attendees to an event) because it's easy to forget you've overridden a private calendar to have a public event. The safer bet is to stick with the default permissions of the calendar type you choose.

Adding Calendars

You have two types of calendars available on the lower-left side of the screen, **My calendars** and **Other calendars**, each of which has an Add link. **My calendars** are calendars that you can view and edit. **Other calendars** are those you can merely view. You add new calendars by clicking the Add link below the desired type of calendar. Your choices will depend on the type of calendar you wish to add. For example, if you want to add a calendar to **My calendars**, you'll see something resembling Figure 10–2.

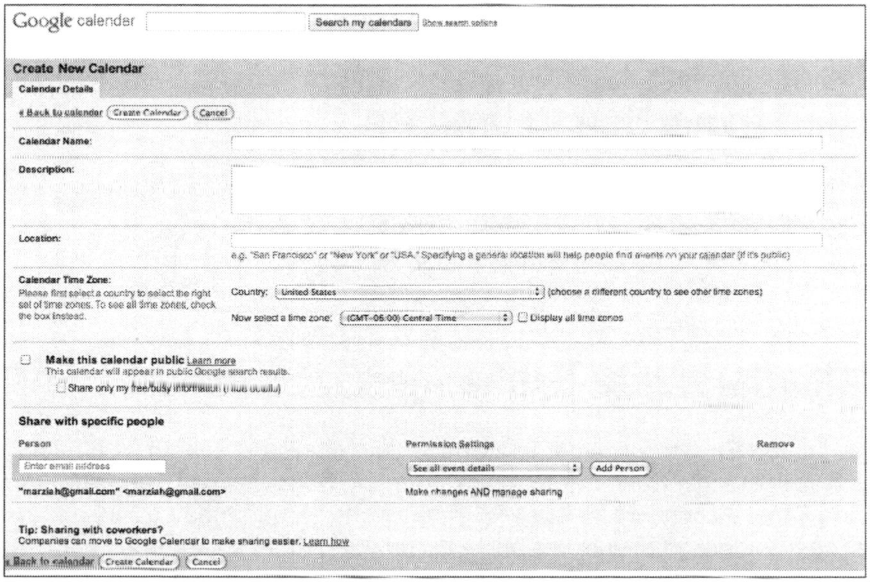

Figure 10–2. *Adding a calendar*

You should add a name and description for each calendar, as well as a location for public calendars (such as City Fine Arts Center). Next, set your calendar's time zone.

That's the basic information; you're now ready to move onto privacy settings.

You must check the specific box to make a calendar public. Otherwise, your calendar is private. You may also share events on a calendar with others by entering an email address in the box labeled, **Share with specific people**. When you add people to your calendar, you can specify whether they can see events; manage events; or both manage events and manage sharing (i.e., manage whether they have permission to add other people to the calendar). If you don't have anyone in mind now, you can always add guests later by editing an event.

You can adjust your sharing and viewing options by clicking the Settings link underneath either **My Calendars** or **Other Calendars**. This gives you a view of all the calendars linked to your account, as shown on the right. You can see the sharing status, hide or display calendars, or unsubscribe from shared or public calendars.

Importing and Exporting Calendars

If you want to get calendar events into or out of Google Calendar, press the **Settings** option just under the **My calendars** list. You'll see a link in the Calendars tab for importing and exporting calendars. Google uses iCalendar (iCal) format to export its calendars; however, it can import calendars in either iCal or CSV format (CSV is the calendar format used by Microsoft Outlook).

Syncing Calendars with Exchange

If you're using a Microsoft Exchange server to manage your company events, you may want to sync it with your Google Calendar to make work and home life easier (see Chapter 4: "Syncing Other Accounts" for specific instructions on adding an Exchange account). Once added, Exchange events will show up on your tablet's **Calendar** app; however, they will *not* show up on Google Calendar when you use it on the Web.

You can sync your calendars in both places by downloading and installing **Google Calendar Sync** from Google at http://dl.google.com/googlecalendarsync/GoogleCalendarSync_Installer.exe. At the time of writing, this utility is compatible with Outlook 2003, 2007, and 2010. It's Windows-only and compatible with Windows XP, Windows Vista, and Windows 7. It does not run on 64-bit editions of Windows.

When you install **Google Calendar Sync**, you can decide if this is a two-way sync, where events are editable in both programs; or a one-way sync, where events are only editable in one program. If you're using an alternative calendar app like **TouchDown**, you may want to just sync in one direction to avoid having everything show up twice.

If you're a Mac user, syncing between Google Calendar and Exchange is trickier. OS 10.5 and higher users can sync between Apple's calendar program (**iCal**) and **Google Calendar** using the CalDAV protocol. However, CalDAV isn't supported in Office 2011. My personal solution is to sync Exchange events through Android and use **iCal** on my Mac laptop, which supports both Exchange and Google Calendar syncing.

TouchDown

Another alternative to the Exchange-syncing conundrum is Nitro's **TouchDown for Tablets**. You can download the trial version for free. The full version costs $19 and allows full Exchange ActiveSync support. **TouchDown** does not sync your Google Calendar and Exchange info – that info is strictly separated. However, **TouchDown** does support Exchange task syncing, while Android does not. You can find **TouchDown for Tablets** at https://market.android.com/details?id=com.nitrodesk.honey.nitroid.

Google Calendar on Tablets

I covered the Web version of Google Calendar in some detail because understanding how that version works will help you understand how it works on your tablet. You can also use Google Calendar's Web version from your browser. It looks great on ten-inch tablets.

> **TIP:** If you launch Google Calendar from your **Browser** app, and you see a clunky mobile version of the interface, just tap the Desktop link at the bottom of the page.

However, the go-to app for using Google Calendar on tablets is the **Calendar** app.

 Many tablets include a shortcut for the **Calendar** app on the **Home** screen. Figure 10–3 shows the basic layout of this app.

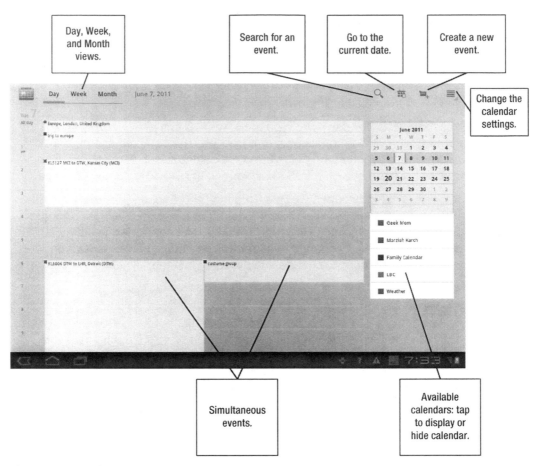

Figure 10–3. *The Calendar app*

As you can see, the layout of the tablet's **Calendar** app is a little different from that of the Web version. It's simplified, clean, and designed to be used by swiping and tapping with your fingers rather than clicking with a mouse.

You can navigate between **Day, Week,** and **Month** views. Notice that there's no **Agenda** or **5 Day** view in the app.

TIP: You navigate between next and previous days and weeks using a side-to-side swiping motion; however, you navigate between next and previous months using an up and down dragging motion.

Adding Events

You can add events to your calendar by tapping the **New event** button ![icon] on the upper-right corner of the screen. You'll need to fill out the options shown in Figure 10–4.

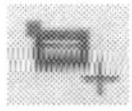

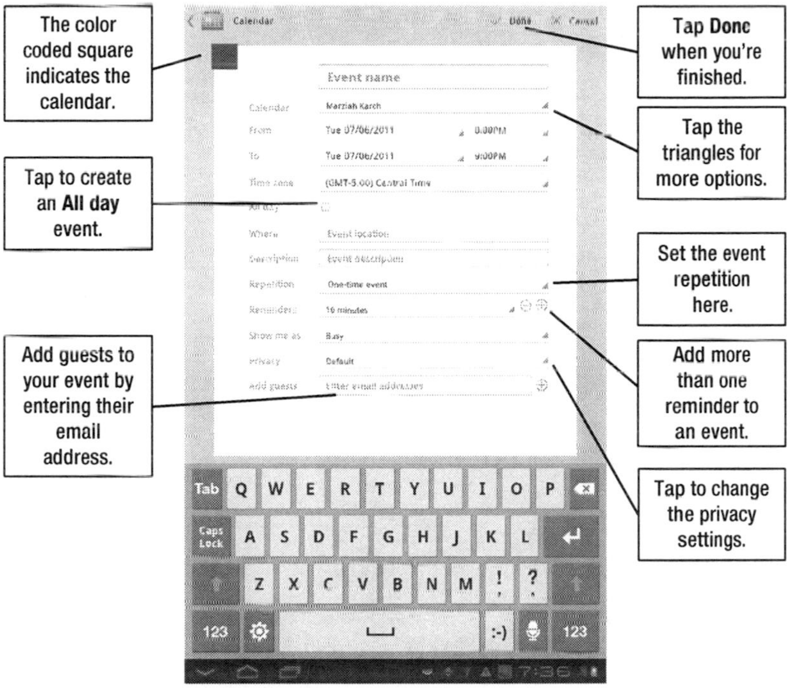

Figure 10–4. *Adding a new calendar event in Honeycomb*

Just as in other apps, the triangle on the bottom-right corner of a field indicates you have additional choices. Simply tap it to view your options. A **Plus** or **Minus** button with a circle indicates a field you can add more of or delete. For instance, you can create multiple reminders for a single event by clicking the **Plus** button for that field.

I do this sometimes for something important, such as a presentation. I set one reminder for the day before, one for the morning of, and one for fifteen minutes before the event. That way, I remember to dress for the occasion and bring all my materials.

You'll also want to pay attention to the time zone of the event if it occurs somewhere other than your current location. Tap **Done** once you're finished adding the event or **Cancel** if you change your mind.

Adding Guests

You may have also noticed the field at the bottom of the list that allows you to add guests. You can add guests to private or public events. People with an email address will receive a notification of the event. People with a Google Calendar account will receive notifications based on their preferences. Guests can indicate whether they're attending, and you can see the results (see Figure 10–5).

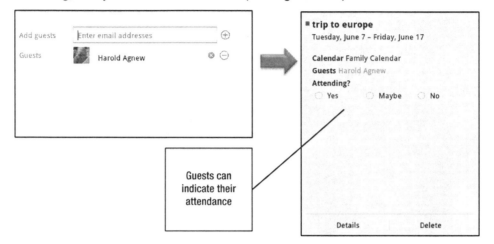

Figure 10–5. *Inviting guests to events*

Changing Your Calendar Settings

You don't have control over all the Web options, but there are a few settings you may want to change in the **Calendar** app. From the **Day**, **Week**, or **Month** view, press the

Menu button ▤ on the upper-right corner of the screen, and then go to settings. As Figure 10–6 shows, you have options for both general settings and account settings. You can also use this option to add an account. For more details on adding accounts, refer to Chapter 4: "Syncing with Google Accounts."

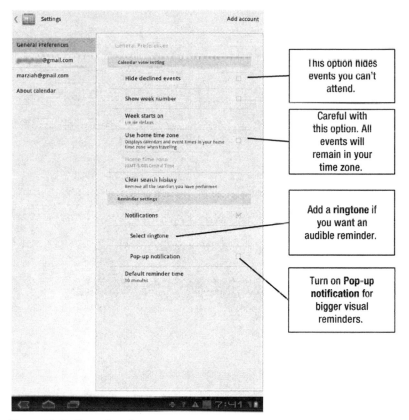

Figure 10–6. *General preferences*

Tap an individual Google account to change the specific calendar settings, as shown in Figure 10–7. Individual accounts simply allow you to change which calendars sync with your account. You can pare down unnecessary calendars to save on battery life and data usage.

Select all calendars to sync. You can hide synced calendars in month, day, and week views, but non-syncing calendars will never appear in those views.

Figure 10–7. *Individual account settings*

Widgets

Google Calendar comes with a widget; and on Honeycomb tablets, that widget (shown on the right) is resizable and interactive. You can click the **New events** button to add new events straight from your **Home** screen, and you can scroll through your events by swiping up and down. You can't hide calendars or change the view on the widget, however.

If you'd like more features, you can try a third-party widget, such as **Pure Calendar Widgets** ($2.14). This widget allows you to sync with **TouchDown**, **Google Calendar**, **Google Tasks**, **GTasks**, and other apps. It offers many size, display, and skinning options. It even lets you display the missing **Agenda** view from Google Calendar. Right now, this isn't a resizable widget; however, the developer has announced plans to release a Honeycomb-optimized version, which will hopefully be available when you read this.

Tasks

You may have noticed on the Web that one of the calendars Google Calendar displays is a Task calendar, as shown on the left. This calendar shows a simple task list that allows you to create collections of tasks, set due dates, add notes, and check off items as they're completed.

However, this feature is not supported in the **Calendar** app on your tablet, yet. That doesn't mean you can't use the feature, however. If you use Google Calendar from the Web, you can create a bookmark to go specifically to the tasks at http://gmail /tasks. My preferred option is to go with third-party apps for this. I use **Dato GTasks** (https://market.android.com/details?id=org.dayup.gtask), which offers a free trial or a $3.99 paid app that syncs with Google Tasks. You could also use a separate task-management tool, such as **Astrid Todo.** Both apps are compatible with **Pure Calendar Widgets**.

Chapter 11

Using Maps

Your tablet is more than a laptop without a keyboard. Depending on the device, it's also a map, compass, GPS navigation system, and a restaurant guide—all rolled into one.

There are a lot of apps that use maps; but in order to do so, those apps have to know where your tablet is. To that end, many Android tablets have GPS units, some have cell phone data, and all of them so far have Wi-Fi.

In general, tablets can be located by the following:

- GPS (global positioning satellites)
- Cell phone towers
- WPS (Wi-Fi positioning system)

There are more than 27 global positioning satellites orbiting the Earth. Your tablet's GPS unit attempts to find the signal from at least three of them and triangulate your position. However, this requires your tablet to have a chip that detects GPS signals and be in an area that can detect them. If you're indoors or around lots of tall buildings, your tablet might not pick up a GPS signal.

Your location can also be estimated using relative positions to cell phone towers. This isn't as accurate as GPS because cell towers are positioned for efficient signal reception, not triangulation, so it's less likely you'll be in a spot with three overlapping points.

The third method of locating your phone comes from using a map of known public Wi-Fi spots. It's a method that works well in urban areas and indoors—precisely the places where GPS does poorly. Because this approach requires only a Wi-Fi signal, it even works on laptops, netbooks, and tablets.

Depending on your hardware, your tablet may use a combination of all three methods to know where it is.

You can enable and disable your tablet's ability to track you by opening the **Settings** panel and then choosing **Location & security**. Figure 11–1 shows the options available on a Wi-Fi Samsung Galaxy Tab 10.1.

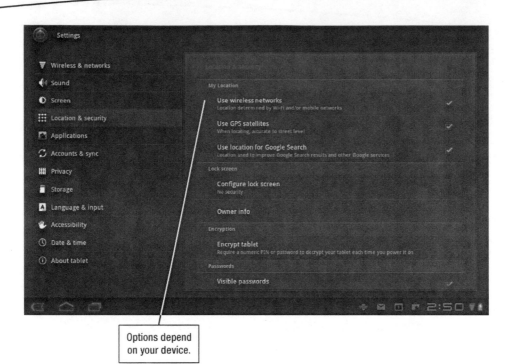

Options depend
on your device.

Figure 11–1. *Location & security options*

You can choose to enable both the **Use GPS satellites** and **Use wireless networks**
options. The latter option uses both Wi-Fi and cellular networks if your tablet is capable
of this. You can also choose to enable or disable the **Use location for Google Search
option**. You can disable this option if you have privacy concerns about Google tracking
your location; however, enabling it gives you better results for local searches.

Understanding Google Maps

By default, Honeycomb tablets come with the **Maps** app, which relies on Google Maps.

Google Maps is also available on the Web, which means you could use your
tablet's **Browser** app to access it; however, the **Maps** app provides a great interface for
tablets, and it includes lots of options. Figure 11–2 shows the basics of using Google
Maps on your tablet.

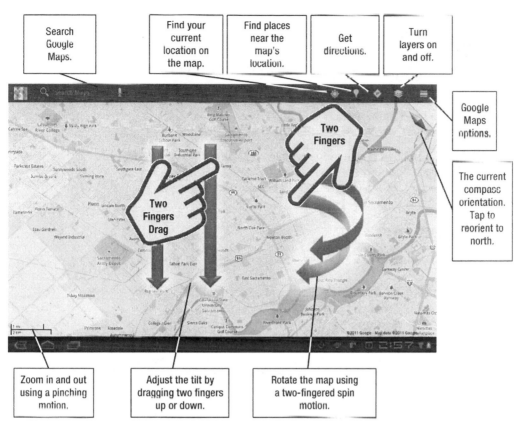

Figure 11–2. *The Maps app's touch interface*

The **Maps** app lets you navigate Google Maps using handy finger gestures:

- Use one finger to slide the map in any direction.

- Tap with one finger to zoom in on a location.

- Tap with two fingers to zoom away from a location.

- Tap a labeled location like a museum, park, or restaurant to see more about the location.

- Drag straight down or up with two fingers to tilt the perspective of the map.

- Twist with two fingers to spin the orientation of the map. Tap the compass to make north up again.

- Pinch or expand with two fingers to zoom in or out of the current map view.

Find Your Location on the Map

If you'd like to find your current location on the map, tap the **Location/Compass** button

in the **Action** menu (see Figure 11–2). You'll see your location on the map as an arrow surrounded by a blue circle. You could be anywhere within that blue circle, so the smaller the circle, the more accurate the location information is.

If your tablet has a built-in compass, you can tap again to enter **Compass** mode. When you do this, the map tilts and stays oriented towards north, even when you tilt and move the tablet. This is handy for trying to get your bearings when you're lost.

Getting Directions

You can find a new location by using the search function at the top of the screen. Once you find a location, you may want to figure out how to get there. You can also skip to the chase and find the location and directions at the same time. With either method, you

start by tapping the **Directions** button on the **Action** menu at the top of the screen (see Figure 11–3).

Figure 11–3. *Getting driving directions in the Maps app*

You'll see fields for **My Location** and **End point** (see Figure 11–3). The **My Location** field assumes that you want directions from your current location. If you want to use a different address, you'll need to enter it into this field.

There's also a handy **Bookmark** button right next to the **My Location** and **End point** fields. This lets you choose from your current location, a place you point to on the map, the address of one of your contacts, or any location you've starred.

You'll also see a series of buttons below these fields that let you choose what mode of transportation you need. You can choose **Car**, **Public transportation**, **Bicycle**, and **Walking** directions. These options can be a lifesaver if you're trying to get anywhere in a big city without a car.

> **NOTE:** Public transportation directions depend on the city and how well a given city has communicated its public transportation options to Google. Some routes will have unnecessary bus transfers and walks simply because Google's database doesn't have the nearby stop listed; however, Google has also added directions for public transportation for more than 400 cities worldwide.

Once you've settled on a start point, an end point, and a means of transportation, tap **Go**. You'll see a text-based list of step-by-step directions (see Figure 11–4).

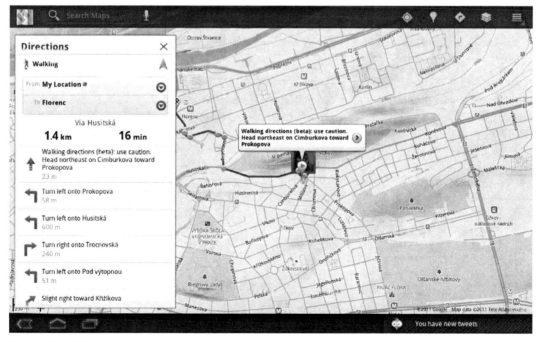

Figure 11–4. *Directions listed*

If you have walking, biking, or driving directions, you can also tap the
Navigation button or select **Navigation** after pushing your phone's **Menu** button to turn
your tablet into a GPS navigation system. Google's Navigation feature will give you turn-
by-turn directions by voice and even attempt to help you avoid traffic jams.

> **CAUTION:** You can only use the Google Navigation feature to get to your destination if you have
> an Internet connection for the whole trip. That means you either need a tablet with a wireless
> data plan or you need to find some other data option, such as a mobile hotspot device.

Just like dedicated GPS navigation systems, Google's Navigation feature will attempt to
compensate if you take a wrong turn or choose to take an alternate road. It also has
text-to-speech, which means you'll hear "Turn left on West Highway 50" and not just
"Turn left in 1000 feet." As with any GPS navigation system, this feature works better for
some roads than others. Sometimes, the Google Maps data will reflect a less commonly
used name for a road, and sometimes the pronunciation will be off.

The Navigation feature displays map information for driving, the length of time it will take
to reach your destination, and the direction of your next turn. As you near your
destination, the Navigation feature will show you a street-level view, so you can glance
(or better yet, have a passenger glance) to see where you're headed. Unlike some
commercial navigation systems, you cannot choose new voices or change the
appearance of your "car" on the map.

Tap the **Back** button to exit the Navigation feature and get back to text-based
directions. From here, you can also press the phone's **Menu** button to get updated
directions, reverse the directions for the trip back, or report a problem with the
directions. You can also use the **Route** options to avoid toll roads or highways.

Map Layers

The **Maps** app for Android works by displaying Google Maps information as a series of information-layer overlays. If you're familiar with Google Earth, it works the same way. You can turn these layers on or off individually by following these steps:

1. Tap the **Layers** button to see some of the available layers, as shown to the right. This list may also scroll.

2. Tap the **More Layers** button to see even more layers.

3. Tap each layer to toggle it on or off. You can turn on more than one of these layers at a time.

Traffic

Much of the information on Google Maps comes from contracts with third parties, and the traffic information is no exception. Traffic information is only available for large cities, and it's shown by color-coding the roads. Green indicates smooth traffic, yellow indicates delays, and red indicates major snarls. Traffic information can change rapidly, so don't expect absolute accuracy. It's also difficult (and dangerous) to check this while you're actually on the road. Google's Navigation feature automatically compensates for typical daily congestion patterns. For example, the directions it provides will have you use alternate routes during rush hour.

Satellite

Satellite info comes from third-party and Google-owned image sources, and those photos are stitched together and superimposed on the map information (see the example shown to the right).

The images are usually great, but sometimes the stitching process distorts the image. Consequently, there are times when an address appears to be in the wrong location, and you'll notice patches of ground with different image quality.

Satellite images are not typically recent, and the photos for any given area could be several years old. Google will often buy new images when something major happens in an area, such as Hurricane Katrina or the earthquake and tsunami in Japan; however, don't be surprised if the satellite image of your house doesn't include your recently built garage.

Google Labs Layers

Google Labs is a collection of experimental features you can turn on and off (see the figure to the right). They're not always reliable, and they don't always last; however, some Google Labs "graduates" have turned into solid and popular features, such as the public transportation directions in Google Maps.

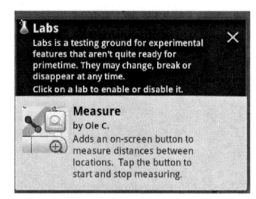

Most significant Google products have their own set of Google Labs experiments, but often those features won't work on your phone (this is true for many Gmail features). Google Maps is an exception to this. Follow these steps to access the Google Labs features in Google Maps:

1. Press the **Menu** button while in Google Maps.

2. Tap **Labs**.

3. Tap individual layers (i.e., additional Google Labs features for Google Maps) to toggle them on or off. You can enable or disable layers at will.

Google uses the relative popularity of Google Labs experiments as one factor in determining what stays and what goes. A Google Buzz layer was recently axed, but there's currently a **Measure** layer for quickly measuring distances between two locations. It may be replaced with something else by the time you read this.

Location Sharing with Latitude

The Latitude feature gives you a way to let your social network know where you are. You can use it to make sure people know you made your flight or to let your contacts know you're in their city.

Currently, you can only share information with mutual friends. This means you must invite your friends to share their Latitude information with you, and they must accept the invitation. You can also use Latitude from a laptop or desktop computer, so the feature doesn't depend on everyone owning a phone. Your four global choices for sharing Latitude location information are as follows:

- **Detect automatically:** You just let your phone report where you are to your friends.

- **Set your location:** You can manually update your location (and lie about where you are if you wish).

- **Hide your location:** Nobody sees your location, but you can still see your friends.

- **Turn Latitude off:** No one sees where you are, and you don't see where your friends are, either.

Keep in mind that your friends are the only ones who can see any of this, and settings for individuals will override global choices. Early after Latitude's release, there was concern that people could be stalked by having this feature turned on without their knowledge, so you may receive an email letting you know you've joined Latitude or that you have turned on location tracking.

To add friends to Latitude from Google Maps, take the following steps:

1. Press the **Menu** button.

2. Tap **Latitude**.

3. Tap the **Add friends** button.

4. Choose people to add through your contact list or by their email address. You can also add from the suggested friends by tapping the **Add friends** button next to their name.

People you invite will receive an email inviting them to join Latitude or to accept your request. When someone sends you an invitation, you'll receive an email asking if you'd like to ignore the request, share your location back, or accept the request and hide your location.

If all of this sounds a bit too personal, you can ratchet it down a notch for more casual business contacts. To manage friends on an individual level, simply tap **Latitude** and then tap a contact's name.

You can see where your friends are on a map, contact them (via email, Google Talk, and so on), get navigation directions to visit them, ping them to request that they check-in, remove them as a friend, and set specific privacy settings.

Tapping **Sharing options** lets you set the following options:

■ **Detect your location:** Latitude uses your device to determine where you are.

■ **Set your location:** This feature enables you to say you are anywhere, but it's generally intended for people without wireless data plans.

■ **Do not update your location:** Nobody can see where you are.

■ **Enable location history:** This is just a personal log of where you've been. Nobody else can see it, but it gives an interesting snapshot of your daily life.

- **Enable automatic check-ins:** You can specify places where you want to check in automatically, so your contacts will know you're there. For example, it might update when you are at your office or your favorite coffee shop.

- **Manage your places:** This is where you can see and remove locations you've set for automatic check-in.

You can change these settings later or tweak them by relationship level. For example, you might let your spouse know your exact location, but let your business contacts know your city only when you travel. You can also globally shut this feature down by hiding or manually entering just your city name when you don't want to broadcast your location.

> **NOTE:** Google+ is a new social-networking tool from Google that also allows location check-ins. At the time this book was going to press, Google+ check-ins were only available through the **Google+** app; however, Google plans on integrating the Google+ feature into more services in the future, so Google+ check-ins may be available through Google Maps by the time you read this.

Places Pages

Do you need more information about a location? If so, then the **Places** page on Google Maps is the place to go. On Android, each location has a well-organized **Details** page. Double-tap a location or tap the location bubble, and you'll see the details about that location, as shown on the right.

Not every location will have as many details as you see for Liberty Hall; what you do see will depend on the information available for a given location.

Some details you can find include reviews, the location's website, a phone number, its hours of operation, an average review, related locations, and a picture of the place.

You can also check in to the location, add a star, or tap the **More** button to share the location on social-networking sites.

Google Places

Rather than randomly finding spots on a map, you can search for nearby attractions by using your tablet's built-in **Places**  app (see Figure 11–5). This app lets you browse for locations by category or search for them individually. One you find a location, you can then go to that location's **Details** page.

> **TIP:** You can also use the **More** button in the **Places** app to download map information within a 10-mile radius of a place. You won't see satellite images or 3D buildings, but the downloaded map information can help you navigate to a place when you're outside of Wi-Fi range. You can also use this app to download maps of your vacation spots before you hit the road. Downloaded maps are deleted from your tablet's cache after 30 days.

Figure 11–5. *The Places app*

Starring Locations

You can also use the **Details** page to add a star to a location. Tap the **Star** icon in the upper-right corner of the screen, and the starred location will display a glowing yellow star to the right of its name. To remove the star, simply tap the **Star** icon again. Using stars is like saving bookmarks for web pages; it enables you to easily find locations you visit frequently or need to find quickly.

Nelson-Atkins Museum of Art
4525 Oak St
Kansas City, MO   0.6 mi
★★★★★ 103 reviews
Open until 4:00pm
www.nelson-atkins.org

You can access your list of starred items in Google Maps in two simple steps:

1. Tap **Menu**.

2. Tap **Starred places**.

> **NOTE:** When you travel for business, put a star on your hotel and your conference's convention center before you arrive. This will give you instant access to the addresses and phone numbers for both locations. It will also give you driving directions between the two locations and a list of nearby restaurants.

Google Street View

Google used cars with mounted cameras and other equipment to take 360-degree photos of roads everywhere in the US and many other countries.

That aside, Google's Street View feature is an amazing tool for figuring out where you need to be, as shown in Figure 11–6. You can use it when you have an appointment at a new location to see what the building for the meeting location looks like before you get there. You can also use this feature to see if there's any parking or tricky intersections along the way.

Figure 11–6. *Google Map's Street View feature*

Follow these steps to get to the Street View feature:

1. Go to a location's **Places** page.

2. Tap the **Street View** button, which looks like a person with a triangle on his chest. Not every location has a Street View; if this button is grayed out, the feature is unavailable at that location.

3. Navigate by dragging your finger around the picture; this will pan around the scene.

4. Go further up or down the road by tapping the arrows. The yellow line shows you the path the Street View car took as it traveled.

5. Exit Street View by tapping **Go to map** on the bottom of the screen.

> **TIP**: Google's Street View uses large pictures and requires some bandwidth, so you should only attempt to use it if you've got a fairly strong signal or are in a Wi-Fi hotspot.

You may also notice that Street View has a **Compass** mode. This feature performs a neat trick: it allows you to see the area around a given Street View by spinning around slowly with your tablet in front of you.

Email and Text Directions

Other apps link to **Google Maps**, and Google provides plenty of alternative ways to find directions and locations. If someone sends you a location in Gmail, Google will sense that the information is an address and attempt to automatically create a **Google Maps** link from it.

Making Your Own Maps

You may have noticed that one of your options in Google Maps is called **My maps**. You're not limited to Google's layers when constructing a map. You can actually create your own map as a layer to Google Maps; however, at this time you'll need to do so on the Web because there's no Honeycomb version of the **My Maps** editor.

All your maps will be available in the **My maps** layer, but only maps you've made public will be visible to other people or available via search.

Third-Party Navigation

Google Maps is a free service, and most tablets ship with an app that lets you access its content; however, it's not the only navigation system in town. If your tablet comes with a data plan, you can explore a variety of navigation tools, such as **CoPilot Live** or **MobileNavigator**. Most of these alternative navigation tools are premium apps, but some of them allow better caching of map information for navigating when you don't have a strong data signal.

Location-Sensing Social Media and Games

I've focused a lot in this chapter on Google Maps specifically. However, one recent trend worth noting is location-sensitive social media. There are restaurant and service guides like Yelp, as well as apps that tag photos or messages with your location. Your tablet's camera can also tag your photos with the location they were taken.

The Latitude, Google+, and Buzz features use some of these geo-tagging features, allowing you to check in directly from Google Maps, as shown on the right. The Twitter and Facebook services also allow you to check in from their apps, but two rising stars in this field are the Gowalla and Foursquare services. Both were created around the same time, and they offer very similar features. Finally, app developers are free to take advantage of the Google Maps library and Android's location-sensing features.

In both Gowalla and Foursquare, the object is to check into locations. You need to use a phone or other location-sensing mobile device, and you can't just manually type in a location. The whole point is to actually *be* there. You can share these check-ins with nobody, your friends, your Facebook page, or the whole world via Twitter.

Both Foursquare and Gowalla are working with businesses and cities to offer features like coupons and specials for users who check in with these services. This unique form of advertising may become very popular because it gives businesses an obvious way to measure the effectiveness of their advertising campaigns.

Foursquare

Foursquare was cofounded by ex-Googler Dennis Crowley, who worked on a similar project, Dodgeball, which was purchased and abandoned by Google. However, Foursquare takes the social network to a new and different level by adding a gaming component. Dennis Crowley described it as a method of combining the act of exploring your city with gaming and a little bit of Boy Scout pride (you earn merit badges and trophies as you do so).

Certain combinations of check-ins in Foursquare earn badges. For example, you can earn badges by checking into the same location three times, finding five karaoke bars, finding three places in Chicago with photo booths, or checking in after 3 a.m. on a school night.

Checking into the same location regularly could also earn you a *mayorship*. The mayor of a location is the person who has checked in the most often in the last two months, so you need to keep checking in to maintain the title.

However, the service doesn't allow rapid checking in because it wants to prevent too many people from gaming the system.

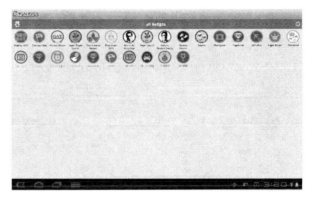

Gowalla

While Foursquare is a bit of a competitive game, Gowalla is more of a personal exploration and virtual geocaching tool. Gowalla lets you earn pins, which are similar to the badges in Foursquare. In this service, you maintain a passport of places you've visited. You can also create and travel on tours of different check-in locations.

Gowalla also gives users a few virtual items they can leave or exchange at locations. Examples might be blankets, avocados, and espresso machines. To the right, you can see the luggage tags left at a location. When you encounter a virtual item at a location, you can see the history of who owned the item; this encourages the frequent exchange of these virtual geocaches.

Rapid check-ins are fine with Gowalla because there's no such concept as a mayorship. The Gowalla service is also much more sensitive to proximity than Foursquare, so you need to be pretty close to a location to check in. This makes Gowalla ideal for walking tours and pub crawls, but not so great for check-ins within a building or anyplace where the GPS will not work well.

Chapter 12

Browsing the Web

Chapter 6 covered how to get your tablet connected to the Internet. Plenty of apps use your Internet connection to do things like check your email or update your calendar; however, you can also use your tablet to surf the Web directly. In this chapter, we'll focus on how to use Android's default **Browser** app and other alternatives.

Chrome and the Android Browser

Google actually has two Web browsers, just as it has two operating systems (Android and Chrome OS). Google makes the **Chrome** web browser, but it also makes the *Chrome OS*, which is built around that browser and designed to run on laptops known as *Chromebooks*. It might appear that Android tablets use the **Chrome** browser, but they actually use a different, Android-specific browser: the **Browser** app (AKA the **Android browser**). Both browsers were based on **Webkit**, which was originally developed by Apple to power **Safari** and is now used in a variety of mobile browsers.

> **NOTE:** The **Android browser** isn't **Chrome**, so you can't run **Chrome** extensions on your Android tablet. However, you can sync bookmarks, which we'll get to later in this chapter.

Android Browser Navigation

Browsers on phones don't give you a lot of screen real estate, so you can't easily do

Browser

things like use tabs for browsing. When you tap to launch the **Browser** app on your 10-inch or larger tablet, you'll see that your browsing experience starts to resemble what you expect when browsing on a laptop. Figure 12–1 shows the basics of navigating the **Browser** app in Android.

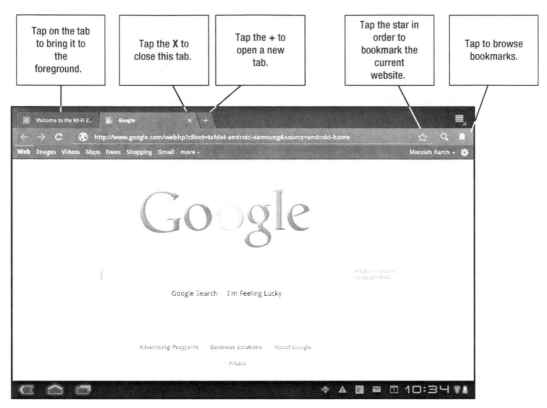

Tap on the tab to bring it to the foreground.

Tap the **X** to close this tab.

Tap the **+** to open a new tab.

Tap the star in order to bookmark the current website.

Tap to browse bookmarks.

Figure 12–1. *Navigating the Browser app*

Multiple-tab browsing means you can quickly navigate between tabs. However, adding too many tabs will cause them to start scrolling off the screen, and you won't be able to navigate between them as quickly. You can see the **Back**, **Forward**, and **Refresh** buttons in the upper left. You can navigate within most pages using the standard gestures, such as dragging to scroll, pinching to zoom, and spreading two fingers apart to zoom out.

> **NOTE:** Smaller tablets that run an earlier version of Android—such as the Nook Color, the HTC Flyer, and the original Samsung Galaxy Tab—use a non-tabbed version of the **Browser** app that is designed for smaller screens. The Kindle Fire uses its own Silk Browser.

Finding a Website

To navigate to a new website, you can either open a new browser tab, or you can tap the URL of the existing tab and type in a new location, as shown in Figure 12–2.

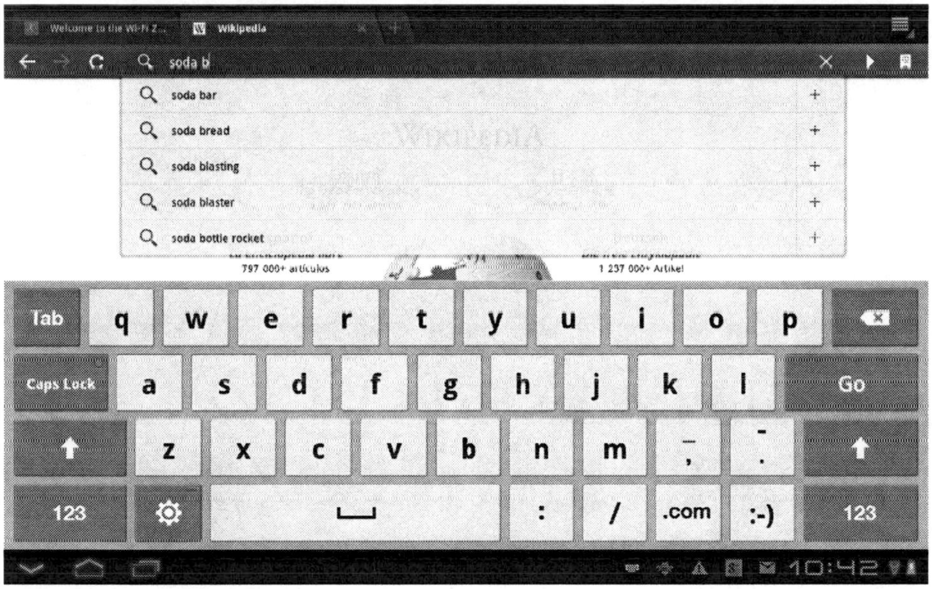

Figure 12–2. *Finding a website*

But what if you don't know the exact URL of the website you want to visit? No problem. Just type in a key phrase instead of a URL, and your browser will search the Web automatically. There is no separate search engine box, and there's no reason to navigate to a search engine before simply searching.

Bookmarking Pages

Rather than repeatedly search for the same words, you probably want to save frequently visited websites as bookmarks. Tap the **Star** icon in the upper-right corner to save a bookmark, as shown in Figure 12–3.

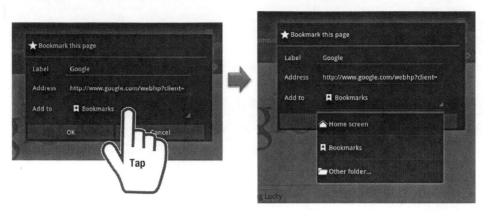

Figure 12–3. *Saving a bookmark*

You can save bookmarks to the **Bookmarks** area (this is the default and easiest option), or you can save a bookmark as a shortcut on your **Home** screen or to another folder.

Using Bookmarks and History

Saving bookmarks is only useful if you can quickly browse to those bookmarks when you need them. Rather than taking up space on your browser's **Navigation** bar,

bookmarks in Android get their own page. Tap the **Bookmarks** button ![bookmark icon] on the upper-right corner of the screen, and you'll see a screen similar to the one shown in Figure 12–4.

Figure 12–4. *The Bookmarks page*

You can swipe with your finger to navigate through the **Bookmarks** page. This page comes pre-populated with some common websites, like CNN and eBay; however, this page also shows any bookmarks you've added, as well as thumbnails for any website you've visited. The **Bookmarks** page is also available as a **Home** screen widget.

In addition to viewing bookmarks, you can also browse your own viewing history. This is a really useful way to get back to a page you know you've visited, but which you've forgotten to bookmark or otherwise can't find again. To view your history, tap the **History** tab on the upper-left side of the **Bookmarks** page (see Figure 12–5).

Figure 12–5. *Viewing the Browser app's History page*

Notice the stars next to each site in the list. These stars indicate whether you've already bookmarked a page; they also let you create a bookmark, if you so desire.

If you don't want your browsing history to show up here, you can tap the **Menu** button and select the option to delete your history.

Syncing with Your Google Account

If you use the **Chrome** browser on your computer, it's handy to sync your bookmarks and browsing history between your tablet and your computer. Follow these steps to do so:

1. Tap the **Menu** button on the upper-right corner of the screen.

2. Select **Settings** from the dropdown list.

3. Under the **General** settings, tap the option labeled **Sync with Google Chrome** (see Figure 12–6).

4. Decide whether to merge existing bookmarks from your tablet or delete them, as shown on the right.

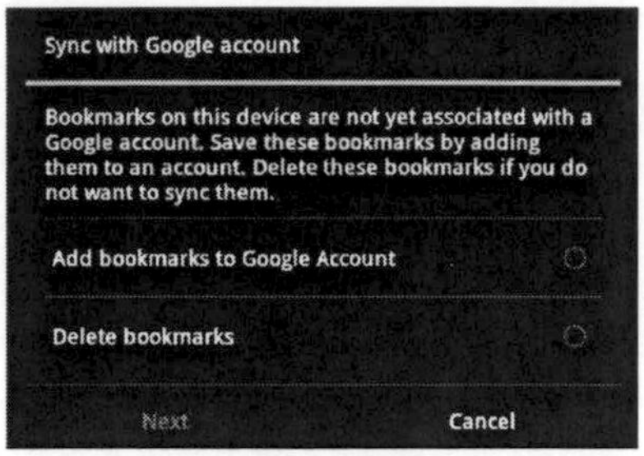

Sync with Google account

Bookmarks on this device are not yet associated with a Google account. Save these bookmarks by adding them to an account. Delete these bookmarks if you do not want to sync them.

Add bookmarks to Google Account   ○

Delete bookmarks   ○

Next   Cancel

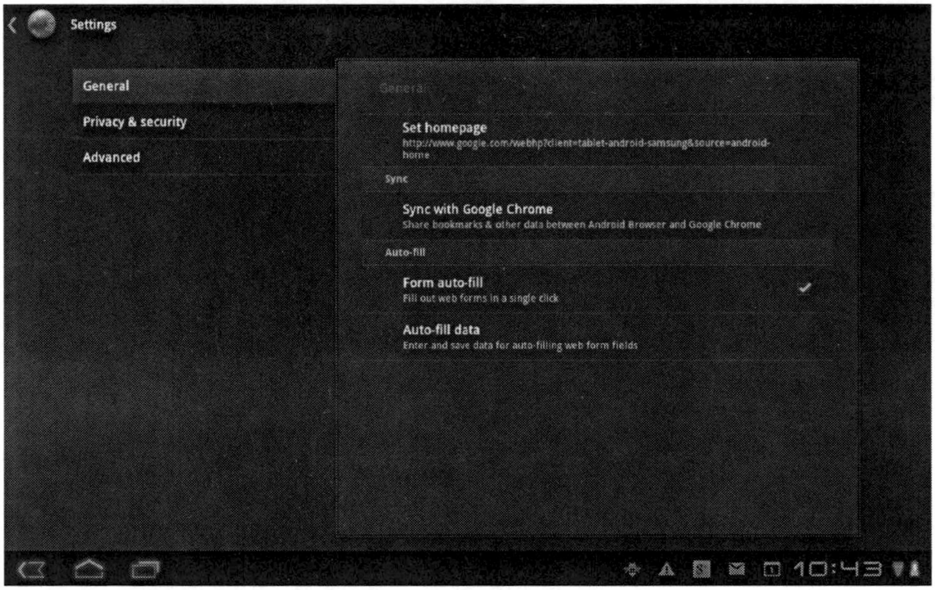

Figure 12–6. *Syncing with Google Chrome's bookmarks*

NOTE: There might be times when you don't want your browsing or search history to show up at all, such as when you borrow a tablet or shop for a gift. I'm sure you can use your imagination to figure out other reasons, as well. For incognito browsing, tap **Menu: New Incognito Tab**. The **Secret Agent** icon 🕵 indicates that websites in this tab will not be saved to your Android's search or browsing history.

Setting Your Search Engine

You may not be a Google search person. If that's the case, then you're not trapped into using Google's search engine If you prefer something else. You may also end up with a tablet that's been set to a different search engine by the device manufacturer. Follow these steps to change your **Browser** app's default search engine:

1. Tap the **Menu** button.

2. Select **Settings.**

3. Go to the **Advanced** area.

4. Tap **Set search engine**.

Flash

Adobe Flash is available as a free download from the Android Market. Once installed, Flash elements will display within the **Browser** app. Honeycomb tablets support Flash elements; however, not every Flash animation or movie will play on a tablet. Some streaming movie sites, such as Hulu, block their player from running on Android tablets without a paid subscription account. If you prefer, you can save bandwidth by setting **Flash** to only display Flash objects on demand:

1. From the **Browser** app, go to **Settings**.

2. Tap **Advanced**.

3. Tap **Enable plug-ins**.

4. Tap **On Demand**.

Google Labs and Quick Controls

Google Labs is an area where you can find experimental features. They may not become permanent features, but part of the analysis for what becomes permanent is how many people use them. If your browser has a **Labs** tab in the **Settings** menu, you can give the experimental features a try. (Only the Xoom tablet had a **Labs** tab at the time of writing, but other tablets may receive this feature in a future update.)

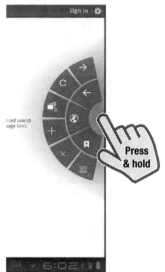

One example Labs option is the **Quick Controls** button. When this is turned on, you no longer see the standard tabbed browser; rather, you press and hold to the right of the screen to make the **Quick Control** bar appear, which gives you access to most controls. This bar frees up space at the top of the screen, but it also tends to be a bit tricky to use.

Desktop and Mobile Versions of Websites

Sometimes when you look at websites, you'll notice that two-finger gesturing does not work, and the display looks sparse and spread out. What you may be seeing is the mobile version of the website, such as the mobile version of Yahoo! shown on the left. It looks fine on a phone, but it's not so pretty on a 10-inch tablet.

Browsers have a *User Agent* that tells websites the type of device you're using. Google specifies that the User Agent for Android tablets is "Android" as opposed to "Android Mobile," which is used for phones. This means websites can treat tablets differently than phones. That's the theory, anyway. In practice, many websites simply have two versions: mobile and desktop.

If you see that you're reading a mobile version of a website, you can usually scroll to the bottom and click a link that says "Desktop Version" or something similar. Not every site will provide this link, so sometimes you'll be stuck with a mobile version of a site.

Unfortunately, the **Browser** app doesn't allow you to change your User Agent in the **Settings** menu. There's a method to enter debugging commands to change it; however, it's complicated, and some users report that the settings don't stick. The easiest way to change your User Agent is to use a browser that supports this change.

Alternative Browsers

You're not locked into the Android browser. You can download alternatives through the Android Market, and you can even set those alternatives as your default browser. **Dolphin HD** is probably the best alternative browser for Honeycomb tablets, and **Opera** is a great choice for smaller tablets. **Firefox** also offers a tablet browser, and it includes the ability to add features through extensions. Figure 12–7 shows the **Dolphin HD** browser, which is available from the Android Market at http://goo.gl/sgU8q.

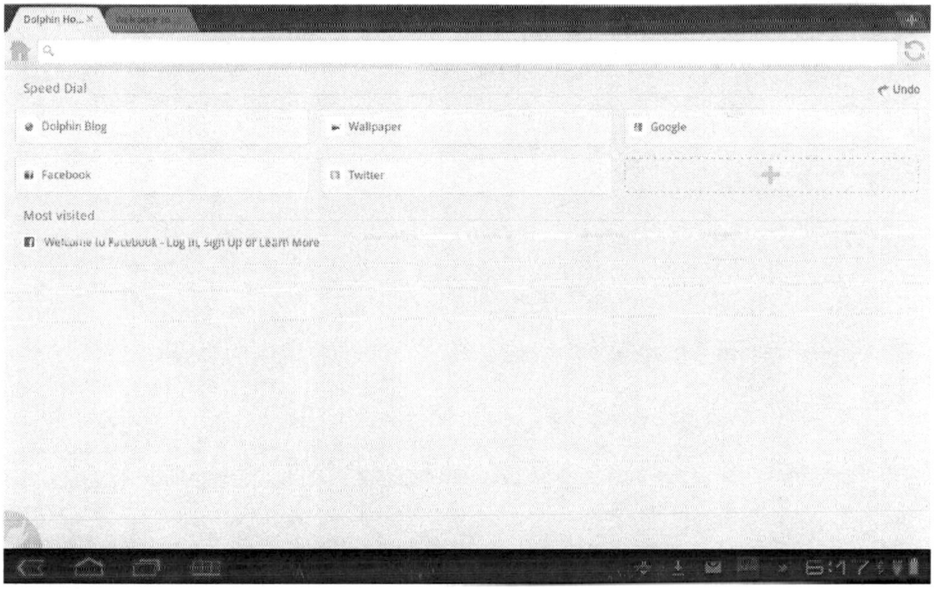

Figure 12–7. *The Dolphin HD browser*

Dolphin HD lets you use gestures to navigate. For example, you can trace the letter "N" to open a new tab. It's also very customizable, and it includes a variety of plug-ins (some of which may work better on some tablets than others).

One feature that makes **Dolphin HD** a great alternative for Honeycomb users is that it lets you easily set your User Agent from the **Settings** menu. Not only can you set it to view websites as a desktop browser, but you can also set it to **iPad** (since more websites have been optimized for iPad display) or a custom value.

User Agent	
Android (default)	◉
Desktop	◉
iPhone	◉
iPad	◉
Custom	◉
Cancel	

Opera is a popular choice for smaller tablets because it has easy-to-use large icons for bookmark browsing. However, it's still not optimized for larger tablets at the time of writing, and it doesn't allow you to change your User Agent. Mozilla Firefox is also available in a mobile version, but it is still relatively new to Android, and reviewers have complained that it is slow and unreliable.

Chapter 13

The Android Market

You can do a lot with the apps that come with your device, but sooner or later you'll want to install something new. This is the chapter where we'll cover downloading and installing both free and paid apps from the Android Market on your tablet. In Chapter 14, we'll discuss downloading apps from other sources.

Introducing the Android Market

Some early tablets didn't support the Android Market because of restrictions imposed by Google. Other tablets don't support the Android Market because they use modified versions of Android, and the device makers have chosen either to disallow apps or to use an alternative app market. However, the Android Market is the default app store for most Android tablets.

The Android Market takes a laissez-faire approach to app approval. Apple's App Store sets high standards and scrutinizes each app before allowing people to download it. The Android Market, by contrast, generally only yanks apps that are malicious or dishonest. It's up to you, the user, to determine whether an app will be worth your while.

> **NOTE:** Google has the power to remove apps from your tablet if it turns out they're harmful. This is rare, but it has happened.

Paying for Apps

Before you start purchasing apps, you should establish your method of payment. If you have a wireless data plan with your tablet, you may be able to pay through your wireless carrier. However, not all carriers offer this option. In most cases, you'll want to pay through the *Google Checkout* service. This is a service through Google that associates your credit card with your Google account, and it allows you to pay for Android apps—and third-party goods and services—through a variety of websites.

You can set up your account by visiting www.google.com/checkout.

Installing Apps from Your Tablet

One easy and intuitive way to install apps is directly from your tablet. Your tablet must be connected to the Internet, either by Wi-Fi or a 3G or 4G signal. Simply tap the **Market** app icon to launch the Android Market or tap the **Shop** button at the top-left corner of the **App** tray.

This will launch the Android Market (see Figure 13–1). In addition to apps, the Android Market on tablets also offers books through Google Books. Some tablets also offer movie rentals; however, we're focusing on apps in this chapter.

Tap on either the **Market** app or the **Shop** button.

Toggle between Apps and Books here.

Search for an app by key phrase or title.

View **My apps** to see apps you've downloaded.

Figure 13–1. *The Android Market tablet interface*

The Android Market has a large scrolling banner at the top. Beneath that, you can browse different types of featured apps, such as **Featured for Tablets**, **Top Paid**, and **Top Free**. You can also scroll through categories, such as **Entertainment**, **Communication**, and **Finance**.

You're not limited to just aimlessly browsing. You can also use the **Search Market** box at the top of the screen to look for apps by title or by key phrase.

Once you've found an app you'd like to examine more closely, tap the link. You'll see a page resembling the one shown in Figure 13–2.

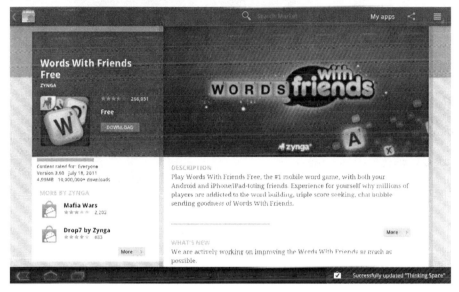

Figure 13–2. *An app's **Details** screen*

Each app has a **Details** screen designed to give you more information. You'll see user reviews, similar apps, screen captures, usage statistics, and more. You'll also see the price of the app on the upper-right corner (in this case, free) and a button to either purchase or download the item.

> **NOTE:** If you can see an app in the Android Market, it should be compatible with your device. Developers specify platform compatibility when they list their apps in the Android Market. However, be sure to read the user reviews to make sure nobody is commenting that the app doesn't work on your tablet.

Once you decide to download an app, you'll see a screen like the one shown in Figure 13–3. This screen outlines the exact permissions this app needs to function as designed. You can choose to click either **OK** or **Cancel**, depending on whether you want to proceed with the installation. If you tap **OK**, the app will start downloading, and you'll see a notification message when the download has completed.

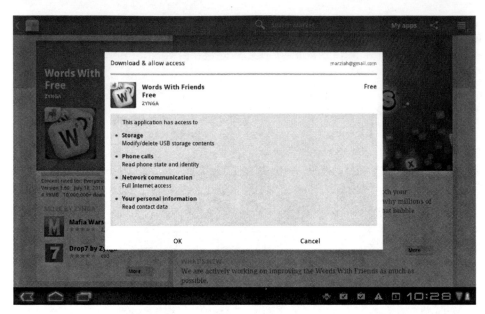

Figure 13–3. *App permissions*

Follow these steps to download a free item from the Android Market directly from your tablet:

Launch the **Android Market** app, either from the desktop or the **App** tray.

1. Navigate to the desired app's **Details** screen.

2. Tap the **Download** button.

3. Review the permissions you're granting the app and press **OK**. This will download the app.

Paying for Apps

There are a lot of great free apps, and it's possible to enjoy a tablet without ever purchasing an app. However, there are also a lot of great paid apps out there. You'll probably want to register for a **Google Checkout** account at www.google.com/checkout. Doing so will make it easier to enter your credit card information without having to worry about tapping it out on a tablet; however, you can still add and change credit card information from your tablet.

Once you've worked out the payment details, purchasing apps is pretty simple. Basically, you follow the same steps required to download free apps. Rather than tapping the **Download** button, however, you tap the **Buy** button. Figure 13–4 shows the process of downloading a purchased app.

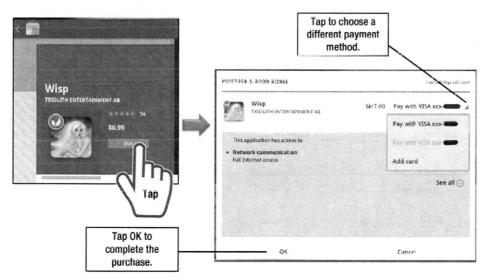

Figure 13–4. *Downloading a purchased app*

Apps in Foreign Currencies

App developers can market their apps to a worldwide audience, and sometimes that means the developer is actually in another country. App prices are actually shown in two ways. When you browse through apps from the US, apps are shown in approximate U.S. dollars. Once you click the **Buy** button, the foreign currency price is listed (see Figure 13–5).

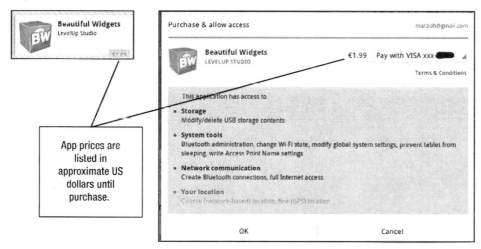

Figure 13–5. *Foreign transactions in the Android Market*

So long as your credit card allows foreign currency transactions, you can purchase the app as usual. Be aware that some credit cards charge transaction fees on top of the cost of the app.

Uninstalling Apps

If you have an app that is defective, takes up too much room, or is no longer useful, then you can uninstall it. One method to uninstall an app is to use the **App** tray:

1. Tap the **App** tray.

2. Long press the app from within the **App** tray.

3. Drag the app to the right corner of the screen where it says **Uninstall** (if it says **Remove**, you're not in the **App** tray).

Another way to uninstall an app is to go to its **Details** page in the Android Market. You'll see an **Uninstall** button, as shown in Figure 13–6. Simply tap it to remove your app.

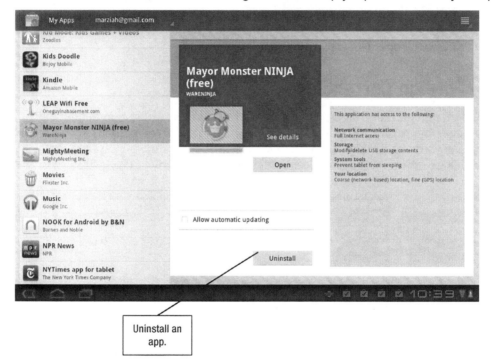

Uninstall an app.

Figure 13–6. *Uninstalling an app*

There's yet another way to uninstall apps, but it's slightly more complicated:

1. Tap the **Notifications** bar.

2. Tap **Settings**.

3. Tap **Applications**.

4. Tap **Manage Applications**.

5. Tap the name of the app you wish to remove.

6. Tap **Uninstall**.

The only advantage of using this method is that it doesn't require a Wi-Fi connection.

Getting a Refund

When you purchase an app, you have exactly 15 minutes from the time you download it to change your mind and request a refund. While that's certainly not enough time to give an app a test drive, it *is* enough time to roll back an accidental download.

To get a refund, simply go to the app's **Details** page within the required timeframe and tap the **Refund** button (see Figure 13–7).

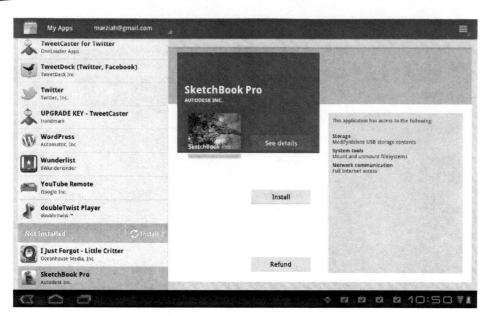

Figure 13–7. *Requesting a refund on a purchase*

Once your fifteen minutes are up, you'll no longer see the **Refund** button. You'll need to contact the app developer directly with any concerns. Fortunately, there's also a button to contact the developer on the app's **Details** page.

Updating Apps

Everyone once in a while, you'll get a notification that one or more of your apps has an update available. You can update an app in one of two ways. First, you can go to the Android Market directly and tap the My Apps link at the top of the screen. Second, you can use the update notification you receive to launch the Android Market.

Once at the Android Market, you'll see the **My apps** area (see Figure 13–8).

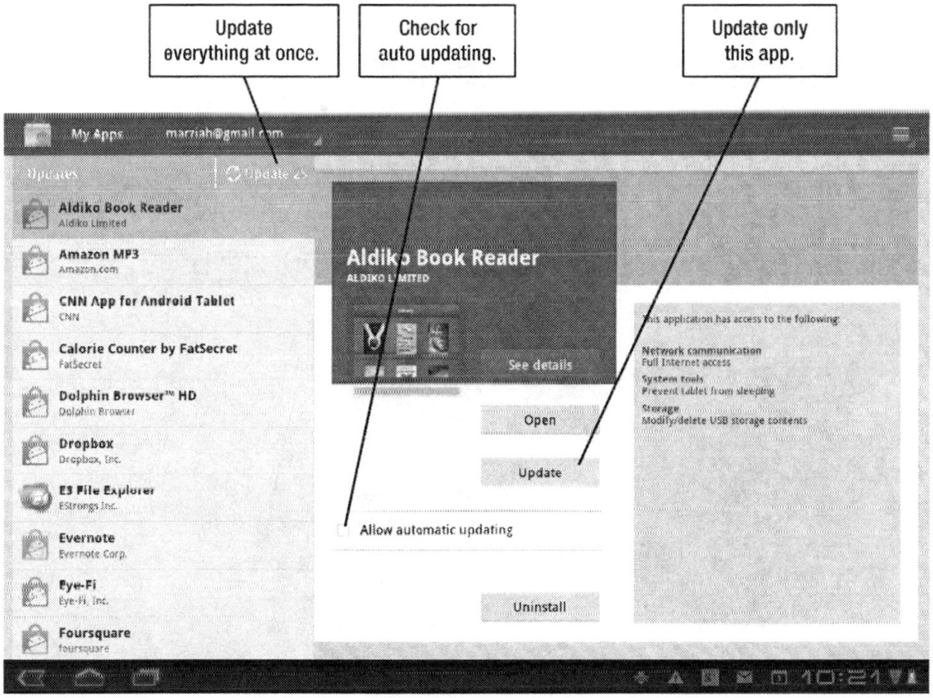

Figure 13–8. *Updating apps on your Android tablet*

You may have more than one app that needs to be updated. If so, you can tap the **Update** button on the upper-left side of this page to update all of your apps at once. You can also update one app at a time by going to that app's **Details** page. This might be useful if you're close to your bandwidth limit on your data plan.

You may also notice the checkbox to allow automatic updating. Selecting this means you'll download the latest update as soon as it's available. There is one scenario that will prevent you from auto-updating an app or updating all of your apps at once: when an app's permission level changes. Any time an app needs different permissions, you'll need to explicitly OK the changes before the app can be updated. Fortunately, you can also do this in a batch, as shown in the image to the right.

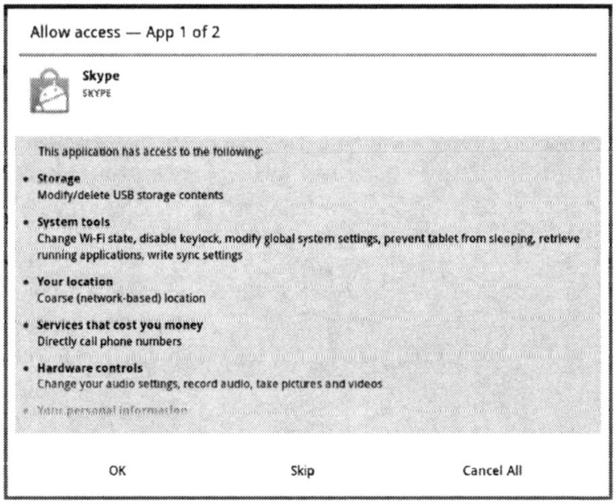

Using the Android Market Website

Now that we've covered the ins and outs of installing apps from your tablet, let's look at how to install them from the Internet. You can go directly to `http://market.android.com` from your laptop or desktop browser to find and install apps without having your tablet in hand.

The Android Market website looks a lot like the tablet version (see Figure 13–9).

Figure 13–9. *The Android Market website*

There are a few differences between the tablet and Web versions of the Android Market. For example, the layout is designed for a bigger screen. The Web version also lets you better fine-tune your searches, and it includes a few more navigational choices. However, the concept is pretty much the same. Simply browse or search for an app you like, and then go to that app's **Details** page.

You'll need to be logged into your Google account to download anything, but you'll be prompted to do so once you click the **Download** button. Once you log in, you'll see a screen resembling the one shown in Figure 13–10.

Figure 13–10. *Downloading apps from the Web*

In addition to displaying permissions, this window prompts you to select a device to send this app to. If you've only got one Android device, there's not much choice, obviously. However, you can use this option to select between many different phones and tablets. You'll only see choices for *compatible* devices you've registered.

After you click **Install**, the app is queued for installation. The next time your tablet is connected to the Internet, it will download and install the app for you.

Once you've downloaded and used an app, be sure to go back and use the website to leave an app review. In the next chapter, we'll look at installing apps from sources other than the Android Market.

Chapter 14

Alternative App Markets

In the last chapter, we discussed the Android Market and how you can download and install both free and paid apps from it. In this chapter, we'll discuss other sources for apps you can acquire. Google doesn't like to lock Android down. Unlike an iPad, your Android lets you install apps from third-party sources without having to *jailbreak* your device. One caveat: Google doesn't lock Android, but that doesn't prevent the device manufacturer (or your carrier) from trying to do so. Some tablets, such as the Nook Color and Kindle Fire, use modified versions of Android that prevent you from installing apps from outside sources. In the Fire and Nook's case, "outside sources" include the Android Market.

There are some clear advantages to using third-party app markets. For example, they enable more competition and innovation. Also, selective app markets may offer a higher quality selection. Then again, they may not offer the same protections that the Android Market provides, including the ability to remove malicious apps. You should only download apps from reputable sources. As always, caveat emptor.

Installing Apps from Unknown Sources

In general, you'll need to enable third-party apps from the **Settings** menu before you can use alternative app markets (see Figure 14–1).

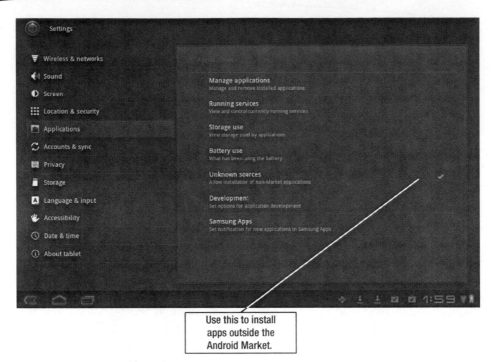

Use this to install apps outside the Android Market.

Figure 14–1. *Enabling third-party apps*

Follow these steps to do so:

1. Go to the **Settings** menu.

2. Tap **Applications**.

3. Tap to check the box labeled **Unknown sources**.

Once you've enabled apps from unknown sources, you can download them from websites, get them as attachments in email, or transfer them to your tablet via USB. All these alternate methods are referred to as *sideloading*.

Once you tap to open a downloaded .apk file, you will see the permissions required for that app. Just as when installing apps from the Android Market, you can click **Install** to proceed with or **Cancel** to abort an installation. For example, you can see the permissions window presented for the **Amazon Appstore** app on the right.

Let's look at that app a little more closely.

The Amazon Appstore

Amazon.com sells books, movies, and Android apps. Using the Amazon Appstore requires that you install the **Amazon Appstore** app, but from that point on it works a lot like the Amazon Market. Follow these steps to install the **Amazon Appstore** app:

1. Enable apps from unknown sources in the **Settings** menu.

2. Go to www.amazon.com on the Web, either from a tablet's browser (as shown on the left) or from any other computer.

3. Enter your email address in the **Get Started** box (see Figure 14-2).

4. You'll get an email with a link to download the app. Click this link to download and install the app.

Figure 14–2. *Downloading the Amazon Appstore app*

Because the Appstore is controlled by an app, you can launch it using the **Amazon Appstore** icon. Once you do, you can find and install apps from your tablet without launching a browser (see Figure 14–3). You use your Amazon.com account to pay for apps you purchase from the Appstore.

Figure 14–3. *Browsing the Appstore*

Once you launch the **Amazon Appstore** app, you can browse apps by category, search by name, and/or take advantage of Amazon's daily specials. The Amazon Appstore is the only app market available for the Kindle Fire.

My Apps

You'll get alerts for app updates you buy from the Appstore through the **Amazon Appstore** app. Just click the alert that pops up, and you'll see the **Updates** section of **My Apps**.

You can also go to the **My Apps** area by tapping the **Menu** button on the bottom of the app's screen (see Figure 14–4). This area lets you manually check for updates. If you have more than one Android device, such as a tablet and a phone, then you can also use this area to download apps you're missing on a particular device. You can also use this area to recover Appstore apps you've purchased previously if you ever need to reset your tablet.

Figure 14–4. *The My Apps area of the Appstore*

Installing Apps from the Web

Nearly every Android app market allows you to install apps from the Web, and the Amazon Appstore is no exception. You can browse and purchase apps on the www.amazon.com website, and they'll be delivered to your device as soon as you launch the **Amazon Appstore** app (see Figure 14–5).

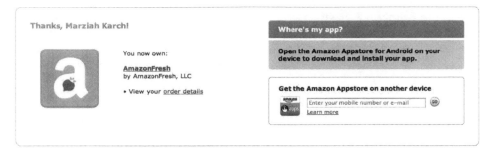

Figure 14–5. *Downloading an app from the* www.amazon.com *website*

The Samsung App Store

Samsung Galaxy Tabs come with the **Samsung** app pre-installed. This app is exclusive to Samsung devices, and it requires a separate account with Samsung. Once launched, it behaves a lot like any other third-party app store (see Figure 14–6).

Figure 14–6. *The Samsung app*

Updates are also delivered through the app, and the **My page** tab offers features similar to the **My Apps** area in the **Amazon Appstore** app.

> **NOTE:** You'll likely see similar pre-installed app stores from carriers on other tablets.

Barnes & Noble Nook Apps

If you've got a Nook Color, you use the Barnes & Noble Nook app store to find and download apps, as shown in Figure 14–7. Because the Nook uses a modified Android, it's harder to install apps outside of this store, and you may find the Nook prices to be more expensive.

Figure 14–7. *Nook apps*

Handmark

Handmark is a website (www.handmark.com) that sells apps for multiple devices. Most apps cost money, but the selection is generally of good quality. All apps from Handmark must be downloaded from its website (see Figure 14–8), not from an app you install on your tablet.

Figure 14–8. *Handmark's website*

If you don't mind being on a mailing list, Handmark regularly sends out specials and coupons to its subscribers.

GetJar

GetJar originally launched in 2004 (before Android) as a place for developer feedback. Today, it's one of the largest truly independent app stores in the world, and it even includes the largest free app store. You can find apps for Android and other platforms by navigating either to the full www.getjar.com site or to its mobile version at m.getjar.com. If you browse GetJar's website from your tablet, it will auto-detect the type of device you have (i.e., an Android tablet). Otherwise, you specify your device on the website (see Figure 14–9).

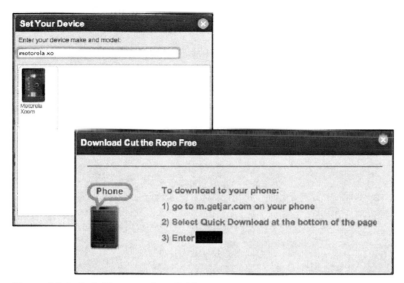

Figure 14–9. *Installing apps from GetJar*

In the case of GetJar, it's easier to install apps directly from your tablet because you still have to launch the website from your tablet and then enter a code to specify the correct app.

Uninstalling Apps

The easiest way to uninstall third-party apps and apps that come from alternative app markets is to go through your tablet's **Settings** menu (see Figure 14–10).

Figure 14–10. *Uninstalling apps*

Follow these steps to uninstall a third-party app:

1. Go to the **Settings** menu.

2. Tap **Applications**.

3. Tap **Manage applications**.

4. Tap the app you wish to uninstall.

5. Tap **Uninstall**.

As you can see, the mechanics of downloading and installing apps is pretty similar, no matter which market you acquire them from.

Chapter 15

Social Media

Tablets are great devices for keeping track of Twitter, Facebook, and other social media. Not only can you use these services to type messages, but you can also use them to sense location, take photos, and even edit movies. In this chapter, you will learn how to share content from your Android with your colleagues, friends, family, and fans.

When you think of social media, you may think of relatively recent websites and services, like Twitter, Facebook, and Google+. While those are certainly great examples of social media services, the Internet has always been social. The whole purpose of linking together computers has been to share information and communicate. What's different now is that communicating via social media has gone mainstream. At the time of writing, Facebook is the single most popular website in the world.

You can use social media not only as a great way to connect with friends and family, but also as a great way to connect with colleagues and customers. Social media done right can be an integral aspect of CRM (customer relationship management). For example, you can use social media to keep your customers updated with your latest projects, keep them excited about your products and services, and let them tell you where you should go next. You can also use social media to network with your colleagues or to find your next opportunity.

Social media done badly can be a disaster. People have been fired for casual remarks they've made to their blog or Facebook page, and inappropriate use of social media has forced the infamous resignation of politicians. You should always use common sense when using social media and never assume anything you say is truly private.

Facebook

The Facebook social network started out as a simple virtual yearbook for college students. Since then, it has morphed into one of the most popular websites in the world. At the time of writing, it's even more popular than Google's main search page in terms of its sheer volume of page views.

Facebook is meant for people to use their actual names instead of pseudonyms. The service enables people to share information with small-to-large circles of acquaintances.

However, Facebook has been facing increasing scrutiny over its privacy policies and confusing security settings; so when you use Facebook, the wisest course of action, as with any website, is to assume anything you say is completely visible to the world.

Facebook allows multiple types of posts—from quick status updates to photos, videos, and longer notes. You can also link to articles, videos, and pictures hosted outside of Facebook and add apps that incorporate games, group reading lists, and more. Facebook didn't invent the *Like* button, but it purchased the company that did, FriendFeed. Since then, Facebook has created a universal **Like** button that can be used on websites outside of Facebook to show your enthusiasm for various websites and brands.

How do you manage both personal and business contacts on Facebook? You can do it a couple of ways. One way I *don't* recommend is to create multiple accounts. If you create multiple accounts using your real name, it will only serve to confuse you and your contacts when they try to add you as a friend.

The two approaches you can take are either to create a *fan page* or to *friend* everyone and assign people to friend groups through your privacy settings. Fan pages (officially, Facebook just calls them *pages*) got their name from the way people used to add other users to their feed. They'd "become a fan" of the page. Facebook has since changed this mechanism to a simple **Like** button, but many people still use the old name.

> **TIP:** Currently Facebook has a 5,000-friend limit on personal accounts; so if you anticipate reaching that limit between clients, fans, and good friends, then you need a fan page. Even if you don't anticipate an overwhelming deluge of clients and business contacts friending you, it may still be disturbing to manage personal and work acquaintances in the same social space.

Creating Fan Pages

You set up fan pages through the Ads and Pages feature. If you don't have any pages, search for "Ads and Pages" from within Facebook. I'd suggest using a desktop browser to set this up.

The advantage of using a fan page is that you can make a fan page an official company presence without needing to be friends with any of the fans of the page, and you can even make posts as if you were that page. The disadvantage is that you do not see the activity fans generate anywhere outside of that page.

Whether or not you want your business contacts mingling with your classmates and relatives is a personal decision; however, you should decide how you want to handle that situation before you get your first friend request. It's a lot easier to establish a separate space in advance than it is to migrate a friend page to a fan page.

> **NOTE:** Whether or not you are Facebook friends with colleagues, business partners, or customers, it's just bad business to badmouth *any* of them. They may not be able to see what you've said, but it's not hard to copy and paste. The last thing you need is for casual gossip to get back to the victim. People have been fired for less.

Facebook Apps

Facebook makes an official **Facebook** app for Android that will work on most Android tablets. The tablet app is handy because it lets you sync your Android contacts with your Facebook contacts, as shown in Figure 15–1.

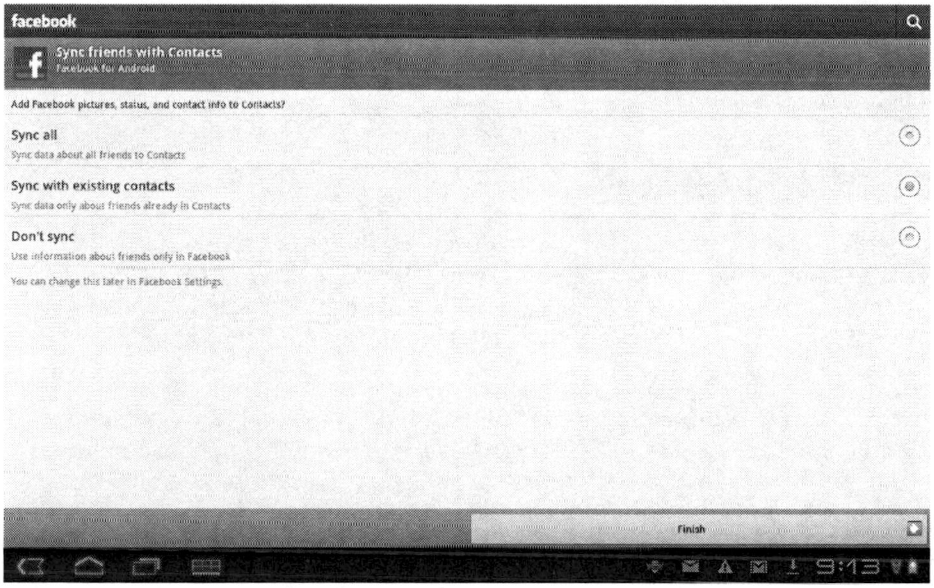

Figure 15–1. *Using Facebook's contact syncing*

Android's **Facebook** app also lets you read your activity stream, record your location, and make posts; but as of this moment, it's still pretty limited. It's really an expanded phone app and not an app that takes advantage of the space and features you have available with a tablet.

Fortunately, there's an easy solution: don't use the app and rely on your browser, instead. As with most sites on the Web, you may need to scroll to the bottom of the page and tap the Desktop link to get the full view of the Facebook site. Once you do, you'll see most of the same features you're used to using on full-size computers (see Figure 15–2). You can also try third-party apps like **Friendcaster**.

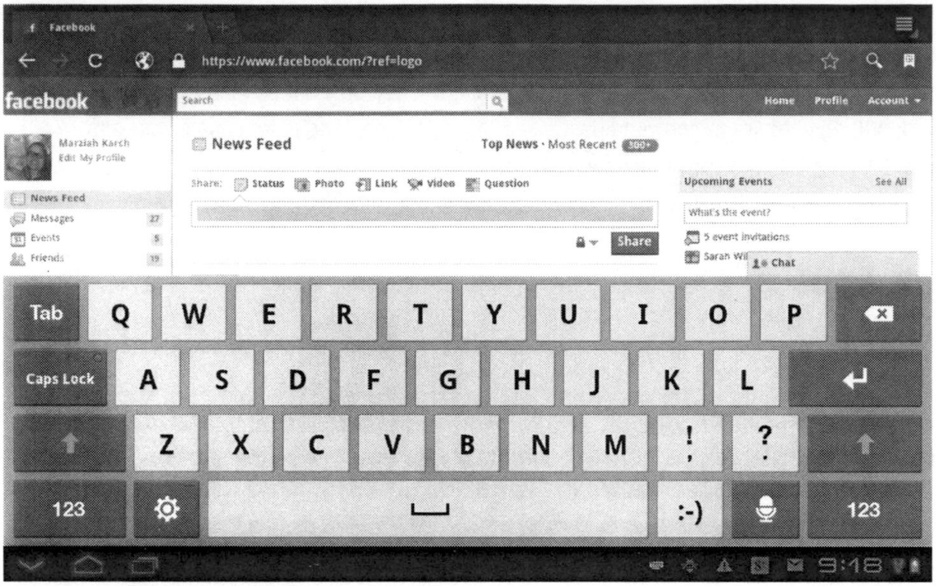

Figure 15–2. *Using Facebook from your browser*

Twitter and Microblogs

Twitter is a popular service used to send short messages. It started around SMS text messaging on phones, so Twitter messages are restricted to no more than 140 characters. Twitter is part of an evolving class of services called *microblogs,* although most other microblogs have given up on the SMS text messaging constraints and allow features beyond the simple text message.

Twitter gained popularity, not only for its ease of use on cellphones, but by allowing a lot of third-party tool and app development around its service. Twitter purchased some of these tools, and others remain popular alternative choices to Twitter's core offering.

Why would you use Twitter? The short messages are great for pointing out items of interest, letting your friends know what you're feeling, or critiquing a conference as it happens. Twitter is good for business, too. If your business is transportation, you can let the riders know about delays. If your business is weather-dependent, you can let your customers know if you need to make cancellations. You can also use Twitter to advertise specials, promote your latest accomplishments, or deepen your customer engagement by having a conversation about their needs. Or, you can just listen to what your customers or colleagues in the industry are saying.

NOTE: Twitter infamously played a role in former U.S. Rep. Anthony Wiener's fall from grace. And off-color Twitter jokes lost comedian Gilbert Gottfried his ongoing role as the voice of the Aflac duck.

If that gives you pause, it should. One of the appeals of Twitter is its immediacy; but unlike a conversation you have at a company party, this conversation is potentially with the entire world.

The Mechanics and Culture of Twitter

Twitter consists of a series of small posts known as *tweets*. Originally these tweets were unconnected and unthreaded, so you had a stream of what looked like totally random posts from all the people you read, or *followed*. This gave Twitter the feel of a noisy party. As you wandered through the party, you could hear snippets of conversations, but you couldn't be sure of who said what. I'm not the only one to make that analogy. There's a book on the topic: *Social Media Is a Cocktail Party*, by Jim Tobin and Lisa Braziel (CreateSpace, 2008).

TIP: If you are already a Twitter user, the sections that follow will be a bit of a review. Feel free to skip ahead to the "Choosing a Twitter App" section later in this chapter.

@Replies

A lot of the social conventions of Twitter were built around its weaknesses. All of these conventions made efficient use of characters because there's a 140-character limit on Twitter. In order to tag the person you were responding to, the convention of the @reply (pronounced "at reply") was introduced. Specifically, you used the @ sign next to the username of the person to whom you were replying. The convention has since been added to Twitter's interface, and it's available in every app I've tested.

Direct Messages

Direct messages are private messages sent between two people who follow each other. For example, DM@*UserName* is the convention for typing a direct message. It may be even simpler in some apps, but you should never assume anything you say is ever truly private.

Retweets and Modified Tweets

You can also repeat, or *retweet,* a clever post using the convention of RT @UserName. Some also use MT @UserName to show that a tweet has the same concept, but has been modified from the original—usually shortened or with added commentary. Twitter built an easy retweet feature into its interface, but many still prefer to use the old convention, so they can add commentary.

Hashtags

Because tweets are not sorted by topic, it's hard to search by category. Also, there's no way to add a tag or label, as you can with many long-form blogs. Hashtags are an elegant solution to the problem. Hashtags consist of a hash sign (#) followed by a label with no spaces, such as #tablets or #Android. This creates an unlikely character combination that can be easily searched. Hashtags are also used for sarcastic commentary.

URL Shorteners

URL shorteners solve the 140-character problem when it comes to website links. These are third-party tools that create a small URL that redirects people to the longer URL you want to point people to. The URL shorteners themselves have become tinier over the years; so rather than using TinyURL.com, many users have switched to bit.ly or ow.ly. Some services also offer added value, like analytics to measure how many people clicked a shortened URL.

> **NOTE:** There are some great reasons for using a shortened URL, but you should avoid casually using one in places where it's unnecessary. Any time you use an URL shortener, you're putting a third party between the user and his or her destination. The service could have an outage or even go out of business and leave users stranded. This happened with Tr.im in 2010.

Picture Services

Twitter didn't originally allow you to embed pictures, but it did allow you to easily *link* to pictures. All sorts of Twitter-related picture services offer storage and easy linking for posting pictures from your phone or tablet. Popular services include Twitpic and Yfrog. Many of these services are built into the apps you use to post.

Lists

You *follow* or *unfollow* other Twitter users to see (or not see) their activity in your stream. You can also list them, which means you add them to a group of other users you follow for reading by category.

Twitter Apps on Your Tablet

Now that we've covered the basic conventions, let's start tweeting. Like Facebook, Twitter has an official Android-specific app with limited capabilities (see Figure 15–3).

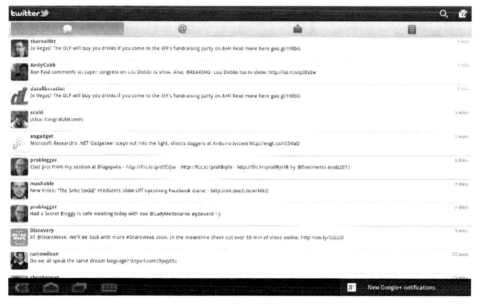

Figure 15–3. *The official Twitter app for Android*

The official **Twitter** app for Android allows you to create tweets, @replies, and direct messages. It also lets you see your stream, search, and view lists. You can use your tablet's browser with Twitter; however, the Twitter website is also limited. The best way to experience Twitter on a tablet at this time is to explore using alternative apps.

Choosing a Twitter App

The Android Market is full of Twitter apps for Android. That's good news for consumers because it means you can try out many apps and decide on the feature set that you like best. One of the things you may want to explore is how well a given app takes advantage of the extra space on your tablet. Right now, there aren't many apps that do more than display a larger version of their phone version. Even the official **Twitter** app is guilty of this. However, many of these third-party alternatives still offer features you can't get from the official app. Interesting features to look for include the following:

- **Delayed Posting:** The HootSuite service allows you to schedule tweets ahead of time. This is important if you're tweeting to promote a business or a blog, and you want to maximize your impact.

- **Multiple Accounts**: Most third-party Twitter apps let you manage more than one Twitter account, and many of them also allow you to manage Facebook and other types of accounts.

- **Cross Posting:** Many Twitter apps allow you to post the same message across multiple accounts and multiple types of accounts, so you can catch your Facebook and Twitter friends with the same announcement.

- **Alerts:** You can find apps that offer enhanced alerts, such as when your user ID or a specific subject is mentioned.

In the rest of this section, we'll look at a few popular apps for Twitter and their features.

Seesmic is both a desktop and mobile Twitter app. It allows you to register multiple Facebook, Twitter, Twitter proxy, Salesforce, and Google Buzz accounts; and then cross-post between them, as shown in Figure 15–4.

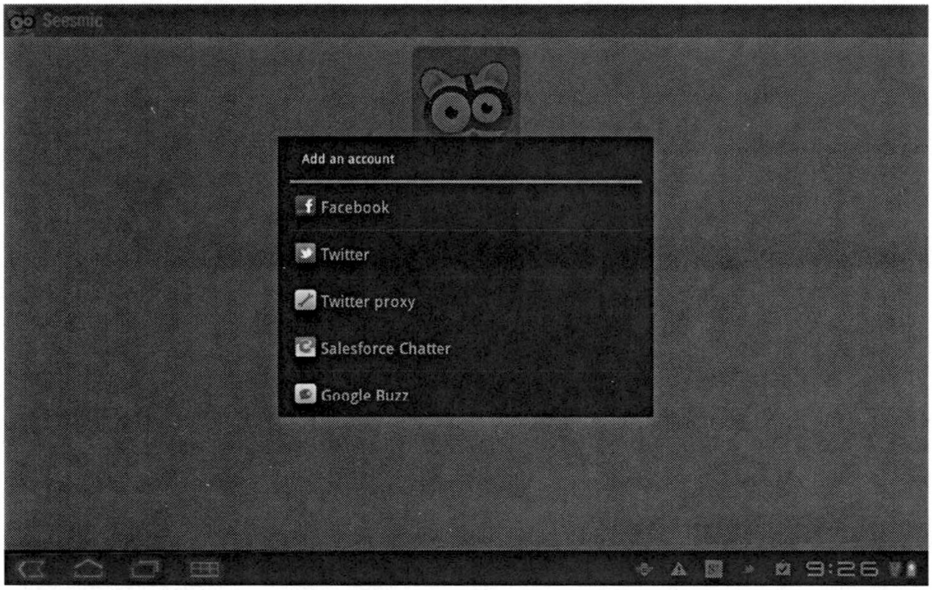

Figure 15–4. *The Seesmic app for Android*

Tweetdeck is both a desktop and mobile app, and the company was purchased by Twitter, so its features may be folded into the official app at some point. **Tweetdeck** allows posting to multiple types of accounts and easy picture posting. The desktop version of this app also features sophisticated search capabilities.

Unfortunately, the Android-version of this app is still stuck in a vertical layout mode. On the other hand, this isn't an issue if you type with your thumbs.

Of all the ways to access Twitter on your Android tablet, my favorite is still the HootSuite service. It's a Web-based service, so you only have to register each account once, but HootSuite will remember all your IDs across all your desktops and mobile devices. In addition to offering the ability to post to multiple Twitter accounts, built-in URL shortening, and easy picture posting, HootSuite also allows you to schedule tweets for later. HootSuite comes in both free and paid versions. Figure 15–5 shows the free version.

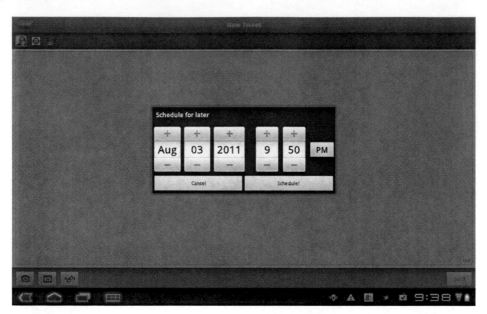

Figure 15–5. *HootSuite*

A few other apps worth examining include **Twicca**, **Twidroyd**, and **Tweetcaster**.

Yammer

If you want the functionality of Twitter but the privacy of a business network, the Yammer service offers a bit of both. You can use Yammer to send small, private, threaded status updates to members of a company that share an email domain. At the time of writing, Yammer clients for Android are rather underwhelming; instead, I recommend you access the service at www.yammer.com directly through your browser for a better user experience.

Salesforce

Salesforce is a popular *CRM* (customer relationship management) suite that resembles Yammer and incorporates social media elements, such as its free Chatter service. Salesforce doesn't currently have any tablet-based clients, but you can use **Seesmic** to post to Salesforce Chatter.

Google+

One of the newer social media services to launch is Google+. This is not Google's first attempt at social media, but so far it appears to be its most promising. Google+ has grown rapidly since its summer 2011 introduction, and Google has put a lot of weight behind developing and promoting the new service. However, it's still a limited beta tool,

LinkedIn

LinkedIn is a social networking site geared toward professionals and career networking. You can post your resume and skills, add professional colleagues, and post updates about your current projects. You may want to stick with using your web browser to read LinkedIn. You can also use the official **LinkedIn** app, which is tablet-optimized and very slick. In fact, It's probably the nicest "official" app out of all the social media site apps I tested.

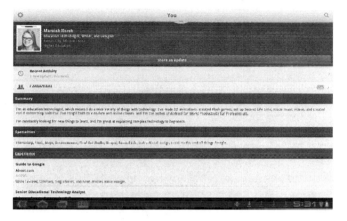

There's also a great third-party app for LinkedIn called **DroidIn** (see Figure 15–7).

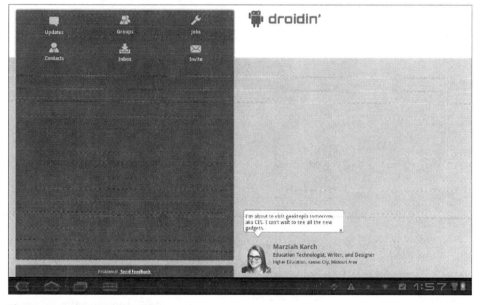

Figure 15–7. *The DroidIn app*

DroidIn sends you notifications when your contacts post status updates, and you can use the app to post your own status updates, check messages, invite users, and monitor interest groups.

Wordpress

Wordpress is a very popular blogging platform. It is available as either a self-hosted blog on your own server or on the commercial Wordpress.com site. Wordpress offers a free app that allows you to post to your blog in either location.

If you plan on doing a lot of blogging from your tablet, you may want to invest in a keyboard accessory; however, the **Wordpress** app is great for editing a quick post or uploading a photo directly from your tablet.

You can use the **Wordpress** app to manage and post to multiple blogs. You can also use your browser to access and post to your blog; however, the **Wordpress** app provides a convenient shortcut, especially for photo posting.

Blogger

The official **Blogger** app lets you post to your blogspot.com blog. This is Google's official blogging service. The app simplifies posting to and editing you blog; it also simplifies uploading photos or videos to it. You can also use **Blogger** with multiple blogs, although you cannot use it to cross-post to multiple blogs at the same time. You also can't use it to adjust your blog's preference and appearance settings. This is strictly a posting app; however, you can switch to your browser to adjust your settings from the Web.

Tumblr

Tumblr is a bit like a multimedia microblog. Blogs created with Tumblr are called *Tumblogs*. Although most posts are short, they aren't restricted by Twitter's 140 character limitation, and they can contain lots of embedded media. Tumblr is really an ideal format for tablet posts since it draws on the strengths of tablets as a multimedia production tool, but without requiring excessive typing.

Tumblr offers an official app for Android tablets (see Figure 15–8), and there are several third-party Tumblr apps available, as well.

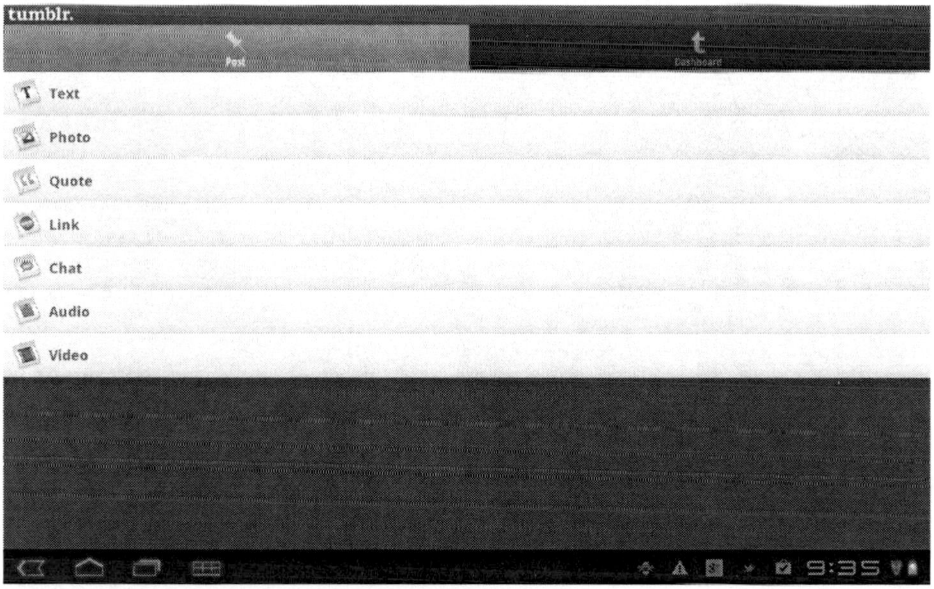

Figure 15–8. *The Tumblr app for Android tablets*

As you can see, the **Tumblr** app lets you easily post text, pictures, movies, audio recordings, and links from your tablet. The orientation is not optimized for tablets, but the app is lightweight enough that this really doesn't hinder using it on your tablet. Tapping the **Dashboard** button brings you to your Tumblog, where you can read your posts and comments.

Chapter 16

Video and Voice Chat

Just because you have a tablet doesn't mean you can't call someone. Modern Voice over Internet Protocol (*VoIP*) tools offer the ability to relay voice calls over the Internet. You can even use your tablet to make calls to people who use telephones.

Tablets with front-facing cameras make ideal video conferencing tools, and there are an increasing number of services that take advantage of mobile tools for video chats. You can use your tablet's native Gmail features, or you can use third-party tools to chat with users on just about any platform. In this chapter, I'll explore a few ways to have live conversations using video or voice, and I'll give you step-by-step instructions for using two commonly used apps: **Talk** and **Skype**. Most other apps use very similar steps to make and receive calls.

Video and Voice Chat with Google Talk

Google Talk is the default video chat app for Honeycomb tablets. You can use it to call contacts with Google Accounts on a wide range of devices, including desktop computers, iPads, iPhones, and Android phones. There's nothing to download for Honeycomb users, and there's no new account to register. You automatically signed up for this Google service when you started using your tablet.

> **NOTE:** Gmail offers a feature that allows you to make phone calls directly from the Web; however, that feature is currently missing from the Android version of the service.

To start chatting with this service, launch the **Talk** app.

Notice how all your contacts have icons. These icons indicate a contact's availability for chat, as shown in Figure 16–1.

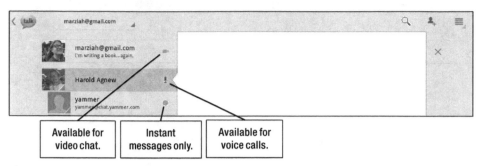

Figure 16–1. *Status messages in Google Talk*

These icons use color and shape to convey info very quickly. Here is a list of colors and the status they indicate:

- **Green**: Available

- **Yellow**: Available but inactive

- **Red:** Busy

- **Gray:** Not logged in or invisible

The shape of the icon conveys the following information:

- **Camera:** Capable of video chat

- **Microphone:** Capable of voice chat

- **Solid circle:** Capable of instant messaging

- **Clock:** User is logged in but inactive

- **X shape:** User is either unavailable or invisible

Setting your status to **invisible** means that you are logged in, but nobody can see that you're available to chat. This is a status you may want to use if you need to chat with a specific person and want to wait until you see him log in.

Setting Your Status Message

In addition to the icons indicating availability, users can also set a status message (see Figure 16–2).

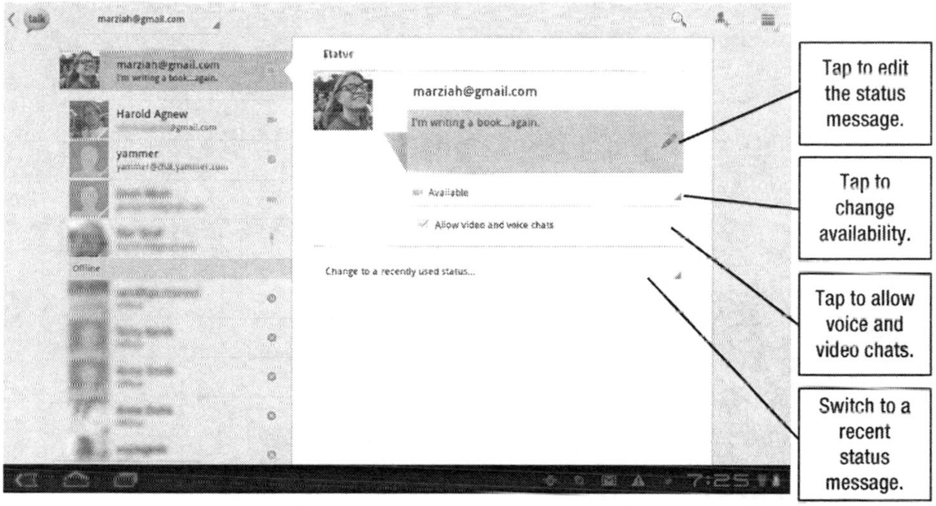

Figure 16–2. *A status message*

Follow these steps to set your status message:

1. Launch the **Google Talk** app.

2. Tap your own name in your Contacts list.

3. Tap the **Pencil** icon near your name to change your status message.

4. Type in a new status message.

Alternatively, you can tap **Change to a recently used status.** You'll see a list of recent status messages for quick switching.

> **TIP:** You can give yourself an easy list of shortcuts by rapidly changing your status messages a few times with things you may use regularly. Typical status messages might include: "I'm available for business-related calls only" or "Please leave a message if I don't answer right away."

Making a Video Call with Google Talk

Follow these steps to make a video call:

1. Tap the **Talk** icon.

2. Find a contact to call—if she has a green **Camera** icon next to her name in the Contacts list, she is available for video chat.

3. Tap the **Camera** icon on the right side of the screen.

4. Wait for the person on the other side to answer and confirm that she wants to video chat.

Once you're both connected, you'll see the other person's image taking up most of the screen and a small preview of your own image (see Figure 16–3).

Figure 16–3. *Video chat through Google Talk*

Making Voice Calls with Google Talk

You can make VoIP calls to other logged in Google Talk users using almost exactly the same steps that you use to make a video call. However, you can't dial a number to an outside phone line through the **Google Talk** app—yet. Follow these steps to make a voice call:

1. Tap the **Talk** icon.

2. Find a contact to call. If he has a green **Camera** or **Microphone** icon next to his name, he can take a voice call.

3. Tap the **Microphone** icon on the right side of the screen.

4. Wait for the person on the other side to answer and confirm that he wants to take your call.

Making Phone Calls with Skype

You can make phone calls using the **Skype** app from your tablet. Calls to other Skype users anywhere in the world are free.

> **CAUTION:** Some phone carriers charge users extra to use Skype or block the service altogether.

The Skype service works on computers and many mobile devices, including iPhones, Android phones, BlackBerry smartphones, and other mobile devices. You will be charged for calls and SMS text messages to mobile phones and land lines, but the rates are reasonable.

Skype is in the process of being acquired by Microsoft at the time of writing; however, Skype officials have stated that the company plans on continuing support for Skype on Android and other devices.

> **NOTE:** Skype is also rolling out video chat features. However, those features are only available on a few devices at the time of writing. Original Galaxy Tabs can use video chat, but tablets with Tegra 2 processors—and this includes just about all Honeycomb tablets—are specifically excluded.

To get started with Skype, you need to download the app from the Android Market at `market.android.com/details?id=com.skype.raider`.

Creating a Skype Account on Your Tablet

If you need to set up your Skype account and have not already done so from your computer, then follow these steps to set up **Skype** on your tablet:

1. Launch **Skype** by tapping its app icon.

2. Tap the **Create Account** button.

3. Enter the requested information, including your name, email, desired username, and password. Entering your phone number is optional.

4. Choose whether to receive Skype news and offers.

5. Tap the **Next** button to create your account.

6. Sync your contacts with existing contacts on your tablet, if desired.

Log into the Skype App

After you create your account, you're ready to log into Skype on your tablet. Follow these steps to do so:

1. If you are not already logged into Skype, tap the **Skype** icon from your **Home** screen.

2. Enter your Skype Name and Password.

3. Tap the **Sign In** button.

4. Once you've signed in, you may also want to tap the **Menu** button on the bottom of the screen.

5. Tap **Settings**.

6. Check the box labeled **Sign in automatically.**

You should not have to enter this login information again; it is saved in the **Skype** app. The next time you tap **Skype**, it will automatically log you in.

Adding Contacts

If you're syncing contacts with your address book, you may already see some contacts; however, you may still want to add a few more. Follow these steps to do so:

1. Tap the **Contacts** button.

2. Tap the **Menu** button.

3. Tap **Add a Contact**.

4. Tap **Search Skype Directory** and then type someone's first and last name or Skype name.

5. Tap the **Magnifying Glass** button to locate that person.

6. Once you see the person you want to add, tap his name.

7. Tap **Add Contact**.

8. Once this person accepts you as a contact, you will see him listed as a contact in your **All Contacts** screen.

TIP: Sometimes you want to get rid of a **Skype** contact. You can remove or block a contact by tapping her name from the contact list. Press the **Menu** button and select either **Remove** or **Block**.

Making Calls with Skype on Your Tablet

So far you have created your account and added your contacts. Now you are ready to finally make that first call with **Skype** on your tablet:

1. If you are not already logged into the **Skype** service, tap the **Skype** icon from your **Home** screen and log in, if asked.

2. Tap the **Contacts** button.

3. Tap the contact name you wish to call.

4. Tap the **Skype call** button.

5. You may see a **Skype** option and a **Mobile** or other phone option. Tap **Skype** to make the free call. Making any other call requires that you pay for it with *Skype Credits*.

6. Wait for the person on the other end to connect.

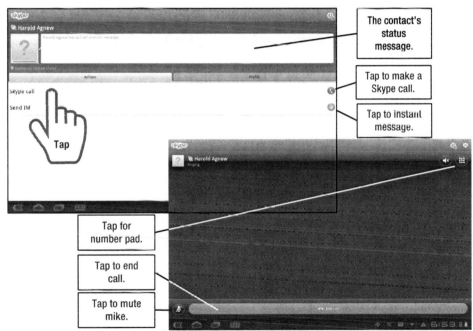

Figure 16–4. *Placing calls from Skype on your tablet*

> **NOTE:** You can call toll-free numbers for free using **Skype Out** on your tablet. The following notice comes from the Skype website at www.skype.com:
>
> "The following countries and number ranges are supported and are free of charge to all users. We're working on the rest of the world. France: +33 800, +33 805, +33 809 Poland: +48 800 UK: +44 500, +44 800, +44 808 USA: +1 800, +1 866, +1 877, +1 888 Taiwan: +886 80"

Receiving Calls with Skype on Your Tablet

You can have **Skype** running in the background and still be able to receive a Skype call when it comes in.

> **TIP:** Not everyone stays logged into her Skype account. If you want to call someone you know who uses Skype, just send her a quick email to let her know you'd like to call her using Skype.

Buying Skype Credits or a Monthly Subscription

Skype-to-Skype calls are free. However, if you want to call people on their land lines or mobile phones from the **Skype** app, then you will need to purchase Skype Credits or purchase a monthly subscription plan. If you try to purchase the credits or subscription from within the **Skype** app, it will take you to the Skype website.

> **TIP:** You may want to start with a limited amount of Skype Credits to try out the service before you sign up for a subscription plan. Subscription plans are the way to go if you plan on using the **Skype** app to call a lot of people who don't use Skype (i.e., people who use regular landlines and mobile phones).

Chatting with Skype

In addition to making phone calls, you can also chat via text with other Skype users from your tablet. Starting a chat is very similar to starting a call; follow these steps to do so:

1. If you are not already logged into Skype, tap the **Skype** icon from your **Home** screen and log in, if asked.
2. Tap the **Contacts** button.
3. Tap the name of the contact.
4. Tap **Send IM.**
5. Type your chat text and press the **Send** button. Your chat will appear at the top of the screen.

Adding Skype to Your Computer

You can use the **Skype** app on your computer, as well. You can also use the **Skype** app to make video calls on your computer if you also have a web cam hooked up.

> **NOTE:** When you call from your computer to a tablet, you will not be able to make a video call until that service is added to tablets.

To create a Skype account and download the **Skype** software for your computer, go to www.skype.com and follow the download instructions.

Fring

Fring is another free VoIP and video calling service that offers voice and video calling features. Although the service may not be as popular as Skype, it does offer video calling from Android tablets. The **Fring** app also offers a group video chat, which is a really nice feature that is only available in a few video chat services. The interface of the **Fring** app is simple and playful, as shown to the right and in Figure 16–5.

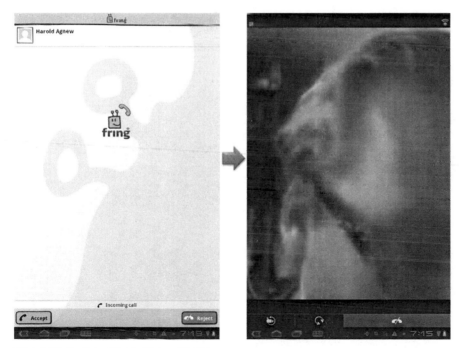

Figure 16–5. *Accepting a video call in Fring*

Qik

Qik —pronounced "quick"—is a video chat service that was acquired by Skype. To use Qik, you must have a separate Qik account (not just a Skype account) and a compatible device. Currently, Qik runs on Motorola Xooms, but not on the Galaxy Tab 10.1.

Video chat in the **Qik** app is similar to what you see in the **Google Talk** and **Fring** apps; however, it does not offer any multi-use video chats at this time.

OoVoo

Another free video and voice chatting service is *ooVoo*. At this point, the **ooVoo** app runs on very few tablets. Compatible devices include the Dell Streak, Motorola Xoom, and original Galaxy Tab; however, you can use the service to make group video calls with up to six participants. You can also make one-on-one video calls and user-to-user voice calls. You can find out more information about the service from company's Facebook page at http://www.facebook.com/oovoo.

Tango

The **Tango** app is compatible with most tablets and Android phones. The PC version is not available yet, but its developers say it's coming soon. Like most services, Tango requires all its users to have an account with Tango. You can register your account after downloading **Tango**, as shown in Figure 16–6.

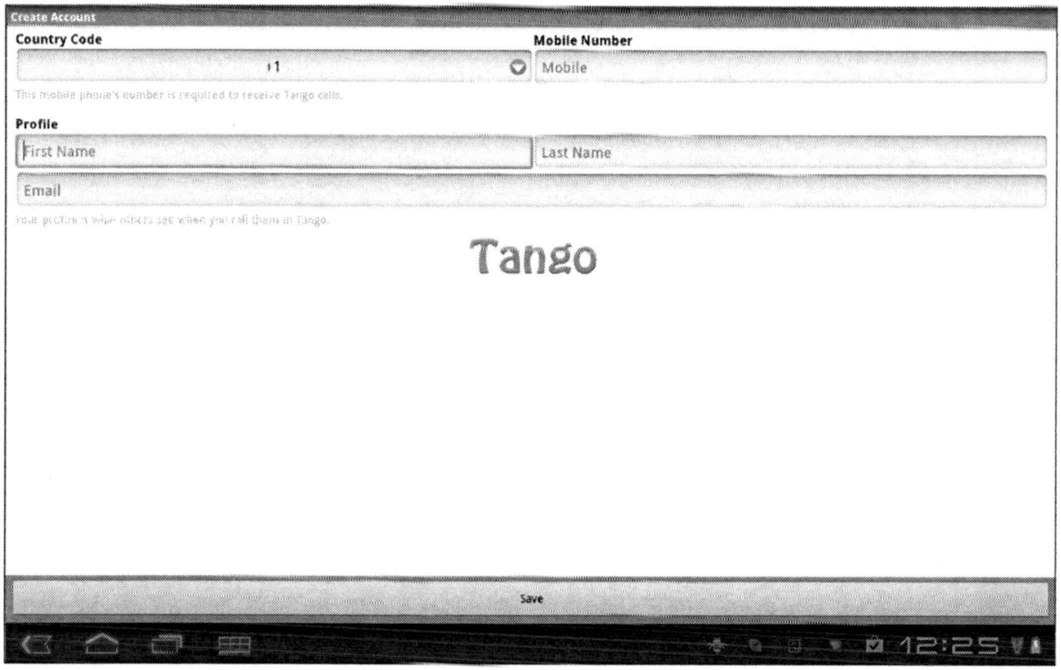

Figure 16–6. *Registering a new Tango account*

One of the nice features of **Tango** is that you can shift from a voice-to-video call while already in the middle of the call. Most other apps demand that you specify the type of call before you make it and stick to only that type of call. You can get more information about Tango by visiting the company's website at www.tango.me.

Chapter 17

Reading E-books, Newspapers, and Magazines

Tablets make fantastic e-book readers. Some tablets, such as the Nook Color, are primarily e-readers that also run apps. You can carry an entire library in a device smaller than a single book; and unlike dedicated e-readers, you're not chained to a single store or app for your reading. There are so many reading apps that I couldn't possibly cover them all in this book. Instead, I'll cover some of the most popular apps for reading books, newspapers, and magazines.

Formats

E-books come in many formats, but there are a few main types you're most likely to see. Amazon Kindle books are usually in .mobi or .azw format (.azw is based on .mobi format). Most other readers use ePUB or Adobe PDF formats (.pdf). All of these book formats can be locked with DRM—*digital rights management*—which is designed to prevent unauthorized copying of the book.

Google Books

Honeycomb and Ice Cream Sandwich tablets come with Google Books already built into the tablet. You can think of this as the Google equivalent to Apple's IBook format. Google Books can be purchased through your Google Checkout account using the same Android Market you use to purchase apps.

Google Books is several things. It is a website (http://books.google.com) that lets you search a vast library of scanned books. At this site, you can shop for books and create your own public profile that shares a list of books you're reading and reviews of books you've read. **Google Books** is also an app, and the Android version of this app taps into part of the Google Books website, but not all of it.

Launch the **Google Books** app by tapping its icon from your **Home** screen or from the app tray. Your view will depend on how you last left the app. If you were reading a book, you'll return to that book. Otherwise, you'll see the library. Google Books displays your books as large **Book** icons arranged in a curve. Swipe your finger left to right to navigate through the books in your library, as shown in Figure 17–1.

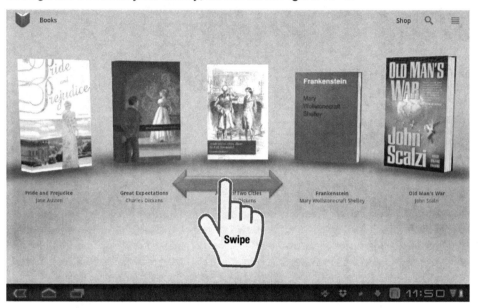

Figure 17–1. *Navigating the Google Books library*

Tap a book to start reading it. You can start as many books as you'd like, and Google Books will keep track of your progress in all of them. Books in Google Books are displayed as single pages when you hold your tablet vertically and double pages when you hold it horizontally. You can turn a page by swiping your finger or pressing the **Volume Up** or **Volume Down** button. Figure 17–2 shows the interface for reading a book.

NOTE: It may be a habit to tap the **Back** button on the bottom of your tablet to return to the main menu of an app; however, this usually doesn't work in e-reading apps, and you'll end up exiting the program instead. The **Library** button is usually on the top of the screen for e-Book readers.

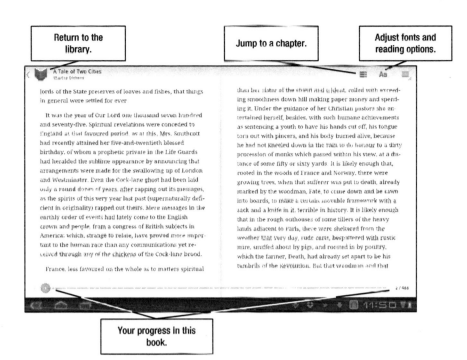

Return to the library.

Jump to a chapter.

Adjust fonts and reading options.

Your progress in this book.

Figure 17–2. *Reading a Google Book*

Adjusting the Reading Options

As shown in Figure 17–2, you tap the **Aa** button on the top of the screen to adjust your reading options. As you can see, there are quite a few choices (see Figure 17–3).

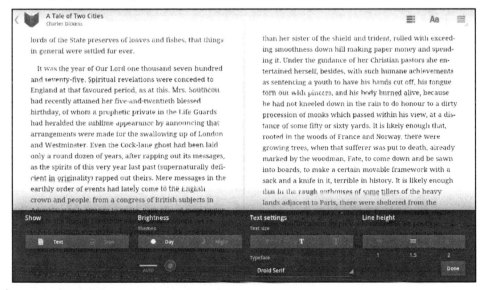

Figure 17–3 *Reading options for Google Books*

The first option, **Show,** is available for some older books. Google originally scanned books from libraries and used software to convert the images to text. This allows you to view easier-to-read electronic text or the original scanned image. Use this option if a passage appears garbled; be aware, however, that including this option causes a book to take longer to download.

The other options—**Brightness**, **Text settings**, and **Line height**—are a little more straightforward. Adjust your settings and tap the **Done** button.

Reading Books Offline

Google Books is a cloud-based reading app. By default, your books are stored online, which means you can read them anywhere you have access to a compatible web browser. However, that also means you're dependent on having an Internet connection. Fortunately, you can make a local copy of your Google Books; follow these steps to do so:

1. Open the book you wish to make a local copy of in the **Google Books** app.

2. Tap the **Menu** button on the upper-right corner of the screen.

3. Tap to check the box labeled **Make available offline.**

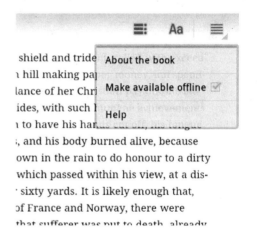

Buying or Downloading Google Books

You can buy Google Books either by tapping the **Shop** button from within the **Google Books** app or through the Android Market. Follow these steps to buy a Google Book from the Android Market:

1. Launch the **Android Market** app from the **Home** screen or from the app tray.

2. Tap the **Books** tab (see Figure 17–4).

Figure 17–4. *Shopping for Google Books*

You can browse for books by category; the **Categories** section is on the right side of the screen. Featured items are shown at the top, and you can browse **New Arrivals**, **Top Selling**, **Top Rated**, and scroll down to the bottom for **Top Free** books. You can also just use the **Search** button on the top of the screen to find books by title, subject, or author.

Once you find a book you'd like to purchase or download, tap the title; you'll see a page resembling the one shown in Figure 17–5.

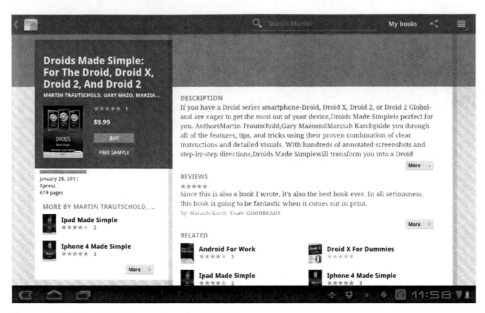

Figure 17–5. *The* ***Details*** *page for a Google Book*

The **Details** page for a Google Book looks pretty similar to what you see when downloading an app. You'll see books by the same author(s), suggestions for similar titles, and reviews of the book. In this case, the reviews come from the Google Books website, public reviews, or Goodreads.com. Currently, there's no way to review a book from within the Android tablet's reader.

TIP: Goodreads (www.goodreads.com) offers an Android app you can use to share reviews and reading recommendations from within your tablet. It even has a built-in barcode scanner that you can use to inventory your physical book library.

If you want to purchase a book, you can tap the **Buy** button. Your purchase will be completed through Google Checkout. However, you can also try a book before you buy it; to do so, press the **Free Sample** button just below the **Buy** button. Most e-book stores now give you some method to read the start of a book before making you commit to a purchase.

Once you buy or try a free sample, you can start reading your book right away. Remember to enable offline reading if you plan on reading this book away from your data connection.

TIP: Google Books comes with a widget you can put on your **Home** screen to let you flip through and open your favorite books quickly.

Google Books Website

You can use your **Browser** app to open and read Google Books. You can also use your **Browser** app to search through books you don't own by going to http://books.google.com. Google has an extensive library of scanned books in its database. You can even find passages within books; the amount of text you see in a given book depends on the agreement Google has with the publisher and whether the book is still under copyright.

The Kindle Reader

The Amazon Kindle is the most popular e-reader on the market, and you can enjoy reading Kindle books on your Android tablet. You can start reading on one device and continue reading on your Android tablet, right where you left off. This is a process Amazon calls *Whispersync*. You don't even have to own a Kindle to use the reader. The Kindle Store carries more than books; you can also order magazines, newspapers, and comic books from the Kindle Store.

The one disadvantage to reading Kindle books is that they currently use a format unique to Amazon. Unfortunately, they don't support the more standard ePUB format, which makes it difficult to buy books from other sellers and read them in your **Kindle** app. That said, it's not impossible to read books in ePUB format on your Kindle app; we'll cover how to use the **Calibre** app to do so in the "Converting Books from One Format to Another" section later in this chapter.

The Kindle Store uses your Amazon account; and on your Android, you can purchase books from the **Kindle** app itself. When you launch the **Kindle** app and register using your Amazon account, you'll see a **Bookshelf** view that resembles Figure 17–6.

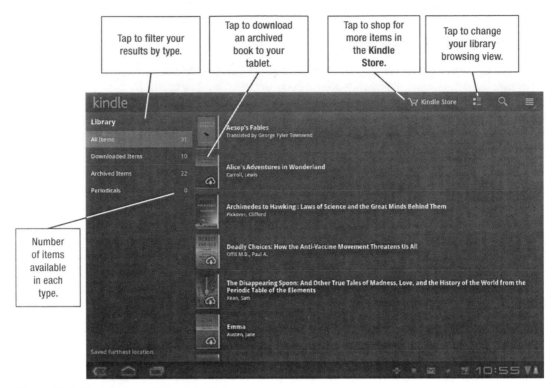

Figure 17–6. *The **Kindle** app's **Bookshelf** view*

If you already have an existing library of Kindle books, they won't be automatically downloaded to your device. You may not be reading them all, so this is done to save space. However, you can tap any archived book to download it to your tablet. Tap a downloaded book to start reading.

Reading Kindle Books

Unlike the **Google Books** reader, the **Kindle** reader does not display a two-page layout when you tilt your tablet horizontally. Instead, it shows a single, wider page. Also, the **Kindle** reader doesn't think of book "pages" the same way traditional books do; however, it does keep track of where you last read. As long as you've got a data connection to keep your books in sync, you can pick up a book where you last stopped reading.

> **NOTE:** Kindle books don't have traditional pages. Your place in the book is tracked by word count. You'll need the Kindle equivalent in order to find a spot in a book someone else references by page number.

Looking up Words

If you want to look up a word, simply long-press the word, and a dictionary definition will appear. The first time you do this, however, you'll be prompted to download a dictionary, as shown in Figure 17-7. Once your dictionary is downloaded, it will work with any of your books.

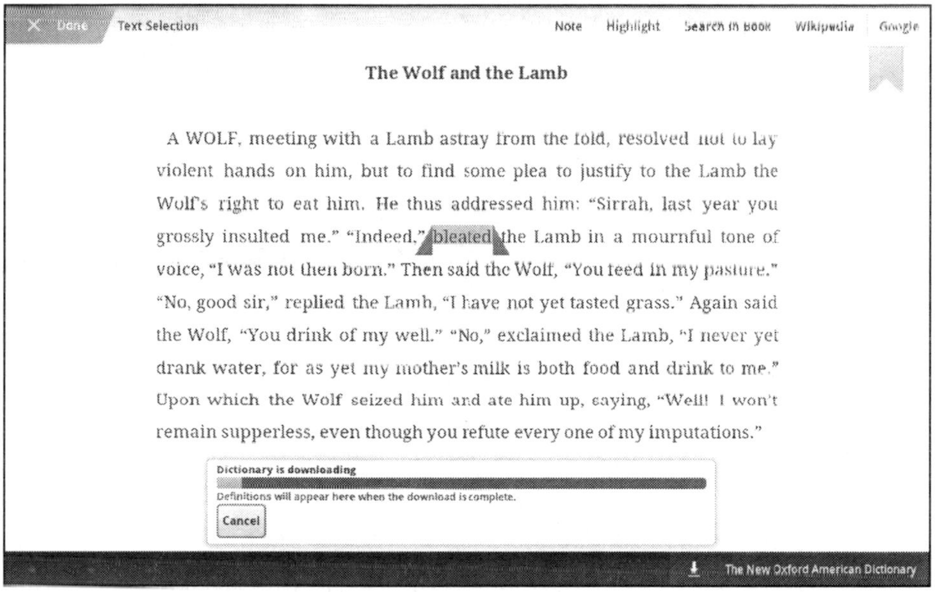

Figure 17-7. *Downloading a dictionary*

You'll notice there are more options than just the dictionary. For example, you can tap the Wikipedia or Google links on the upper right to look up a word or phrase on the Web using your tablet's **Browser** app.

Saving Bookmarks and Taking Notes

The **Kindle** reader automatically syncs your current location, but you may want to bookmark a particular passage in a book. Follow these steps to do so:

1. Tap in the middle of your page or long-press a particular word.

2. Tap the **Bookmark** icon that appears on the upper-right corner of the screen.

3. The **Bookmark** icon will turn blue to indicate you've bookmarked the section.

You can follow the same steps and then tap **Highlight** to highlight the word in the text instead. The process for taking notes is similar. Notes and bookmarks are actually stored online. Follow these steps to highlight text:

1. Long-press a word within a publication.

2. Tap **Note** on the top of the screen to take a text note.

3. Type your note and press **Save.**

Follow these steps to navigate to a previously saved note or bookmark:

1. Tap in the center of a page.

2. Tap the **Menu** button on the upper-right corner of the screen.

3. Tap **View My Notes & Marks**.

4. Tap the **Bookmark** or **Note** icon to view the bookmark or note and navigate to that location.

Adjusting Your Kindle Reading Options

If you find the "print" is too small on your Kindle, you can adjust the font size. You can also adjust the screen brightness. Tap the screen once, and then tap the **Font** or **Contrast** button on the top of the screen, as shown in Figure 17–8.

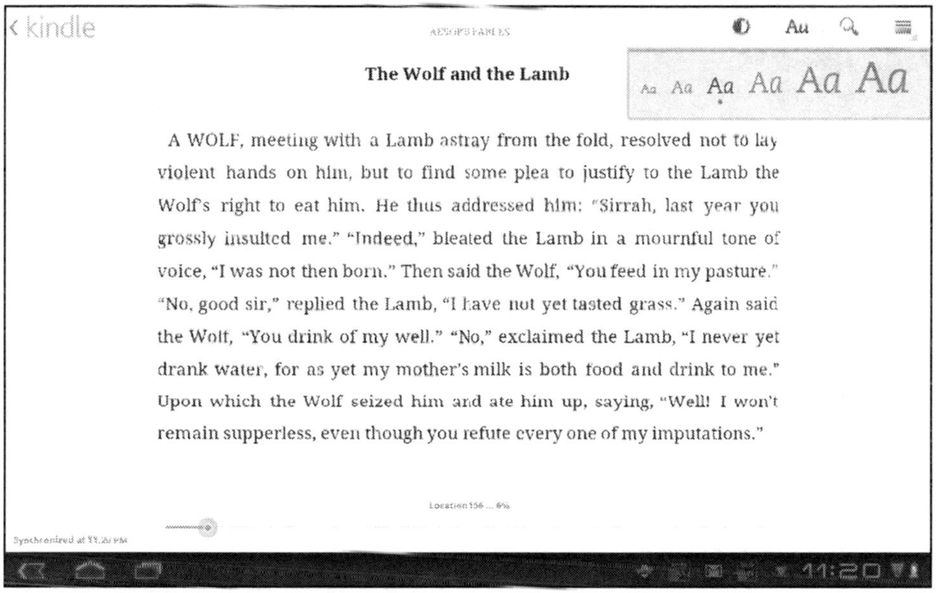

Figure 17–8 *Adjusting the font size*

Purchasing Items for Kindle

You can purchase Kindle books through the **Kindle** app whenever you're connected to the Internet. If you're looking at the **Bookshelf** view, tap the **Kindle Store** button on the top of the screen to view items in Amazon's Kindle Store. If you're reading a book, follow these steps to visit the store:

1. Tap the middle of the screen.

2. Tap the **Menu** button.

3. Select **Shop in Kindle Store**.

You can browse by category, search by author or keyword, or find publications by type. Amazon sells books, magazines, comic books, and newspapers for Kindle. Once you find an item, you can tap it to view a description, details, and customer reviews, as shown in Figure 17–9.

Figure 17–9. *A book in Amazon's Kindle Store*

If you want to buy the book, click the **Buy** button. Or you can click the **Try a Sample** button to download a preview of the book, so you can decide whether you want to purchase it. Once you click **Buy**, you can process your payment through your Amazon account, and your book will download to your device.

You can also browse for items through the Amazon.com website and have them delivered to your tablet or any other device.

TIP: When you download a sample and later purchase the book, you end up with two different copies of the book. Be sure to note your place in the sample version at the bottom of the page, so you can navigate directly to that number in your purchased version of the book. Follow these steps to jump to your current location in the book:

1.   Tap the **Menu** button on the upper-right corner of the screen.

2.   Tap **Go To.**

3.   Select **Location**.

4.   Type in the numeric location.

Buying Magazines or Newspapers

You use the same process to purchase newspapers and magazines from Amazon. The key difference is that you can buy a single issue or a subscription. Figure 17-10 shows the process. Both individual and subscription prices are listed in the Kindle Store. Subscription charges are recurring, usually monthly. When you subscribe to a newspaper or magazine, you'll automatically receive the latest digital edition as soon as you're in wireless range. If you want to cancel your subscription, go online to www.amazon.com/manageyourkindlesubscriptions using either your tablet's **Browser** app or any other computer connected to the Internet.

Figure 17–10. *Subscribing to a magazine*

What does a Kindle newspaper look like? It's much easier to manage than a traditional newspaper. There are no folds, and your hands won't get dirty with ink. You can also navigate directly to the content areas that interest you, and a Kindle newspaper isn't filled with bouncing ads like a newspaper website. Figure 17–11 shows a sample issue of the Kansas City Star.

Figure 17–11. *The Kindle edition of the Kansas City Star*

Kindle magazines and journals have a look and feel similar to Kindle newspapers.

Shelfari

If you'd like to socialize with other Kindle book readers, you can use Amazon's social site, *Shelfari* (www.shelfari.com). If you create a profile on this site, you can import your Amazon purchases, display your current reading activity, rate books, and even share the notes and bookmarks you've saved on Kindle books you're reading on your tablet.

Follow these steps to view Shelfari information (see Figure 17–12):

1. Launch the **Kindle** app.

2. Go to your **Bookshelf** view.

3. Long-press a book.

4. Tap **Shelfari book extras.**

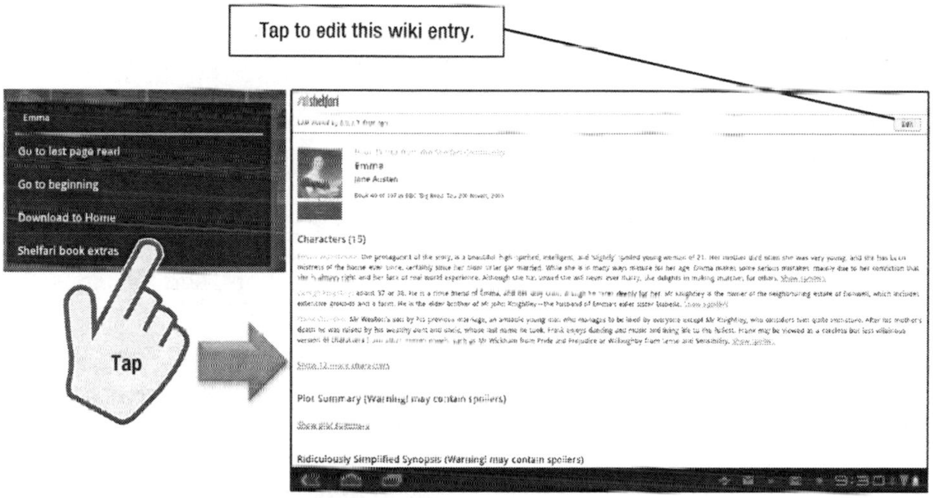

Tap to edit this wiki entry.

Figure 17–12. *Viewing Shelfari information*

Not every book has Shelfari extras, but most do. You'll notice that each Shelfari entry is a *wiki*. Any user can edit the information. For example, you can edit and share information about characters, plots, reviews, and so on. All edits and additions are publicly visible.

Sideloading Kindle Books

If you've got a book you want to read on your tablet using the **Kindle** app, you can do so by *sideloading* it:

> **NOTE:** A book must be in .mobi format before you can sideload it.

1. Mount your tablet's SD card to your computer by using the USB cable or an app like **ES File Explorer.**

2. Open the **Kindle** folder on your card.

3. Place your .mobi file inside this folder.

The Barnes & Noble Nook

While the Amazon Kindle is the most popular e-book reader, the Nook is a close second. The **Nook** app also has the distinct advantage of being an Android app first. Nook e-readers are actually modified Android tablets, and the Nook Color even runs apps.

You don't need a Nook Color to read Nook books, magazines, and newspapers. You can download the **Nook** app from the Android Market; and because it supports the ePUB format, you can use it to sideload books you've downloaded directly from the book publisher's website.

Nook books are purchased through the Barnes & Noble Nook Shop, as shown to the left. You can register for an account at www.barnesandnoble.com. You need to provide credit card information in order to purchase books through the store; however, once you've registered for an account, you can purchase books directly through the **Nook** app on your tablet.

The **Nook** app's **Library** view is shown in Figure 17–13.

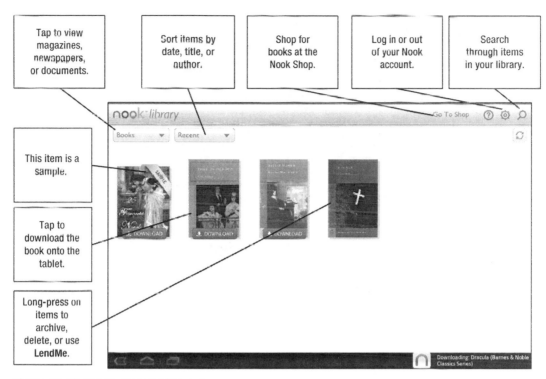

Tap to view magazines, newspapers, or documents.

Sort items by date, title, or author.

Shop for books at the Nook Shop.

Log in or out of your Nook account.

Search through items in your library.

This item is a sample.

Tap to download the book onto the tablet.

Long-press on items to archive, delete, or use LendMe.

Figure 17–13. *The Nook app's Library view*

NOTE: The **Nook** app is one of the few e-readers that uses the **Back** button on the bottom to navigate back to **Library** view.

Reading Nook Books

Tap a book in the Nook's **Library** view to open it. You'll immediately see the **Settings** menu at the bottom of the screen, as shown in Figure 17–14. You can use the **Settings** menu to navigate, adjust the font size and screen contrast, or view the book's **Details** page. If you don't want to adjust any settings, then do nothing or tap in the center of the book. This will cause the screen to fade in a few seconds.

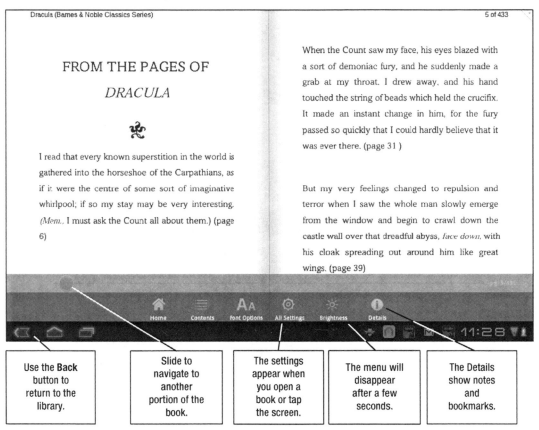

Figure 17–14. *Reading a Nook book*

Saving Bookmarks, Taking Notes, and Researching Words

You can save bookmarks and notes on Nook books, just as you can with Kindle books. You bookmark a page by tapping the upper-right corner of the page; this is a visual metaphor that signifies bending down the corner of a book to mark a page.

You can also save notes; highlight selections; and look up words by long-pressing a word or phrase, and then selecting the appropriate option (see Figure 17–15).

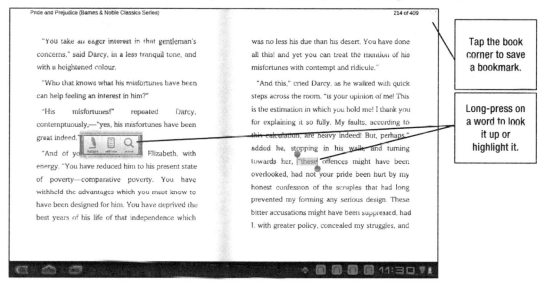

Figure 17–15. *Working with book text on a Nook*

Follow these steps to review your notes (see Figure 17–16):

1. Open a Nook book.

2. Tap the **Details** button.

3. Tap the **Notes**, **Highlights**, **Bookmarks** tab.

Figure 17–16. *The Nook app's Details page*

LendMe Books

You can lend most Nook books to other users for two weeks using the LendMe option. In order to use this option, you need to register on the Barnes & Noble website and use the **Manage My Nook** area to add friends, as shown in Figure 17–17. Once your friends have confirmed, both you and your contacts have the option to lend each other books that can be read on each other's tablets.

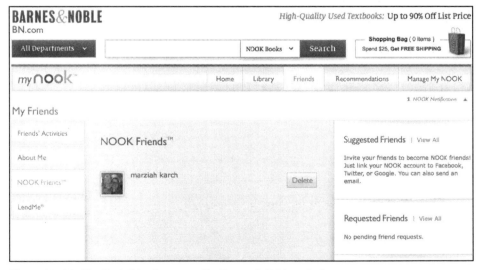

Figure 17–17. *The Nook Friends area on the Barnes & Noble website*

There are a few things to keep in mind about the LendMe option:

- Only books in your library labeled with the LendMe logo are eligible for lending.

- You can only lend a book once.

- You can't read the book yourself while it's being borrowed.

- LendMe books return to the owner in 14 days.

Once you've registered for an account and confirmed friendship with other Barnes & Noble customers, you can use the LendMe option from your tablet by long-pressing any eligible book in your library and selecting **LendMe**.

Sideloading Nook Books

If you own an ePUB book that you didn't purchase through Barnes & Noble, you can still use the Nook app to read it by sideloading the file:

1. Mount your tablet's SD card to your computer by using the USB cable or an app like **ES File Explorer**.

2. Open the Nook folder on your card.

3. Open the My Documents folder.

4. Place your ePUB file inside this folder.

Your books will be listed as "My Documents" rather than books in the library; however, you can read them just like any other book. Books you've sideloaded can't be used with the LendMe option.

Kobo

Kobo is an online e-Book store. It offers dedicated e-ink readers and apps for major computer and mobile platforms. You can connect your Kobo account to Facebook to share what you read with other Kobo users without registering for a separate social reading site. Of all the apps I've tried, the Android version of the **Kobo** app provides the easiest interface for importing third-party ePUB books.

> **NOTE:** Borders was one of the early investors in Kobo; however, it held a minority share, so the Kobo store continued in spite of Borders' financial woes. Borders' customers were able to transfer their e-Book library to Kobo after Borders went bankrupt.

You can register for a Kobo account online at www.kobobooks.com. You do not need to provide credit card information to download free books. The **Kobo** app's **I'm Reading** library uses a **Bookshelf** metaphor view to display your books, as shown in Figure 17–18. You can change this to a **List** view by using the **Menu** button on the bottom of the screen.

Figure 17–18 *The Kobo app's Bookshelf view*

Unlike the **Kindle** and **Nook** apps, the **Kobo** app does not separate items by their type of publication (e.g., book vs. magazine vs. newspaper). The **Discover** and **Browse** buttons both go to the Kobo bookstore and allow you to find and purchase apps using your Kobo account.

Reading Life

The **Kobo** reader includes both social and gaming aspects. As you read, you'll occasionally be awarded badges, such as the Fanatic badge for owning five books by the same author. If you tap the **Reading Life** button from your **Library** view, you'll first see your notifications, and then you'll see the badges you've been awarded thus far (see Figure 17–19). Badges you've yet to earn are gray.

Figure 17–19 *Reading Life badges*

Tap the **STATS** button to see your reading progress; you'll see how long you've spent reading and how many pages you've read.

Note that your stats will only apply to the book you've opened most recently.

Tap a book in your library to start reading it. Like the **Kindle** app, the **Kobo** reader doesn't offer a two-page view of books when you hold the tablet horizontally. And like the **Nook** app, the **Kobo** app sends you back to the **Library** view when you press the **Back** button on the bottom-left corner of the screen.

To adjust the settings of the **Kobo** app, tap the **Menu** button on the bottom-left corner of the screen, as shown in Figure 17–20.

AGNES GREY

hands, it should bring him in cent. per cent. The small patrimony was speedily sold, and the whole of its price was deposited in the hands of the friendly merchant; who as promptly proceeded to ship his cargo, and prepare for his voyage.

My father was delighted, so were we all, with our brightening prospects. For the present, it is true, we were reduced to the narrow income of the curacy; but my father seemed to think there was no necessity for scrupulously restricting our expenditure to that; so, with a standing bill at Mr. Jackson's, another at Smith's, and a third at Hobson's, we got along even more comfortably than before: though my mother affirmed we had better keep within bounds, for our prospects of wealth were but precarious, after all; and if my father would only trust everything to her management, he should never feel himself stinted: but he, for once, was incorrigible.

What happy hours Mary and I have passed while sitting at our work by the fire, or wandering on the heath-clad hills, or idling under the weeping birch (the only considerable tree in the garden), talking of future happiness to ourselves and our parents, of what we would do, and see, and possess; with no firmer foundation for our goodly superstructure than the riches that were expected to flow in upon us from the success of the worthy merchant's speculations. Our father was nearly as bad as ourselves; only that he affected not to be so much in earnest: expressing his bright hopes and sanguine expectations in jests and playful sallies, that always struck me as being exceedingly witty and pleasant. Our mother laughed with delight to see him so hopeful and happy: but still she feared he was setting his heart too much upon the matter; and once I heard her whisper as she left the room, 'God grant he be not disappointed! I know not how he would bear it.'

Disappointed he was; and bitterly, too. It came like a thunder-clap on us all, that the vessel which contained our fortune had been wrecked, and gone to the bottom with all its stores, together with several of the crew, and the unfortunate merchant himself. I was grieved for him; I was grieved for the overthrow of all our air-built castles; but, with the elasticity of youth, I soon recovered the shock.

Though riches had charms, poverty had no terrors for an inexperienced girl like me. Indeed, to say the truth, there was something exhilarating in the idea of being drive... papa, mamma, and Mary were all of the same mind as myself; and then, i... work to remedy them; and the greater the difficulties, the harder ou... dure the latter, and our vigour to

f Share to Facebook	**Aa** Select Text	
⚙ Notifications Settings	**✕** Close this Book	

Figure 17–20. *Adjusting settings in the Kobo app*

Highlighting Text and Adding Notes

to give to the poor, according to his means: or, as some migh

;ested to him a means of doubling his private property at on
riend was a merchant, a man of enterprising spirit and und
or want of capital; but generously proposed to give my fathe
pare; and he thought he might safely promise that whatever
r cent. The small patrimony was speedily sold, and the whol
iptly proceeded to ship his cargo, and prepare for his voyage

ill, with our brightening prospects. For the present, it is true
emed to think there was no necessity for scrupulously restr
at Smith's, and a third at Hobson's, we got along even more
vithin bounds, for our prospect of wealth were but precario
ent, he should never feel... en stinted: but he, for once, w

issed while sitting at our work by the fire, or wandering on t
tree in the garden), talking of future happiness to ourselves
oundation for our goodly superstructure than the riches that
speculations. Our father was nearly as bad as ourselves; only
nd sanguine expectations in jests and playful sallies, that alw
ed with delight to see him so hopeful and happy: but still she
rd her whisper as she left the room, 'God grant he be not dis

. It came like a thunder- clap on us all, that the vessel which

| ✏ Highlight | 📑 Add Note | 📕 Share | ✕ |

Unfortunately, the **Kobo** reader has a more convoluted procedure for adding notes or highlighting text. On the other hand, it also has one of the better ways to view the notes you've taken:

1. Tap the **Menu** button on the bottom of the screen.

2. Tap **Select Text**.

3. The screen will turn yellow, and you'll see a selection area. Expand this area to include your text. Tap either **Highlight** or **Add Note**.

4. Finally, tap **Share** if you want to post your note to Facebook.

Once you take a note, your selected text will be highlighted, and you'll see a **Note** icon on the bottom right of the screen on the page where you took the note. Tap the icon and you'll see your note. You can also tap **Share** to share your note to Facebook.

Importing Books

If you have third-party ePUB books you want to read, all you have to do is save them to your tablet. Someone could email them to you, or you could download them from a website in your **Browser** app. It doesn't matter, as long as you have the books on your tablet. Follow these steps to import ePUb books into your **Kobo** reader (see Figure 17–21):

1. Start at the **Library** view and tap the **Menu** button on the bottom of the screen.

2. Tap **Import Content.**

3. A dialog box will appear. Tap **Start** to begin.

4. The **Kobo** app will search your memory card for ePUB books.

5. You'll see a list of all new books that were found. Place a mark in the checkbox next to each book in the list you want to import; similarly, make sure books you do not want to import do not have a mark in the checkbox.

6. Tap **Import Selected.**

7. Decide whether you want to leave a copy of the books in their old location or delete them in order to save space.

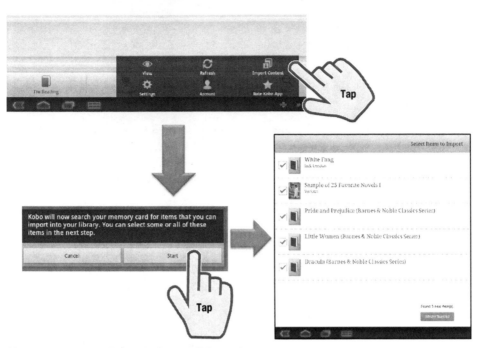

Figure 17–21. *Importing books into the Kobo reader*

Reading PDF Books

We've covered the most popular e-Book reading apps for Android tablets, but none of these apps support importing PDF books at this time. They only support reading PDF books you purchase through the reader's bookstore. PDFs are easy to make and popular formats for distributing files. If you'd like to read an Adobe PDF file, you can use the **Adobe PDF Reader** app, or you can use a third party e-book reading app like **Aldiko.**

Converting Books from One Format to Another

If you've got an ePUB copy of *Moby Dick* (or other DRM-free books), and you'd prefer to read it on your Kindle, then you can do so using the free **Calibre** app for your Macintosh, Linux, or Windows computer (see Figure 17–22).

calibre version 0.8.14 created by Kovid Goyal

Figure 17–22. *Library management in the Calibre app*

Calibre can convert many formats to other formats, such as .PDF to .Mobi or .Mobi to ePUB. You can also use it to manage wireless syncing between **Calibre** and the **Books WordPlayer** apps. Unfortunately, the **WordPlayer** reader is not designed for tablet use yet, so it's mostly useful as an intermediate step before importing books into another reading app.

Chapter 18

Taking Notes and Working with Documents

Remember when nobody lugged a heavy laptop to meetings? You can experience that freedom again. One of the reasons to use a tablet instead of a smartphone is because it makes it easier to work with documents. You may want to take notes at a business meeting, edit a **Microsoft Office** file, or even write a new document—and you can do all that with your Android tablet. This chapter will explore note taking, document editing, and other valuable skills for productivity.

Google Docs

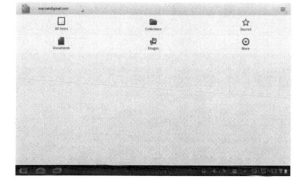

One of the most obvious ways to share documents is to use Google Docs. You can use your Google account to log into http://docs.google.com. Google Docs can be used to upload Microsoft Office files as well as **OpenOffice**, **Adobe PDF**, images, and other files. You can also create original text documents, spreadsheets, drawings, and slide presentations; and you can share those presentations with others.

To get started with Google Docs on your tablet, you should download the **Google Docs** app from the Android Market. You could just use your tablet's browser, but the running the app from your computer makes it a little easier. In any case, you'll need to be connected to the Internet in order to open and modify files. When you launch the

Google Docs app, you'll see a simple screen that allows you to view items by type. *Collections* are items you've stored in folders.

> **TIP:** If you have several documents you want to share with a group, you can allow sharing for a folder and add items to that folder instead of changing sharing preferences for individual files.

Tap the **More** button for more options, including the ability to create a new text document. If you tap the **All Items** button, you'll see a list of your current documents, sorted by the date they were last modified. Different items have different icons, as shown in Figure 18–1.

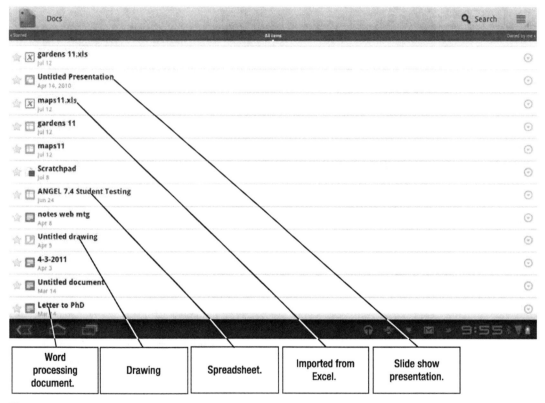

Figure labels: Word processing document. | Drawing | Spreadsheet. | Imported from Excel. | Slide show presentation.

Figure 18–1. *The List view in the Google Docs app*

The **Google Docs** app allows you to create and upload text documents, spreadsheets, slide presentations, images, PDF files, drawings, and other types of files. Text documents, spreadsheets, slides, and drawings are editable from within the app.

Follow these steps to edit a document in the **Google Docs** app:

1. Launch the **Google Docs** app.

2. Tap **All Items** or otherwise navigate to the desired document.

3. Tap the document to open it.

4. Tap **Edit** in the upper-left corner (see Figure 18–2).

5. Your changes will be automatically saved, but you can tap the **Refresh** button to hasten the process.

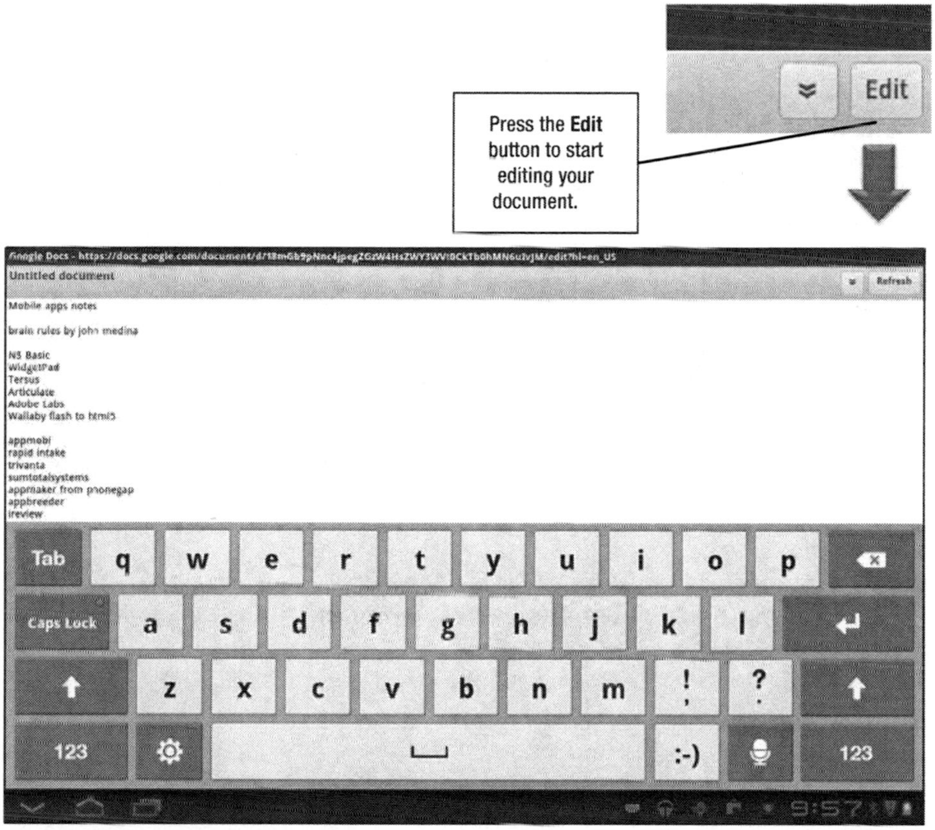

Press the **Edit** button to start editing your document.

Figure 18–2. *Editing a file in the Google Docs app*

You can close the keyboard by pressing the **Down Arrow** icon on the lower-left corner of the screen, and you can return to the document list by pressing the **Back** button.

Editing Spreadsheets

Editing spreadsheets is similar to editing text documents. However, instead of tapping an **Edit** button, you just have to double-tap on a row to start editing it, as shown in Figure 18–3.

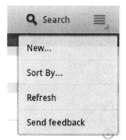

30	Edit	ID	Type	Description	Debit	Credit	Time	Resident/	Ending B	Region
31	Edit	11667483	Upload Charge			10	2008-10-	SYSTEM	5188	
32	Edit	11616021	Upload Charge			10	2008-10-	SYSTEM	7153	
33	Edit	11616020	Upload Charge			10	2008-10-	SYSTEM	7163	
34	Edit	11616019	Upload Charge			10	2008-10-	SYSTEM	7173	
35	Edit	11486314	Upload Charge			10	2008-10-(	SYSTEM	6277	
36	Edit	11483301	Upload Charge			10	2008-10-(	SYSTEM	6287	
37	Edit	11483300	Upload Charge			10	2008-10-(	SYSTEM	6297	
38	Edit	11483299	Upload Charge			10	2008-10-(	SYSTEM	6307	
39	Edit	11483298	Upload Charge			10	2008-10-(	SYSTEM	6317	
40	Submit Cancel	11483 29789	Upload Charge		10		2008- 10-05 17:05: 40	SYSTE M	6327	

Figure 18–3. *Editing a spreadsheet*

Editing Presentations

You can also create and edit presentations using the **Google Docs** app. Either tap to open an existing item or use the **Action** menu button on the upper-right corner to create a new presentation.

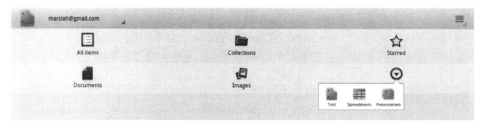

You can also create new documents from the **More** menu when you first launch **Google Docs** (see Figure 18–4).

Figure 18–4. *Creating a new document*

When you create a new presentation, you'll automatically start in **Editing** mode. If you open an existing presentation, you'll start in **Presentation** mode. That's handy if you're carrying your tablet with you to a business meeting.

NOTE: You navigate through presentations by using the **Back Arrow** and **Forward Arrow**. Google introduced transition animations, but most presentations don't use them.

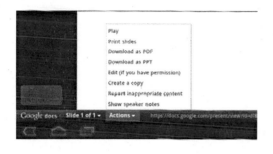

If you want to start editing an existing presentation, tap the **Actions** tab on the bottom of the screen. You can edit a presentation document if you have permission. Notice that you can also download the presentation as a PowerPoint (PPT) or PDF file. That means you can start creating a presentation on your tablet and download the PPT or PDF as a backup to either send to someone else or use locally on your tablet when your Internet connection is down.

Presentations in the **Google Docs** app look a lot like light version of **Microsoft PowerPoint**; and rather than a tablet-specific editing interface, **Google Docs** gives you the same view you'd see from the **Browser** app. Some items may not be fully compatible while using an Android browser. Figure 18–5 shows basic editing options, most of which are similar to **PowerPoint**.

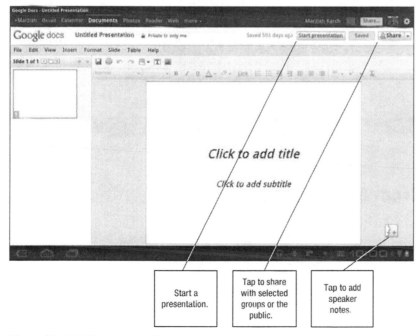

Figure 18–5. *Editing presentations*

Themes

Presentations can have themes, but it's difficult to change the themes beyond the default offerings when using a tablet. Follow these steps to change a theme:

1. Tap **Format**.

2. Tap **Presentation** settings.

3. Tap **Change Theme**.

4. Tap a theme to apply it to your slides (see Figure 18–6).

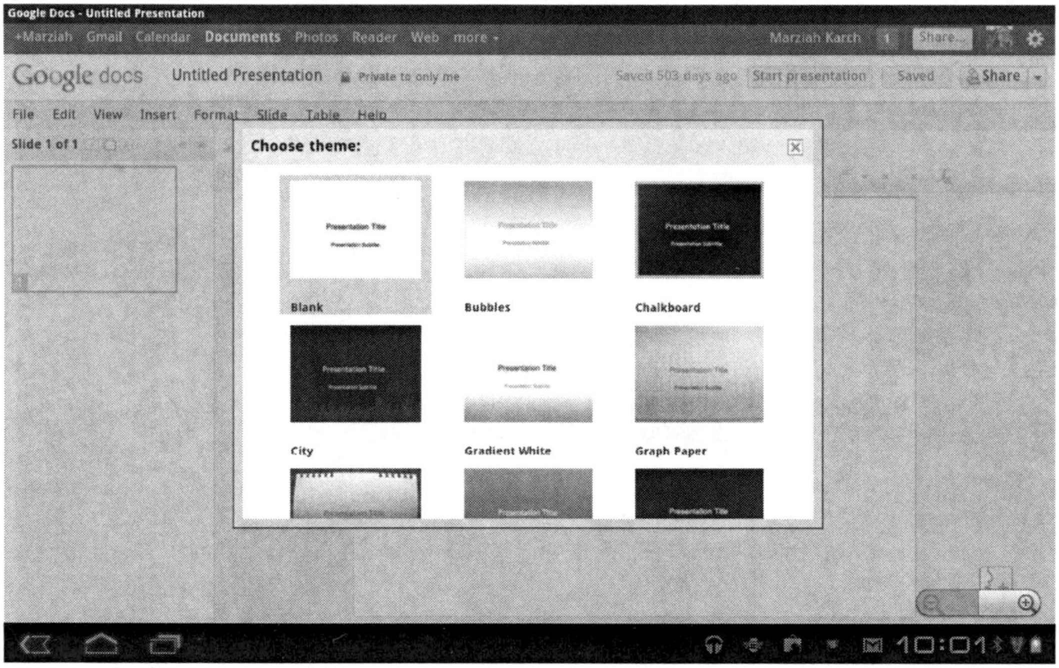

Figure 18–6. *Applying a new theme*

Downloading from Google Docs

You may want to download items from Google Docs to your tablet. This allows you to edit them offline or use a different app to edit them. Follow these steps to do so:

1. In the document's **List** view, tap the **Arrow** icon next to the item.

2. Tap **More**.

3. Tap **Open With** (see Figure 18–7).

4. Your item will download. Next, select an app from the list of available options to start editing your item.

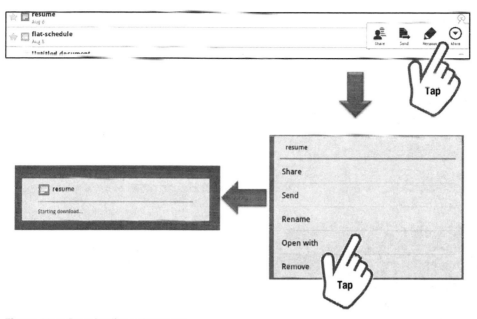

Figure 18–7 *Downloading a document*

Microsoft Live

You can also view many Office Live Documents using your Android's **Browser** app. However, you can't do any editing right now. You'll need to download a given document from http://skydrive.live.com in order to make any changes.

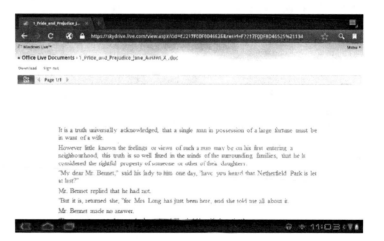

Documents to Go

Another option for editing **Microsoft Word, PowerPoint,** and **Excel** files is **Documents to Go.** This app ships with some devices, so check to see if you already have it installed. You can use the free version of the app to view documents or the US $14.99 paid app to edit them. The paid version also includes PDF support. I recommend trying the free version first, to make sure it is compatible with your tablet and displays your documents correctly.

You can also use **Documents to Go** to edit items you've uploaded to Google Docs. Connect the app to your Google account by tapping the appropriate button (see Figure 18–8), and you can browse through items on Google Docs whenever your tablet is connected to the Internet.

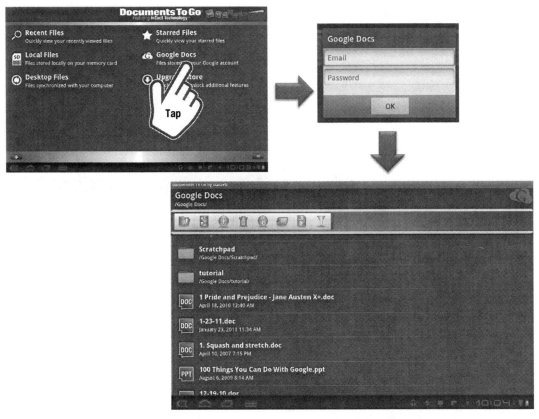

Figure 18–8. *The Documents to Go app*

Whether you're browsing items stored locally or on your Google Docs account, you can tap an item to open it. If you have the Pro version, you can also tap the **Menu** button on the bottom-left corner to start editing, as shown in Figure 18–9.

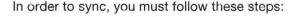

Word To Go - 1 Pride and Prejudice - Jane Austen X*.doc

It is a truth universally acknowledged, that a single man in possession of a large fortune must be in want of a wife.

However little known the feelings or views of such a man may be on his first entering a neighbourhood, this truth is so well fixed in the minds of the surrounding families, that he is considered the rightful property of someone or other of their daughters.

"My dear Mr. Bennet," said his lady to him one day, "have you heard that Netherfield Park is let at last?"

Mr. Bennet replied that he had not.

"But it is, returned she: "for Mrs. Long has just been here, and she told me all about it.

Mr. Bennet made no answer.

"Do you not want to know who has taken it?" cried his wife impatiently.

"YOU want to tell me, and I have no objection to hearing it."

This was invitation enough.

"Why, my dear, you must know, Mrs. Long says that Netherfield is taken by a young man of large fortune from the north of England; that he came down on Monday in a chaise and four to see the place, and was so much delighted with it, that he agreed with Mr. Morris immediately; that he is to take possession before Michaelmas, and some of his servants are to be in the house by the end of next week."

"What is his name?"

"Bingley."

"Is he married or single?"

"Oh! Single, my dear, to be sure! A single man of large fortune: four or five thousand a year. What a fine thing for our girls!"

"How so? How can it affect them?"

"My dear Mr. Bennet," replied his wife, "how can you be so tiresome! You must know that I am thinking of his marrying one of them."

"Is that his design in settling here?"

Figure 18–9. *Editing in* ***Documents To Go***

Documents to Go was designed primarily for people who are not using wireless keyboards to edit documents. You can still use it either way, but you'll find there's a lot more tapping involved than there is with text items in the **Google Docs** app.

Syncing Documents To Go

If you use a Windows PC, you can download the **Documents To Go** desktop app for syncing between your tablet and your computer. Changes you make to an item in either location will be reflected on the other device.

In order to sync, you must follow these steps:

1. Install the **Documents To Go** desktop app. You can download it from www.dataviz.com.

2. Mount your tablet to your PC using the USB cable in **Storage** mode.

3. Open **Documents To Go** on Android and on your PC.

4. Follow the instructions on the screen.

QuickOffice

Chances are, if your tablet didn't ship with **Documents To Go**, it probably came with **QuickOffice.** Like **Documents To Go,** the **QuickOffice** app comes in both free and paid versions; however, the Pro (paid) version ships with a lot of devices. The Pro version allows you to sync with your Google Account. It also offers an impressive number of other syncing options, such as **Dropbox**, **SugarSync**, and **MobileMe**.

To initiate syncing, tap the **Cloud** icon on the upper-right corner of the screen in **QuickOffice** (see Figure 18–10).

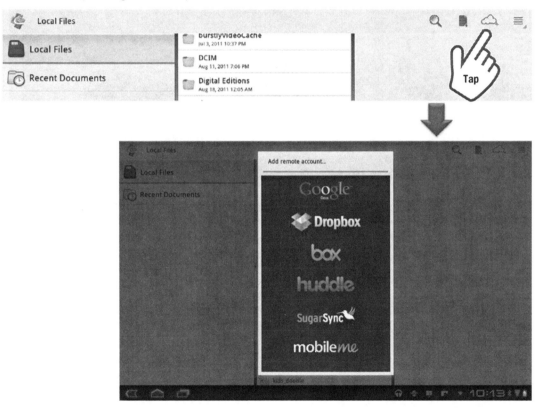

Figure 18–10. *Adding cloud syncing to QuickOffice*

You can add multiple remote accounts, but you must be connected to the Internet to browse files. Figure 18–11 shows the ease of browsing through multiple remote accounts. If you only sync word processing documents and similar files, it may save you storage space to skip installing separate apps like **Dropbox.**

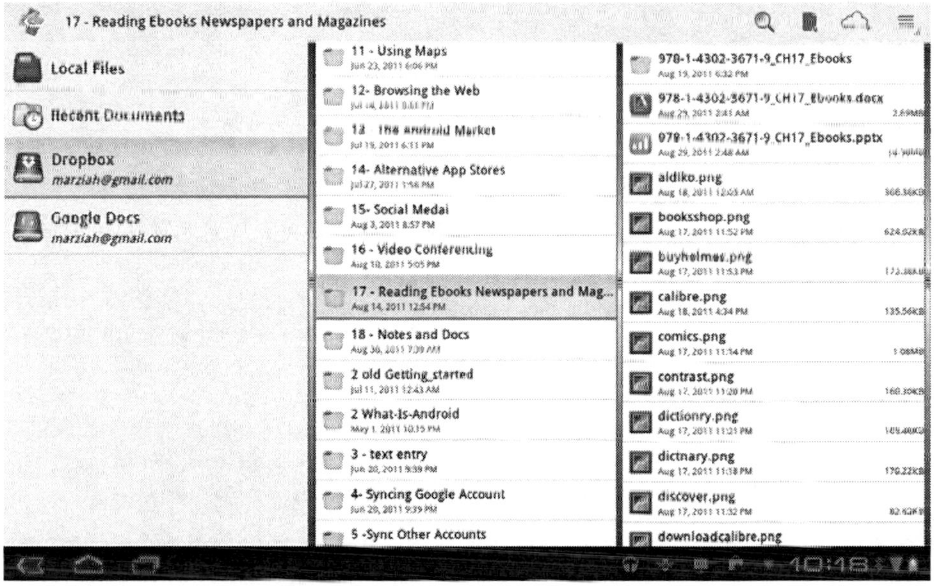

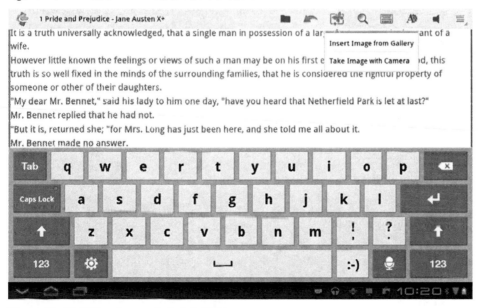

Figure 18–11. *Browsing remote files*

Editing Documents in QuickOffice

In **Documents To Go**, you start editing by clicking the **Menu** button on the bottom of the screen. In **QuickOffice**, all the editing action is on the top of the screen, as shown in figure 18–12. There's even an **Undo** button.

Figure 18–12 *Editing documents in* **QuickOffice**

> **NOTE: Polaris Office** ships with the Asus Transformer. This competent office-editing suite is compatible with **Microsoft Office** and Google Docs. However, it's not available for the Android Market at the time of writing. If your tablet didn't come with it, you're out of luck.

Printing Documents from Your Tablet

You may have noticed that some Google Docs files have a **Print** button. It's true. You can print Google Docs using a service called *Google Cloud Print*. You may be able to print directly to a wireless printer. Otherwise, you may need to have a desktop computer connected to a printer. If you're printing through another computer, you'll need to install Google Cloud Printer on your computer (see www.google.com/support/cloudprint/ for information on setting up a printer). Other apps also support Google Cloud Print, but neither **QuickOffice** nor **Documents To Go** supports it at the time of writing.

PrinterShare is another option. This is a commercial app available in both a free version that requires a desktop computer and a US $12.95 paid app that supports wireless printing. It also supports Google Cloud Print, which means you can print locally stored items you were editing with **QuickOffice** or **Documents To Go**.

Sticky Notes

Sometimes you might not want all the complications of Microsoft-compatible word processing apps. In those cases, it can be nice to just make a sticky note. **ColorNote** is a simple, free app that allows you to make text sticky notes and task lists. **ColorNote** is shown in Figure 18–13. Tap in the middle of a note to edit it, and tap the color swath on the upper right to change the note color. There's also a widget if you'd like to leave a virtual sticky note to yourself.

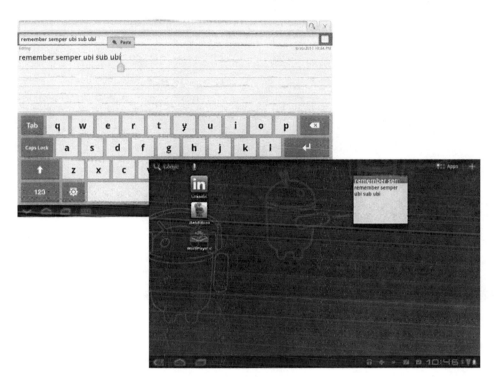

Figure 18–13. *Making sticky notes with the **ColorNote** app*

ColorNote is not the only sticky note app available—you can explore the Android Market to find more options.

Evernote

Evernote is my favorite note-taking app. It's free and syncs to your computer or phone. You can use it to store text notes, photos, voice memos, and even your location. Why is your location important? You might want to keep track of where you parked or the location of a store you visited. Register for an Evernote account at www.evernote.com.

Items in **Evernote** can be organized in many ways. You can assign tags, organize by date, or simply search through the content in your notes. When you launch the **Evernote** app in Android, by default all your notes are organized by date with a large **Calendar** view, as shown in Figure 18–14.

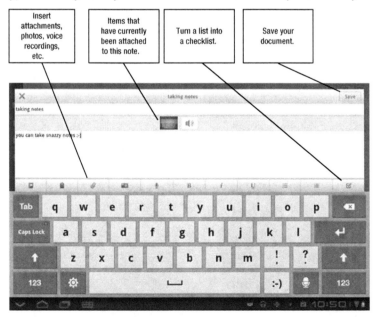

Figure 18–14. *The Evernote app*

Notice that the navigation options are to the side and top. Tap the **Tag** button on the left to browse by tag. You can also tap on a note within the calendar to edit that item.

To add a new note, tap the **New Note** button on the upper-right corner of the screen. As Figure 18–15 illustrates, you can enter text, add formatting, and attach a wide variety of file types directly from your tablet. Your item will be synced with your Evernote account online.

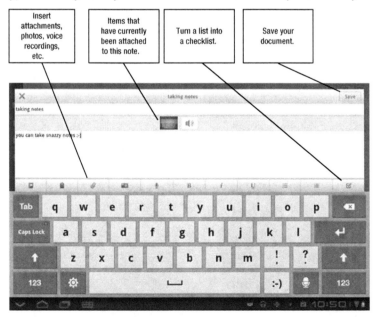

Figure 18–15. *Adding a note in* **Evernote**

Evernote Premium

The **Evernote** app isn't without limits. You can create as many notes as you wish, but you're limited on file size. If you upload a lot of large files, you may run into storage limits and need to purchase a Premium account. The Premium account is US $5 per month or US $45 per year, and it offers increased upload space, as well as support for more file types and offline editing.

Chapter 19

Viewing Videos and Movies on Your Tablet

Your tablet is a self-contained movie showcase. It can display high definition videos to entertain you or your kids on a car trip, or it can display rented videos while traveling on a plane. You can even use your tablet as a portable movie player that you hook up to a TV to bring your movies to your friends. In the next chapter, we'll discuss how to create video; but in this chapter, we'll pop some popcorn and enjoy the show.

CAUTION: Downloading and streaming movies takes a lot of bandwidth. If you pay for a limited 3G or 4G data connection, you'll want to make sure you're connected to Wi-Fi when you watch movies, or you may end up with a nasty surprise when your bill comes.

Adobe Flash

Many websites use **Adobe Flash** to display video. You may need to download the app from the Android Market if it is not already installed on your tablet. Tablets running older versions of Android may have trouble displaying **Flash** video.

YouTube

The first source of videos you think about on a Google-made operating system is probably YouTube. Honeycomb tablets ship with a built-in **YouTube** app that is optimized for tablets. This app is easier to navigate by touch, and it lets you browse by topic, as well as suggestions based on your viewing history. The more you use this app, the more accurate those suggestions will become (see Figure 19–1).

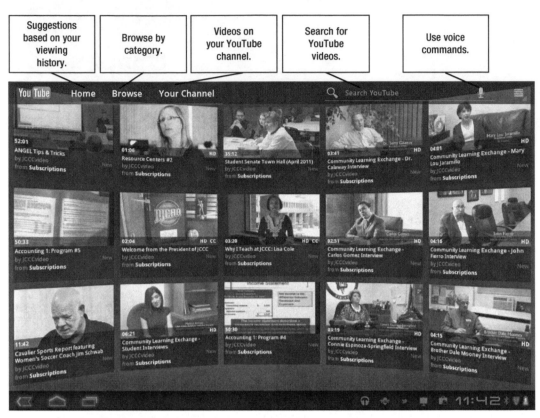

Figure 19–1. *Browsing the YouTube app*

The disadvantage to YouTube is that you must have a strong data connection in order to view your videos. It's also lacking in (legal) long-form entertainment. For example, you're unlikely to find a legitimate upload of your favorite TV show, although you can probably find a short clip or advertisement for it.

Android Movie Rentals

Google has a video rental service attached to the new Android Market. You can rent movies through the Market and watch them on the Web, your phone, your tablet, or even hook up your tablet to your TV using your tablet's HDMI connections.

This market lets you purchase movies just as you purchase apps or books.

At the time of writing, the Android Market is available on several tablets, and Google is adding more. In order to play those movies on your tablet, you must have the **Videos**

app from Google installed.

This app allows you to play both rented videos and personal videos you own. Rented videos can be downloaded to your device for offline playing, but they are copy protected and will expire when the rental period is over. The **Video** app is only available on tablets with an upgraded Android Market.

Rental Period

The rental period for most movies is 30 days to *start* watching the movie and 24 hours to *finish* a video you have started watching.

That gives you enough time to download a few movies for an airplane or road trip somewhere, and it gives you time to watch any movies you didn't get around to starting on the way up. The 24-hour grace period also gives you time to find a better Internet connection or download a movie if you start watching it and find that your connection is too slow.

That said, 24 hours is 24 hours, so be sure to check the terms of a movie before you start renting, and be careful not to start playing a movie before you're ready to watch it.

The terms and conditions of a movie are shown during the first stage of the check-out process. Figure 19–2 shows a movie being purchased from Android Market on the Web.

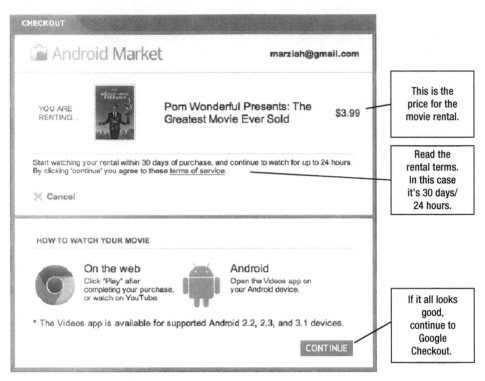

Figure 19–2. *The Android Market's terms and conditions for a movie rental*

Downloading (Pinning) Movies

As mentioned earlier, you can download rented movies to your tablet, so you don't have to rely on Internet access for viewing. Downloading movies through the Android market is called *pinning* the movie.

> **NOTE:** When you pin a movie to your tablet, it's not available for streaming or viewing from other devices like a phone or desktop computer. It's pinned explicitly to the device you downloaded it to.

Follow these steps to download a movie from the **Android Market** app on your tablet (not the Android Market website):

1. Tap a movie you've rented to see that movie's information page. This is similar to the information page you'd see on an app.

2. On the right side of the screen, you'll see two buttons: **Play** and **Download**. Tap the **Download** button; this will launch the **Videos** app and pin your video.

3. From the **Videos** app, tap the **Menu** button on the upper-right corner of the screen.

4. Tap **Manage Offline Rentals.**

5. Tap the **Pin** button (it is literally shaped like a pin).

6. Tap the **Done** button on the lower=right corner of the screen. Your movie will start downloading.

> **NOTE:** Movies are big files, and they'll generally take about 90 minutes to download. If you plan on watching a movie on an airplane trip, make sure you set aside time to download it well before you leave.

Using Your Tablet to Display a Show on Your TV

As mentioned earlier, you can view videos you rent from YouTube or the Android Market on an HDTV. However, there are a few requirements for doing so. First, you must use the **Video** app, even if you rented the movie from YouTube instead of the Android Market. Second, you need to have an HDTV that supports *HDCP* (high bandwidth digital content protection). Third, you must have the proper HDMI cable to connect your tablet to your TV. Fortunately, most recent HDTVs are capable of this.

Once you've connected your tablet to an HDTV, you should see the same thing on both screens. If you can't hear any audio, make sure your TV is set to use the HDMI as the TV input.

> **NOTE:** The display port on the Motorola Xoom only outputs 720p, even if your video source is 1080p.

Channel Apps

The Syfy channel has an example of an app dedicated to programming on a specific channel. The purpose of the app is to encourage you to view shows on TV, so the **Video** button only shows promotional clips instead of full videos. You can use the **Schedule** button to view upcoming episodes and put them on your tablet's calendar as events (see Figure 19–3).

Figure 19–3. *The Syfy channel app*

Similar apps are available for other channels, including the Discovery Channel, Animal Planet, Cartoon Network, and even local stations.

A few channel apps, such as the Smithsonian Channel, allow you to watch full episodes directly from your tablet.

TWiT

TWiT, which stands for "This Week in Tech." It is a free channel full of different technology ad science programming, including shows like "All About Android" and "Dr Kiki's Science Hour." Some of the podcasts are videos, and some are audios. The **TWiT** app, shown in Figure 19–4, isn't the only way to watch TWiT.TV. You can also watch the channel's shows directly from the Web. However, the app makes it easier to browse and download episodes.

The channels' episodes use *netcast*, or *podcast*. Therefore, when you view a show, you're actually temporarily downloading it, rather than streaming. That's actually good news for your subway ride if you need something to watch on the way.

Figure 19–4. *The TWiT app*

iPlayer

The BBC channel in the UK allows viewers in the UK to use the **iPlayer** app on their desktops and mobile devices to stream full shows from the BBC. The channel has announced plans to introduce this app to the US, starting with an iPad app; however, it has also said it intends to support Android down the road. This is projected to be a paid subscription service that will allow you to view BBC original TV series, not movies and other programming.

Netflix

The **Netflix** app is available for Android phones and some tablets running Android 2.2 and later. This app allows you to stream content from the Netflix library. It requires a data connection of at least 3G in order to stream, but you may find buffering issues when traveling, since your connection may fade in and out. Netflix's website uses **Silverlight** instead of **Flash**, so visiting the Netflix website will not solve the problem.

Amazon Videos

Amazon.com also offers video content. Some videos are available for purchase; some are available for rental; and the Amazon Prime membership ($79 a year) allows you to watch some videos for free.

If you purchase a movie, you can download that movie to your desktop computer. However, you cannot download and play it from your tablet at this time. Tablets can only stream videos. That means you need a data connection. However, you can view your shows in HD quality over a Wi-Fi connection.

Rather than downloading an app to view these videos, you use your **Browser** app. Go directly to **Your Video Library** on the Amazon.com website and view your videos in the browser window. Next, tap the **Expand** button on the lower-right corner to view your videos full screen (see Figure 19–5).

Tap to view the video in full screen mode.

Figure 19–5. *Watching Amazon videos*

Watch Directly From the Web

Watching shows directly from a website also works for many other TV channels and sources, including CBS and PBS. Most freely available streaming TV content uses **Adobe Flash**. As long as the website isn't actively blocking Android tablets from viewing the content, you can view streaming video on your tablet, just as you would with any other computer. Apps like **TV.com** can help you find free, available streaming videos.

Hulu+

Hulu is a popular streaming service for TV shows, and it hosts content from multiple networks. However, Hulu does not allow streaming on tablets. If you try browsing to the Hulu website (www.hulu.com) from your tablet, you'll see an error message resembling the one shown in Figure 19–6.

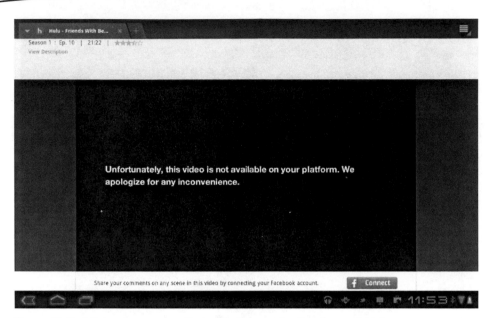

Figure 19–6. *A Hulu error message displayed when viewing the site on a tablet*

Hulu also has a subscription service called *Hulu+*; unfortunately, this service is not available for tablets, yet. This service *is* available on some Android phones, and Hulu says that it is working on rolling the service out to more devices. Once it does, you'll be able to download the **Hulu+** app; and for $7.99 a month, you'll be able to watch Hulu shows on your tablet, as well as watch full seasons of many shows, instead of just the last three episodes. Note that the **Hulu+** app does not take away the commercials.

PlayOn

One way to get around the current restrictions on services like Netflix, Hulu+, and other websites that block Android tablets is to use a real-time transcoding service like PlayOn. *Realtime transcoding* converts a video on-the-fly from one video format to another, changing it to a format your tablet can view. Follow these steps to use the PlayOn service on your tablet:

1. You must install the **PlayOn** app on a Windows machine that must remain on. You can find the software at *www.playon.tv*.

2. Download and install the **PlayOn** app for your tablet from the Android Market.

3. You must be using the same network as your PlayOn Windows machine in order to connect to PlayOn with your tablet; as long as this is true, your machine will automatically be connected.

The PlayOn service currently runs $5 per month, or $39 per year.

Using Your Tablet As the Remote

YouTube Leanback is a personalized display designed for large screens like computers hooked up to TVs or large monitors. You can access this service at www.youtube.com/leanback. If you're using this service, you can use the **YouTube Remote** app to control your experience. You can also download remote apps that control Boxee, Roku, Dish, GoogleTV, and other connected devices. Most of these apps use the Internet to control your devices, instead of relying on Bluetooth or infrared signals.

Your tablet can serve as both your remote and your schedule. The **TV Listings** app (on the left) will give you a location-based list of shows both over the air and through cable. It won't let you view any of the shows, but it's a great tool to use if you still watch most of your shows on a TV.

Chapter 20

Creating Photos, Videos, and Art

In the last chapter, we learned how to view videos from commercial sources. Now it's time to use your tablet for creative expression. Depending on which tablet you have, you can use it to snap and edit photos, film, and publish movies, and even use your tablet as a canvas for painting pixel artwork.

Tablet Differences

It's important to point out that not all tablets are the same. I'll use two tablets as examples: the Motorola Xoom and the Samsung Galaxy Tab 10.1. However, you'll need to consult with your user manual to find the specifics for your device's camera, to see if it differs from what you see in this chapter. In fact, this chapter may have the most variation between what you see in the screen captures and what you see on your tablet. That's because there are many differences in the types of cameras used in various tablet devices, and device makers have to tweak Android to compensate for this. That said, the standard Honeycomb camera interface looks like the Xoom, and most tablets use something very close to it, even when they present different options.

Taking Photos with the Camera App

Most—if not all—Honeycomb tablets have two cameras. The first is a front-facing camera you can use for taking pictures of yourself or video conferencing. The second is a rear-facing camera you can use to shoot pictures or videos at higher quality. You use the **Camera** app to control all of it. The Xoom uses the basic Honeycomb camera interface, and the basic controls are shown in Figure 20–1.

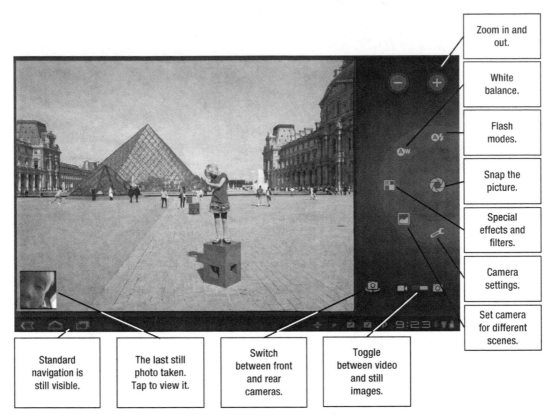

Zoom in and out.

White balance.

Flash modes.

Snap the picture.

Special effects and filters.

Camera settings.

Set camera for different scenes.

Standard navigation is still visible.

The last still photo taken. Tap to view it.

Switch between front and rear cameras.

Toggle between video and still images.

Figure 20–1. *Using the camera on the Xoom*

The Galaxy Tab offers mostly the same options, but the layout is slightly different. You can also tap to focus on a specific part of a picture, which is a feature not offered on the Xoom.

The Galaxy Tab camera doesn't use standard Android navigation. Once you're using the camera, the only way to exit the **Camera** app is by using the **Back** button, as shown in Figure 20–2.

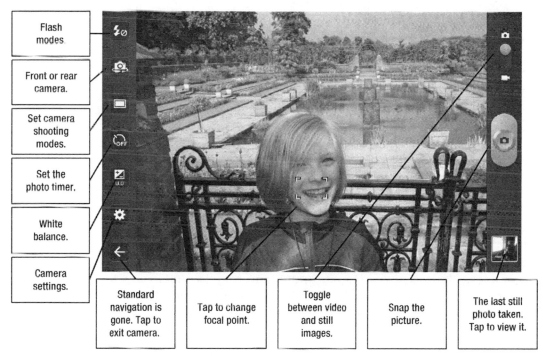

| Flash modes. |
| Front or rear camera. |
| Set camera shooting modes. |
| Set the photo timer. |
| White balance. |
| Camera settings. |

| Standard navigation is gone. Tap to exit camera. | Tap to change focal point. | Toggle between video and still images. | Snap the picture. | The last still photo taken. Tap to view it. |

Figure 20–2. *Using the camera on the Galaxy Tab*

If your tablet has a front-facing camera, you won't have the same camera options as you do when using the rear camera. That's because front-facing cameras usually have a lower resolution and don't have a flash. That means you'll want to stick to well-lit areas for shooting photos and video, and you won't see the options for features you don't have (see Figure 20–3).

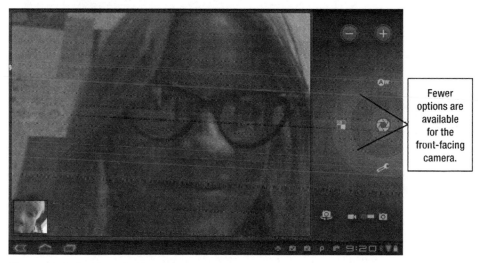

| Fewer options are available for the front-facing camera. |

Figure 20–3. *The front-facing camera on a Xoom*

Follow these steps to snap a photo:

1. Launch the **Camera** app.

2. Select the front- or rear-facing camera by tapping the toggle.

3. Focus the camera on your subject.

4. Tap the **Shutter** button.

> **TIP:** It's easy to shake the tablet when you snap a photo, so try positioning your thumb over the shutter button and using both hands to hold the tablet steady.

Special Features

Each tablet can come with its own set of special features for shooting everything from 3D photos to panoramas (see Figure 20–4). You'll need to refer to your tablet's user manual to see the specific features available or just play around with the various settings and effects. Android Ice Cream Sandwich includes panorama abilities as a standard feature.

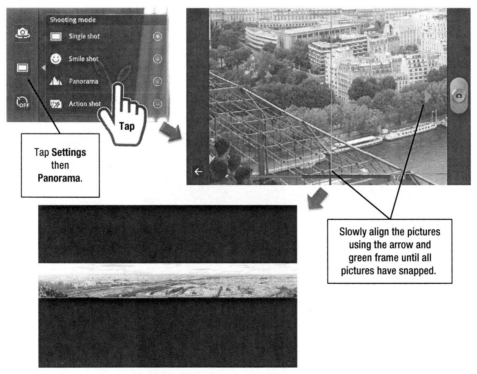

Figure 20–4. *Shooting a panorama using the Galaxy Tab 10.1*

GPS

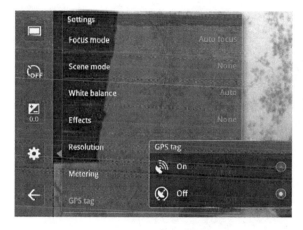

Most tablets offer you the chance to save location data with your photos. This is handy for remembering where you took a photo for things like vacation shots. You can toggle GPS tagging on and off using the **Settings** menu, and most photo sharing apps allow you to choose whether to display locations with the photo.

You can also take photos you've tagged with location data and upload them for submission to Google Earth using an app called **Panaramio**. Google generally only uses good quality photos that show the location without any portraits of people in them.

> **TIP:** Although many tablet cameras allow you to apply color effects to your pictures, you may want to shoot the photos normally and then use a third-party photo editing tool to apply an effect. That way, you're not committed to the shot if it doesn't work out as well as you'd hoped.

Reviewing Pictures

Once you snap a picture, you can tap the small preview picture shown in Figures 20–1 and 20–2 to review your shot using the **Gallery** app. You can also review any other photos you've taken on your tablet, and then share, delete, or rotate them. You can even edit them if you have a third-party editing app installed. Figure 20–5 shows different ways to manipulate the photos you take.

Figure 20–5. *Reviewing photos in the* **Gallery** *app*

> **NOTE:** When you're using your tablet's still camera, you'll see only still images for review. When you're shooting video, you'll only see videos for review.

You can use two-fingered pinching and expanding gestures on the photo itself to zoom in and out and to inspect the photo's elements. Tap the **Gallery** button on the upper-left corner to view the whole album.

Deleting Photos

While you're reviewing your work, it's a good idea to delete any blurry or otherwise bad shots, so you don't have to sort through them later. Follow these steps to do so:

1. Tap the unwanted photo.
2. Tap the **Trashcan** icon on the top of the screen.
3. Tap **Confirm delete**.

Shooting Video

In order to use your tablet as a video camera, you need to toggle it from **Still Image** to **Video** mode. The interface for these two modes look nearly identical, with only a few options changed (see Figure 20–6).

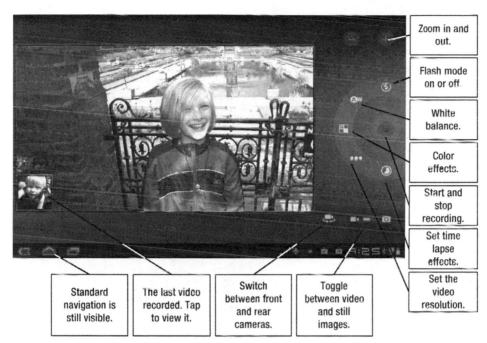

Figure 20–6. *Shooting video on the Xoom*

You can see the Galaxy Tab interface for capturing video in Figure 20–7. It's also largely unchanged from the still camera interface.

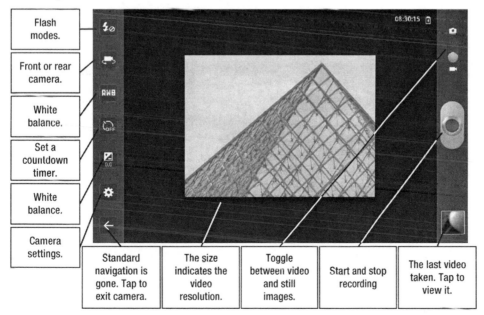

Figure 20–7. *Video on the Galaxy Tab 10.1*

Time Lapse vs. Timers

Here are a couple features that distinguish various tablets: some tablets have a *timer* to count down to when a picture is shot or a video starts being recorded, and some tablets have a **Time Lapse** mode that controls the interval at which video is shot.

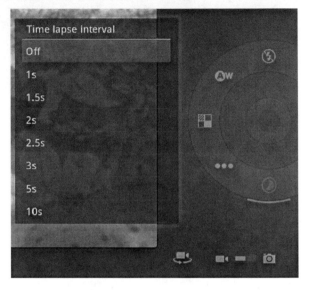

If you set a timer, your tablet will count down for the set number of seconds before it starts recording. This lets you set the camera and run into position before it starts.

If you set a time-lapse interval, as shown on the right, the video will shoot one frame for each specified interval.

Normal video resolution is 30 frames per second for most tablet cameras. That means the one-second interval will shoot video that will play back 30 times faster than real-time; similarly, a 10-second interval will play back 300 times as fast.

The Gallery App

While you can review your photos immediately after shooting them, the **Gallery** app gives you even more options for reviewing, sorting, and sharing your photos. Depending on your Google Account sync settings, the **Gallery** app can also pull in photos from Picasa Web Albums, a Google photo-hosting service. You can also view pictures stored in folders on your tablet. You may have imported these photos or created them in other programs.

The icon at the bottom corner of each album indicates the app that is the source of the picture, as shown in Figure 20–8.

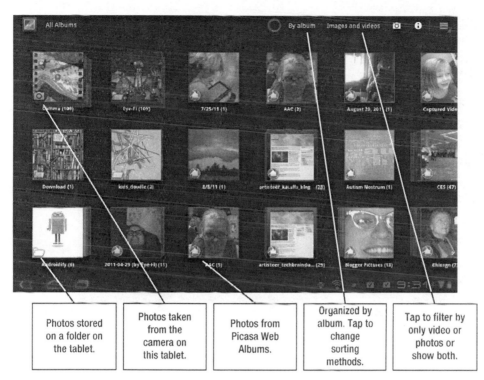

Photos stored on a folder on the tablet.

Photos taken from the camera on this tablet.

Photos from Picasa Web Albums.

Organized by album. Tap to change sorting methods.

Tap to filter by only video or photos or show both.

Figure 20–8. *Album view in the Gallery app*

TIP: Moving your tablet also moves the photos and videos stacked in an album.

The default view for the **Gallery** app is by album. If you'd like to sort your photos in a different order, tap **By album** on the top of the screen and choose a different sorting method. You can sort by date, location, tags (mostly useful for Picasa photos), and size. Sorting by location is shown in Figure 20–9.

Figure 20–9. *Sorting by location*

Photos are organized in stacks whenever possible. Figure 20–9 shows a few stacks of photos taken at the same location. Tapping a stack opens it and lets you navigate it by album, date, location, or tag. Tapping an individual item brings up the familiar view you see when reviewing a photo you've taken (see Figure 20–5 earlier in the chapter). Tap the **Gallery** button on the upper-left corner to go back and view the album or stack.

Sharing Photos and Videos

As long as you're connected to the Internet or using your data plan, you can easily share your photos and videos to online services. Follow these steps to share a photo or video to such a service:

1. Launch the **Gallery** app.

2. Navigate to the photo or video you want to share.

3. Tap the Sharing icon at the top of the screen.

4. Pick a service and share.

The services you have available will depend on the apps you have installed and whether or not you're sharing a photo or a video. In the example on the right, this is a still video. When you share videos, your options are generally limited to YouTube and email.

Third-Party Photo Apps

You can edit and share your photos using a wide variety of third-party photo apps. For example, even Adobe has a free **Photoshop Express** app for Android. The app, which is shown in Figure 20–10, does not have all the features and tools you might be familiar with from desktop versions of similar software. However, it does allow you to apply quick effects and upload and share photos through www.photoshop.com.

Figure 20–10. *Adobe Photoshop Express*

Photobucket users will appreciate the **Snapbucket** app. It allows you to snap photos with a custom-camera interface or import existing photos. You can use it to apply a wide variety of filters, and then upload your photos to your Photobucket account.

At the time of writing, the app is not optimized for tablets; for example, it still somewhat stubbornly offers all its features in a vertical interface.

One of my favorite photo-editing apps is **PicSay Pro**. This app is available in both free trial and paid versions; the paid version costs US $4.13. You can use this app to make serious photo corrections, such as red-eye reduction or sepia filters; however, you can also add word balloons, hats, fake mustaches, and other fun items to pictures, and then export them back to the **Gallery** app or a photo-sharing site (see Figure 20–11).

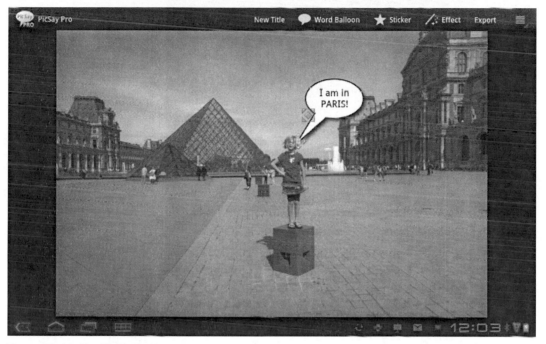

Figure 20–11. *The PicSay Prol app*

> **NOTE:** You can also use Google's web-based photo-editing app, **Picnik**; however, there isn't a separate, local client for this app, so you'll need to upload your photos to Picasa or Flickr before you can edit them with **Picnik**.

Editing Video

Honeycomb tablets come with a great video-editing app called **Movie Studio**. **Movie Studio** allows you to shoot a video from your tablet, do some basic editing, and then export the video to YouTube. You can also import a series of pictures and create a slideshow to upload to YouTube.

If you've ever used video-editing software, **Movie Studio** will be pretty familiar. If you haven't, this app may look intimidating; however, it's actually fairly easy to use once you get the hang of it. Figure 20–12 shows the app's basic interface.

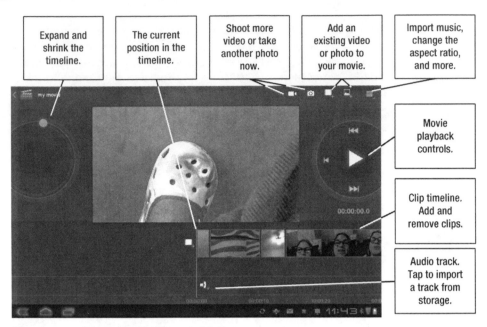

Figure 20–12. *The Movie Studio app's interface*

Movie Studio shows your movie in the middle of the screen. Below it, you'll see the collection of clips that make up your movie in a timeline. On the right, you'll see basic video controls, and to the left you'll see a round ring that lets you expand and shrink the preview icons of the clips showing in the timeline. This lets you edit larger or smaller sections of video.

Long-press a clip on the timeline to edit that clip directly, as shown in Figure 20–13.

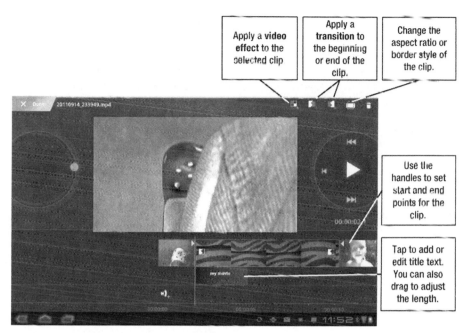

Figure 20-13. *Long-press options in* **Movie Studio**

Transitions

Movie Studio also lets you add basic *transitions* between clips, such as slides and cross-dissolves:

1. Long-press the desired clip.

2. You'll see a green outline around the clip, and you'll see transition symbols on either side of the clip. You can either tap the **Transition** button on the clip itself or tap the buttons on the top of the screen.

3. Choose a transition.

4. You'll see a tiny box between the clips. This is your transition for editing purposes. However, when you view the movie, you'll see the transition.

Video Effects and Adjustments

You can also apply video effects to individual clips within a movie, such as the negative effect shown in Figure 20-13:

1. Long-press on the desired clip.

2. Tap the **effects** button on the top of the screen.

3. Select the desired effect.

You may also find that you have video with different aspect ratios or resolutions. This happens if you've shot the video using different cameras, such as one part using the front-facing camera and another part using the rear camera. You can add letterboxing or change the resolution of some or all of the clips. To do this, follow the steps for applying effects; and instead of tapping the **Effects** button, use the **Border and Aspect Ratio** button.

Adding Titles

The layer immediately underneath the clips is for title text. You can't add anything highly detailed, but it's a simple matter to add a title or basic caption:

1. Tap directly underneath the clip you want to add a title for.

2. You'll see a **+FIN** button. Tap it.

3. Choose your title style and add your text.

Uploading to YouTube

If you already have a YouTube account tied to your Google account, uploading to YouTube is a snap. However, if you're using a data plan on your tablet, you'll probably want to make sure you use Wi-Fi to save on data usage fees. Follow these steps to upload a video to YouTube:

1. Once you've finished your movie, tap the **Menu** button on the top of the screen.

2. Select **Share movie**.

3. Select **YouTube**.

4. Enter the video title and any other desired settings.

5. Tap **Upload**.

By default, YouTube videos are public, so you'll need to override this setting if you prefer any other setting.

Using a Different Camera

Just because your tablet comes with a camera doesn't mean that you're stuck with only using your tablet's camera. For example, you could transfer photos taken on another camera to your tablet for slideshows or editing via USB. If you've got a better camera that supports SD cards, you can use an Eye-Fi brand card and the free **Eye-Fi** Android app to transfer your photos directly to your tablet and upload them to Photobucket, Flickr, or Picasa whenever your tablet has an Internet connection. The photos in Figure 20–14 were taken with a separate camera and wirelessly loaded onto the tablet.

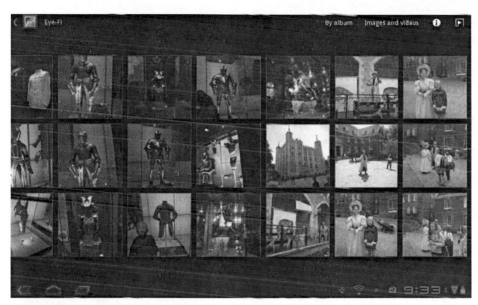

Figure 20–14. *Eye-Fi card and Android*

Using Your Tablet for Art

One big advantage tablets have over phones is their extra screen real estate. Tablets have enough space to really allow you to finger paint or use a capacitive stylus accessory to draw on the screen. For example, the **Autodesk SketchBook** app comes in both free and US $4.99 Pro versions (see Figure 20–15).

Figure 20–15. *The **Autodesk SketchBook** app*

SketchBook offers features you'd expect to find in a desktop-drawing app. It supports layers, a large selection of naturalistic brushes, and the ability to import photos.

> **NOTE:** If you want a stylus to use with most Android tablets, you'll need to find a *capacitive* stylus designed for use with phones and tablets. A stylus marketed for iPads will work fine. The important part is that this stylus must allow the small electrical charge from your fingers to transfer to the tablet. Styluses for Nintendo DS or similar devices won't work with most Android tablets. Those are designed for *resistive* screens, where an electrical charge isn't necessary.

Printing Photos

Once you've created a photo or work of art, how do you print it? There are a variety of ways. You may be able to print to some Bluetooth printers through the **Share** menu.

If you don't have that option for your printer and want to print directly from your tablet, you can use an app like **Printbot** or **PrinterShare** to print. In some cases, you may need to install an app on a desktop computer hooked up to a printer. Once installed, **PrinterShare** will show up as a sharing option in the **Gallery** app, as shown to the right.

You can also upload your photos to many photo printing websites. It's often easier to first share your photo to Picasa, Photobucket, or Flicker, and then order prints from the website you uploaded your photo to. Some tablets may even have built-in print ordering.

Chapter 21

Listening to Music

Your tablet is a combined computer and compact entertainment center. You don't need to carry a separate music player when your tablet has the storage and hardware capabilities to play your music as you read an eBook or surf the Web, and you don't need to keep track of different music libraries you've loaded onto different computers. You can sync them all. In this chapter, we'll explore a few ways to enjoy music on your tablet. This chapter is by no means an exhaustive resource on the available music options for your tablet—there are just too many quality music apps out there to try to cover them all here. However, we'll touch on a few highlights.

Google Music

Google introduced Google Music at the 2011 Google I/O developer's conference. At the time of writing, this service is available by invitation only; however, you can sign up to receive an invitation at http://music.google.com. Xoom owners are sent invitations without signing up.

The Google Music service uses your Google account to store music on the Internet—*in the cloud*—and that music is available from any device with a modern Internet browser. On Android 2.2 and higher, there's also a **Google Music** app.

Getting Music to Google

Once you get your invitation and start your Google Music account, you'll need to transfer your music collection to Google. You don't have unlimited storage, but Google estimates you've got room for up to 20,000 songs. Those songs may be on different computers, but you can still get them into Google Music.

NOTE: Google Music won't import songs that are protected by *digital rights management* (DRM). This includes some songs you may have purchased from iTunes or other music services. Sometimes, you can remove the DRM from iTunes files by burning a song to CD and then reimporting the file into iTunes.

Follow these steps to import your music into Google Music:

1. Log into Google Music from your desktop computer at `www.google.com/music`.

2. Download and launch the **Music Manager** desktop app from Google.

3. Specify your music location. You can choose from your iTunes folder or another location where you store music files.

4. Choose which songs and playlists to upload. You can specify some or all songs or playlists; you can also specify whether to include podcasts. The app can also watch those folders for new music.

5. Choose whether to allow **Music Manager** to upload songs from your watched folders. If you choose **Yes**, any new (non-DRM) songs you download will be automatically imported into Google Music in the background.

Music Manager might take several hours or even days to upload your music to Google Music; however, you can continue to use your computer or even stream the currently uploaded files on Google Music while you wait. Repeat this process on any computers where you store music files. Figure 21–1 illustrates the steps required to upload your music to Google Music.

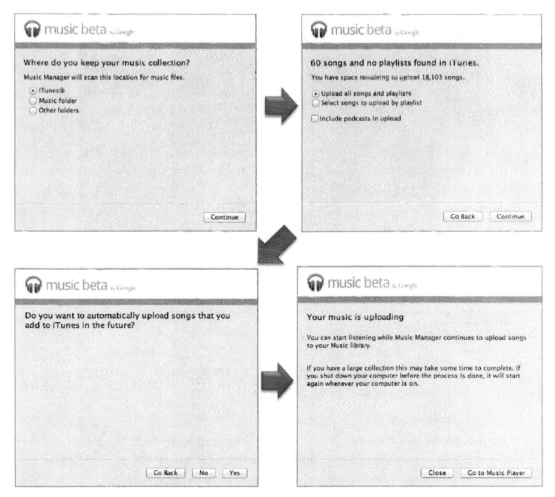

Figure 21-1. *Using Music Manager*

Using Google Music on Your Tablet

Once you've set up Google Music and populated it with your songs and playlists, you're

ready to play with the **Google Music** app on your tablet. You can download the app from the Android Market. Figure 21-2 shows the slide carousel–like interface of the **New and recent** view.

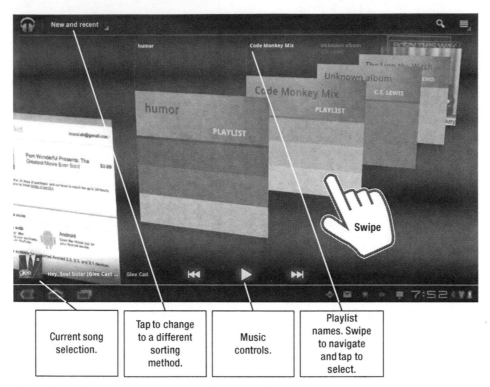

| Current song selection. | Tap to change to a different sorting method. | Music controls. | Playlist names. Swipe to navigate and tap to select. |

Figure 21–2. *The New and recent view in the Google Music app*

> **NOTE:** The **Google Music** app will detect album artwork for most music. Some things don't have album covers, like playlists, and some just aren't in the database. You can add or change album covers on the Web version of Google Music, but not in the Android version of the app.

The different views are really just sorting methods to find your music faster, just as they are in iTunes. To change views, simply tap the upper left of the screen next to the headphones and pick a new view from the list.

While each view has a slightly different graphic display, each view also allows you to drag and scroll to find your music or a group of musical files.

A few different views are shown in Figure 21–3.

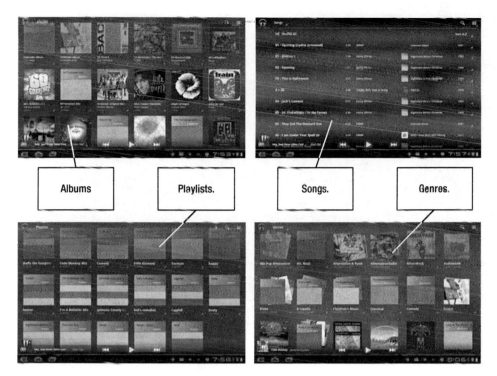

Figure 21-3 *Different views in Google Music*

> **NOTE:** If you see a **Triangle** icon on the bottom corner of an item, that means you can tap it for choices of what to do with that item, such as playing it or adding it to a playlist.

Playing Songs on Google Music

If you tap through any of the sorting choices, you'll eventually see a list of individual songs. Tap any song, and you'll start playing that song and any other song within that group, whether it's a playlist, album, or genre. Sometimes a group can contain one song. The controls for an individual song are shown in Figure 21–4.

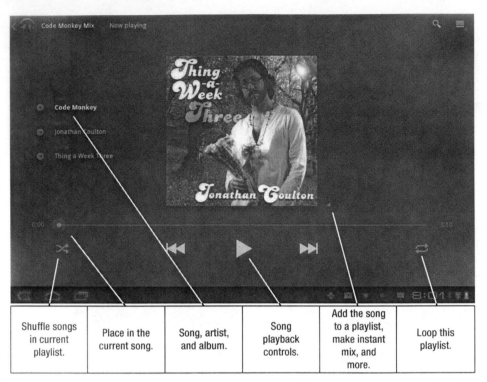

| Shuffle songs in current playlist. | Place in the current song. | Song, artist, and album. | Song playback controls. | Add the song to a playlist, make instant mix, and more. | Loop this playlist. |

Figure 21–4. *Google Music controls for a song*

Adding a Song to a Playlist

If you imported your music from iTunes, you imported your playlists, too; however, you may want to rearrange your playlists or make new ones as you buy more music. Follow these steps to do so (see Figure 21–5):

1. Tap the **Triangle** icon on the bottom corner of a song.

2. Choose **Add to playlist.**

3. Select from your existing playlists, or tap **New playlist**... to create one.

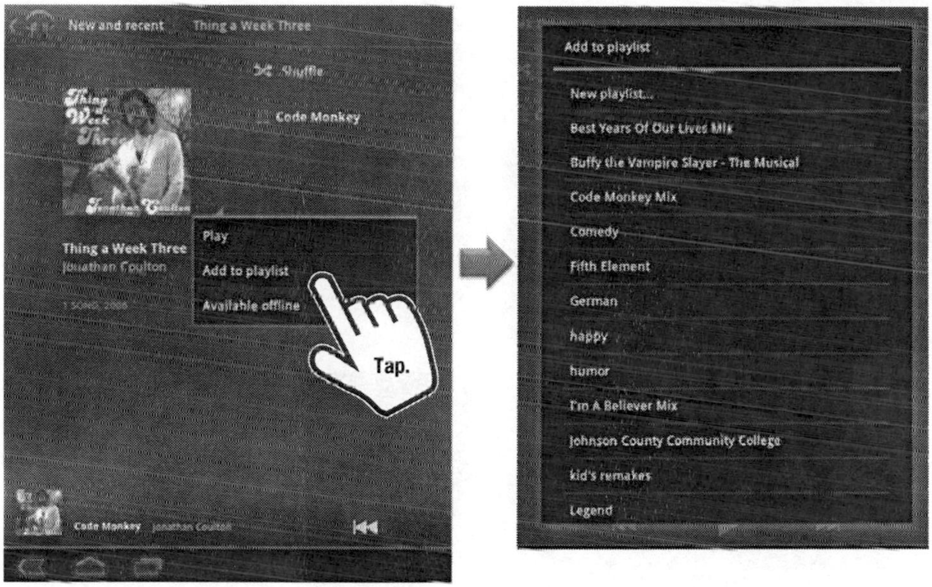

Figure 21–5. *Adding music to a playlist*

Instant Playlists

Rather than individually adding songs to a playlist, you can automatically generate a playlist around a single song. This works better on some songs than others, so you may need to remove a few odd choices once this is done. Follow these steps to do so (see Figure 21–6):

1. Tap through your playlist, album, or genre until you're viewing an individual song.

2. Tap the bottom corner of the album artwork.

3. Tap **Make instant mix**.

4. Your mix will be created. Tap the corner of individual items to remove them from the playlist.

Figure 21–6. *Instant playlists*

Listening Offline

Playing music from Google Music works great while you're connected to the Internet; however, what happens when you hit the road? The good news is that the **Google Music** app automatically downloads the music you've listened to recently, so you can keep listening to those songs. However, you may want to plan in advance for a trip and download a few songs before you leave.

In order to download a song, tap **Available offline**. You'll see a bright green **Pin** symbol in the menu for that item once it has downloaded. Unlike pinning rental movies from the Android Market, you can still stream your song from other devices. This is just a download to a specific device.

The number of songs you can download depends on the space you have available on your device.

Shopping for Music

If you like an artist and want to buy more, you can tap the **More by artist** menu option (see Figure 21–7). This will launch your **Browser** app with a search for shopping items related to that artist. If you buy and download new music to your tablet, it will be added to your Google Music selection; however, not all the items listed here are available as instant downloads. For example, some of the items listed are physical CDs. The items listed here are also on separate stores, not Google or the Android Market; therefore, you should check the individual reputation of the retailer before proceeding.

Figure 21–7. *Shopping for more music by the artist*

TIP: You can get free music for Google Music by visiting Magnifier at
http://magnifier.blogspot.com. If you're logged into your Google account, songs are imported into your Google Music account with one click.

Amazon MP3s and Cloud Player

Amazon.com sells MP3s on its website, as well as the ability to store those files and play them from any connected device, just as you can with Google Music (Amazon's service actually predates Google's offering). Amazon's streaming music service is called *Cloud*

Player; and, as with Google Music, you can download a desktop app on your computer to transfer your non-DRM iTunes and other music files to Amazon's music hosting service.

On Android tablets, you may find the experience of using and playing music with Cloud Player to be a little less satisfying. At the time of writing, the **Amazon MP3** app is not optimized for tablets; however, you're not stuck with Cloud Player as your only playback option. You can purchase songs from Amazon and download them to your tablet, where they'll play in **Google Music** and many other music apps.

When you launch **Amazon MP3** , you'll need to log into your Amazon account. Once you've done that, select **Go to Cloud Drive** to use the music player (see Figure 21–8).

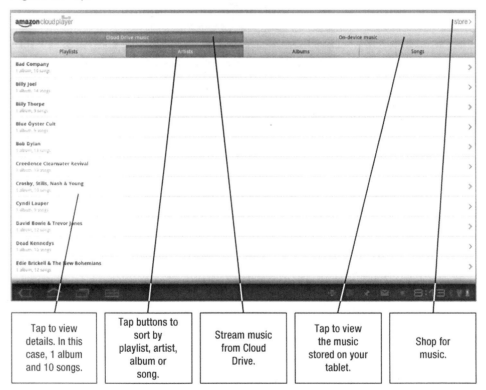

Figure 21–8. *The Amazon Cloud Player service*

Amazon MP3 divides your music into two locations: Cloud Drive music and On-device music. You could potentially have songs in both locations, but Cloud Drive music requires an Internet connection to play, while on-device files require storage space.

Downloading Files

Amazon is far more interested in selling you music than it is in tying you to its music player. Therefore, you can download your files at any time by playlist, song, or album. Tap the **Download** button to start downloading the selected song or group of songs (see Figure 21–9).

Figure 21–9. *Downloading a playlist in Amazon Cloud Player*

Purchasing Music from Amazon

To start shopping, simply tap the **Store** button located conveniently on the top-right corner of any view in **Amazon MP3**. You can search for music by song or album, and you can browse by popularity.

If you find a song you're interested in, tap once to preview, as shown in Figure 21–10.

Tap once to preview.

Figure 21-10. *Previewing music in Amazon MP3*

Once you've previewed the song, tap it again, and the price will turn into a green **BUY** button. Tap yet again to complete your purchase. You'll need to log into your Amazon account and enter your password to confirm the purchase. If you check the box next to **Remember me for future purchases**, you won't have to enter your password again; however, you may want to uncheck the box to avoid accidental purchases (see Figure 21-11).

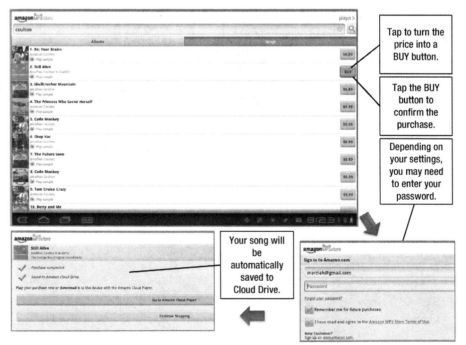

Tap to turn the price into a BUY button.

Tap the BUY button to confirm the purchase.

Depending on your settings, you may need to enter your password.

Your song will be automatically saved to Cloud Drive.

Figure 21-11. *Purchasing a song*

Automatic Downloads

If you tap the **Download** button for your new purchase, you'll be asked if you want to do this automatically for every MP3 you purchase in the future. If you tap **Yes,** all future purchases from Amazon, whether you make them from your tablet or the Web, will be downloaded to your tablet.

Automatic downloads make it easy to buy music from Amazon and upload it to Google Music without tapping any extra buttons. The next time you launch the **Google Music** app, it will find the new music files stored on your tablet and automatically upload them to Google's servers.

Pre-Installed Music Players

Your tablet may have shipped with its own specialized music app. In most cases, such apps can play music installed on your device and connect to a store. The attached music store may offer promotional songs or sales. If the files are not protected by DRM and are being downloaded to your tablet, you can use whichever player is most convenient for you. Figure 21–12 shows the **Music Hub** app that ships with Galaxy Tab devices.

Figure 21–12. *The Music Hub app*

Pandora

Pandora is an Internet radio station that creates custom playlists based on a song or artist you like. You can't pick exact songs or groups, but you can indicate whether or not you like or dislike the choices Pandora makes for you. You can register for a free account at www.pandora.com. Free accounts are sponsored by ads and require you to occasionally tap something to indicate you're still listening. Pandora also offers paid accounts for US $36 per year. Paid accounts offer unlimited listening and higher quality audio files.

The Android version of the app doesn't yet support creating your own playlist, but you can visit Pandora from your tablet's browser and create new playlists that way.

The biggest disadvantage of Pandora is that it is *only* streaming. You can purchase songs by tapping the **Menu** button, but you can't use the app itself without an Internet connection. If you're using a 3G or 4G connection, that could get expensive, so be careful. Pandora is shown in Figure 21–13.

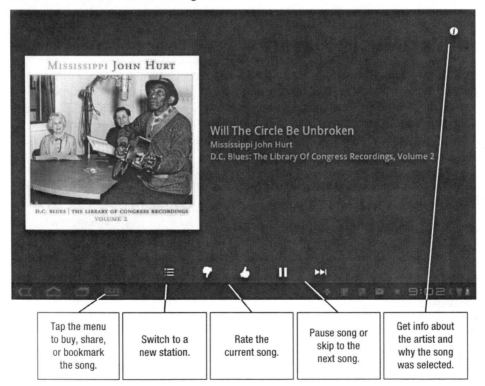

Figure 21–13. *Playing music with Pandora, the Internet radio service*

Spotify

Spotify is an Internet music service that originated in Europe and was recently introduced in the US. Although you can get a free Spotify account, it's really not as useful on Android unless you subscribe to a paid account. Paid accounts run US $5 and $10 monthly and offer unlimited, ad-free listening to an amazing collection of songs and artists. You can also create playlists that you can share with other users through Facebook. When you install the **Spotify** app on a computer, it scans that computer to find any music you already own, and then adds your music and playlists to your available collection.

Although you can't stream any music from Spotify on your Android without a paid account, you can still use the service to play files already stored on your device (see Figure 21–14).

Figure 21–14. *The Spotify music service*

Finding Music When You Don't Know the Name

It used to be that if you had an earworm, you'd have to hum it to someone else or search for a line of what you thought were the lyrics to figure out the name of the song and artist—but not anymore. There are several apps you can now use specifically to find the name of a song by using your tablet's microphone and recording a snippet of a song. Sometimes you can even sing a few bars yourself to find the answer.

Figure 21–15 shows one solution, the **SoundHound** app. Another popular app is **Shazam.**

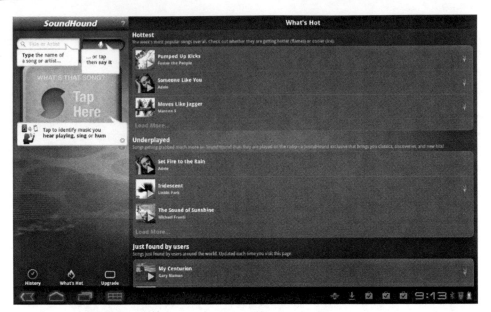

Figure 21–15. *The SoundHound app*

Beyond Listening

Tablets don't limit you to listening to the music of others; you can also create your own. Several musical instrument apps allow you to play virtual pianos or other musical instruments, although the quality of the music you create tends more toward novelty than artistry at this time. One free app, **Perfect Ear**, is designed to train your voice (see Figure 21–16). You can use it to improve your ability to sing notes on key or identify intervals and chords.

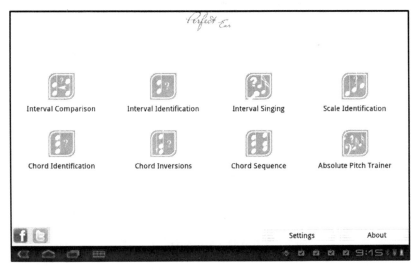

Figure 21–16. *Playing with the Perfect Ear app*

Chapter 22

Fun and Games

We've already discussed books, movies, and music, so now we'll look at games on the tablet. Starting with Honeycomb, Android tablets got a lot faster with dual-core processors. And many of these Honeycomb tablets have sharp screens that allow high-quality graphics displays optimized for **Adobe Flash** playback.

One thing to check before starting a game is whether it requires an Internet connection. Some games play just fine without one, but some require a connection for any sort of game play.

Favorites on a Bigger Screen

Many games are based on games that first hit phones or computers, but now have improved or enlarged graphics that take advantage of your tablet's larger display. The mechanics for the games remain the same, but many of them force a vertical orientation. Some games are simply variations of games that have been computer favorites for a while.

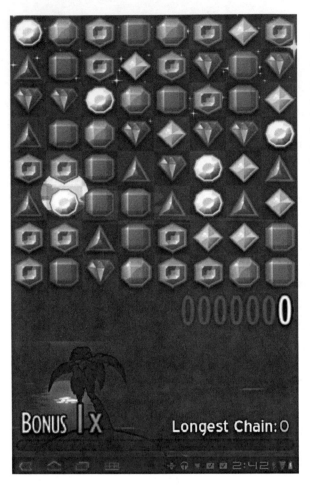

Match-Three Games

The basic match-three puzzle game has been around for a while, and you can find many variations for Android tablets. The rules are simple: match three or more colors in a row by exchanging two adjacent pieces. The matched colors will disappear, and new items will fall in to replace them. One typical example shown to the left is **Jewels** from MHGames.

This is one of many variations on the Russian computer game, **Shariki**. The game is more familiar to American players in the jewel-matching variation called **Bejeweled**. PopCap introduced the popular **Bejeweled** game for desktop computers before the age of phone apps. Electronic Arts offers an official Android version of **Bejeweled**, but it's not available for tablets at the time of writing.

There are other variations on **Shariki** involving bubbles or other shapes that also rely on the match-three mechanics.

NOTE: Beware of games that haven't been updated for tablets. If a game only displays a small rectangle on your large screen, it hasn't been optimized for tablets. Search for the app to see if there are two versions. Typically, the tablet version will be called the *HD* version after the high definition screen; however, just because you don't see HD in the name doesn't mean the app isn't optimized for tablets. Ice Cream Sandwich makes it easier to create tablet optimized apps.

Angry Birds

Angry Birds launched on iOS devices in 2009 as a paid app, and it became a huge hit. Rovio later made the game a free, ad-sponsored download, partially because of inconsistencies with the Android Market and paid apps; however, the company has gone on to introduce multiple variations of **Angry Birds** on just about every small and large computing and mobile platform available. There's even an Angry Birds board game, as well as a line of stuffed animals. There have been more than 350 million downloads so far.

If you've never played this highly addictive game, it's easy to start. You've got a slingshot, some angry birds, a pile of things stacked, and some happy green pigs. Hurl the angry birds at the stacked objects to knock them over and "pop" the pigs (see Figure 22–1).

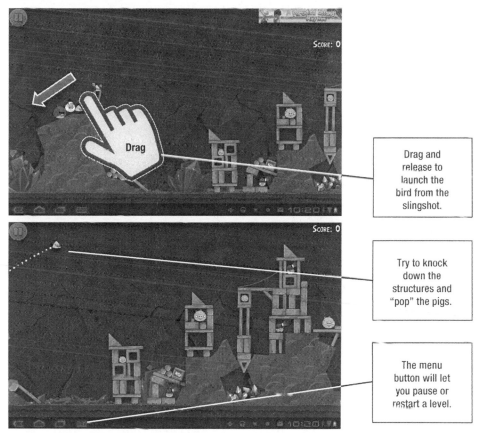

Drag and release to launch the bird from the slingshot.

Try to knock down the structures and "pop" the pigs.

The menu button will let you pause or restart a level.

Figure 22–1. *Angry Birds by Rovio*

Arcade Classics

Another typical type of game is the nostalgic arcade classic. It's even a category in the Android Market. There are both paid and free apps in this category, and there are both official and unofficial remakes of classic arcade games. There are several unofficial remakes of **Space Invaders** and pinball games of all stripes; and Namco has made official versions of **PAC-MAN** and **Ms. PAC-MAN**, although you'll need to double check to make sure they're compatible with your device.

> **NOTE:** Read the review comments and check for a free version before downloading a paid app. Otherwise, you may be burned by an app that doesn't work, doesn't scale well, or isn't as fun as you'd imagined.

Tetris

One classic arcade game that has made a great comeback is **Tetris** by Electronic Arts. EA makes both a free and US $2.99 paid version of the app.

It may take a few rounds to get used to tapping and dragging to manipulate the tiles into position; however, the game is as addictive on a tablet as it was in arcades and on desktop computers.

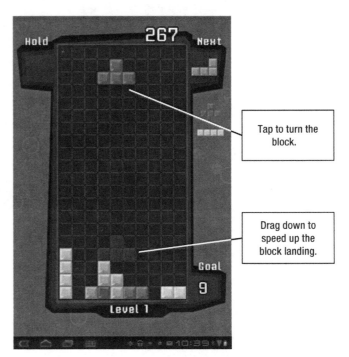

Tap to turn the block.

Drag down to speed up the block landing.

Tower Defense

One popular genre for computer games is the *tower defense* game. This is a type of strategy game—usually solitaire—where the player tries to install static weapons to prevent an enemy from breaching his or her defenses. Each destroyed enemy is worth points that can be used to purchase more defenses or upgrade existing installations.

Drag weapons onto the screen to defend.

Pause or fast forward the game.

Defeat all the enemies to win and open new maps.

One example of the genre that works well on tablets is shown to the left. This is Lupis Labs' **Robo Defense.** It's a fairly a standard tower defense with robots, tanks, helicopters, and jets trying to breach your defenses. One cool aspect of this game is that it is optimized for a variety of screen sizes. You can try the free version, which has one map and eleven levels. If you find the strategy to be strangely addictive, the paid version is only US $2.99 and allows you to choose more maps. US $2.99 is also a typical price for tower defense games.

Other tower defense games include the following:

- **Nexus Defense HD**: Defend against science fiction attackers.

- **ZDefense HD**: Defend along a hexagonal grid using arcade-style graphics.

- **Grave Defense HD**: Defend against a horde of zombies and monsters.

Board Games

The Internet is breathing new life into classic board games, and not just checkers and chess. Of course, you can play checkers and chess if you want to. But you can also play poker, solitaire, and just about any other card game you can imagine. Some involve other players, and some allow you to play opponents on the Internet.

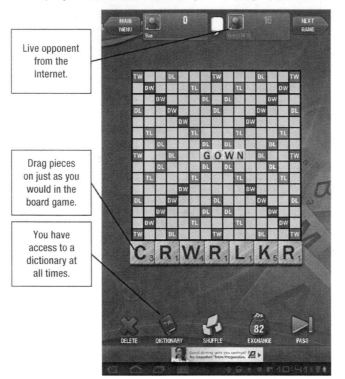

Live opponent from the Internet.

Drag pieces on just as you would in the board game.

You have access to a dictionary at all times.

Gameloft makes a licensed version of the Mattel classic Uno for US $2.99. The **Uno** app allows you to play with other online players around the world.

Electronic Arts makes the officially licensed version of Scrabble. This free game, shown to the left, allows you to play the popular word puzzle game on your tablet.

You can test your wits and luck against strangers, play friends from a list of contacts, or play against computer-generated opponents. Play can occur on many different platforms, so you don't need to restrict yourself to just players with tablets.

Games can sometimes take a long time to play online, but you can quit and nudge each other to make the next move.

Another Scrabble-like variation is the popular Zynga game called **Words With Friends**, which allows you to challenge your Facebook contacts.

> **NOTE:** There are tons of Scrabble-like games, but there are also tons of cheating-app companions. Many apps will allow you to instantly find the word worth the most points for the space available. That takes the fun out of it, so I tend to play only friends I know won't cheat.

Sports Games

If you play a sport, there's probably an app for that. You can track your favorite real life teams, but you can also use ESPN's free **Fantasy Football** app to track your imaginary teams. **Pocket Soccer** from RasterGrid is a game that combines soccer with a bit of air hockey mechanics to make an enjoyable game for soccer fans. Just fling your marble-like players at the ball and try to score goals. You can play one- or two-player versions.

The app on the right is the free **3D Bowling** by Italy Games. Drag the bowling ball toward the pins to see how well you do. You'll see extra fanfare for moves like strikes and turkeys.

This game can also be used to explain bowling to new players, who may not understand how scores work.

Using Tablet Features

Android games can go beyond simply porting a game from a computer and converting it to use touch controls. Tablets often have hardware that computers do not. For instance, the **Labyrinth Lite** game from Illusion Labs mimics a 3D marble labyrinth game (see Figure 22–2). The motion sensors in tablets allow you to play this game by holding and tilting the tablet, and the graphics move and change as you play. This combination of tilting and moving your tablet to move the marble greatly enhances the illusion of 3D depth.

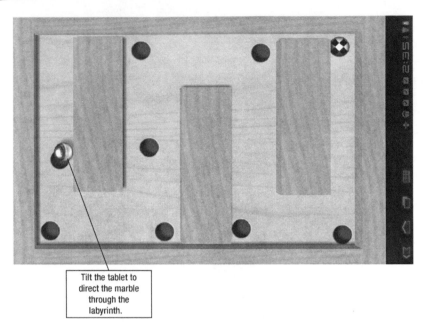

Tilt the tablet to
direct the marble
through the
labyrinth.

Figure 22–2. *Labyrinth Lite by Illusion Labs*

Racing games are another area where motion sensors work well. Many racing games allow you to hold your tablet out like it's a steering wheel and use the tilting motion to steer the car. In some cases, you can control the acceleration by using a thumb on one side of the screen. Figure 22–3 shows the free **Drag Racing** app by Creative Mobile.

Hold the tablet in
front of you and
tilt it like a
steering wheel.

Figure 22–3. *Drag Racing by Creative Mobile*

> **NOTE**: Game-like elements are also combined into items that aren't really games. For example, social networking apps like **Foursquare** award badges for check-ins, and you can play games from within Facebook.

Mystery Adventure Games

Sometimes you want to escape, and sometimes you want a challenge. You could engage in word and memory games, but there are also quite a few puzzle adventure games available for tablets that feature great graphics and involving story lines. If you like **Myst**, this is the sort of genre you might gravitate towards.

One example of this genre is **The Mystery of the Crystal Portal** by G5 Entertainment (see Figure 22–4). In this game, you help a young reporter named Nicole resolve the mystery of her missing father by solving a series of puzzles and mini games.

Tap items to get clues and solve the mystery.

Figure 22–4. *The Mystery of the Crystal Portal by G5 Entertainment*

G5 Entertainment also created **Paranormal Agency**, which features a different story line but similar mechanics.

MMOPRGs

MMOPRG stands for *massively multiplayer online role-playing game*. If you like **World of Warcraft**, this is your genre. Until recently, this was also the sort of game that mobile devices simply couldn't handle. Even laptops would struggle with the graphics and speed required, and phones were both too small and too slow to keep up. Things are changing rapidly, however.

Downloading Data

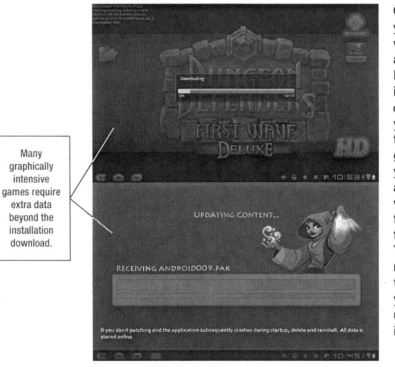

Many graphically intensive games require extra data beyond the installation download.

One of the things you may run into with some games— and especially with MMOPRG games— is that you need to *download* them after you've *installed* them. Be sure you've got plenty of room in your tablet's storage and be prepared to wait a few minutes for your game to finish installation. You'll sometimes need to go through this process again if you pay for an upgrade through an in-app purchase.

Pocket Legends

Pocket Legends is an MMOPRG by Spacetime Studios (see Figure 22–5) that is designed to run on mobile devices. It requires a data connection of some sort, and it will work under slower 3G speeds. Be warned that MMOPRGs take a lot of data, so consider carefully before connecting over anything but Wi-Fi.

Virtual joystick navigation.

Figure 22–5. *Pocket Legends by Spacetime Studios*

Pocket Legends uses a virtual joystick on the corner of the screen for navigation; this feature has become an MMOPRG standard for tablets. You can also use some two-finger navigation such as pinch-to-zoom gestures, and you can communicate with other players using text chat.

Pocket Legends is free to download and play, but purchasing a membership gels you additional features, such as exclusive adventure areas and items. You may notice that the graphics are not as high definition in this game. The lower definition graphics enable faster rendering time over slower connections and devices.

Dungeon Defenders

Trendy Entertainment publishes **Dungeon Defenders** and describes it as a combination of MMOPRG and tower defense. It was one of the first tablet-optimized games released on the market. That's because Nvidia, the manufacturer of the dual-core chip inside the Xoom and many other Android tablets, paid Trendy Entertainment to adapt its game for tablets. The game ships for free on the Xoom.

Dungeon Defenders is a game that tablet players can play right alongside console and desktop computer players, although the game was released on mobile platforms first. The cross-compatibility means you can start playing on one platform and continue playing on another. Figure 22–6 shows the basic layout of this game.

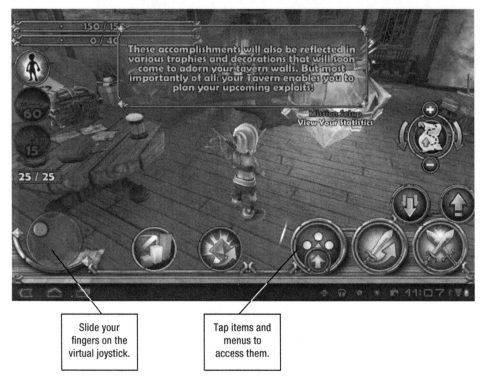

Slide your fingers on the virtual joystick.

Tap items and menus to access them.

Figure 22–6. *Dungeon Defenders by Trendy Entertainment*

The graphics in **Dungeon Defenders** are higher quality than those in **Pocket Legends**, but the tablet requirements are also higher. **Dungeon Defenders** takes advantage of the **Flash** optimization in the Nvidia chips, so it won't work as well on tablets with different processors.

Like **Pocket Legends**, **Dungeon Defenders** is free, but you can upgrade it through in-app purchases. If this game didn't ship with your tablet, you can download it from the Android Market.

Virtual Simulations

Many games allow you to own a virtual business, care for a virtual pet, or grow food on a virtual farm. They use a combination of skill, strategy, and luck; and many people find them quite addictive. G5 Entertainment has a whole series of games along this line, including the example in Figure 26–7, **Stand O'Food,** which lets you open a series of virtual restaurants.

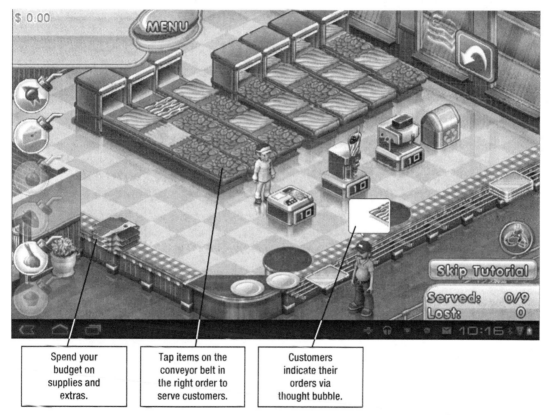

| Spend your budget on supplies and extras. | Tap items on the conveyor belt in the right order to serve customers. | Customers indicate their orders via thought bubble. |

Figure 22–7. *Stand O'Food by G5 Entertainment*

Serving customers requires tapping the correct sequence of food items, and you make decisions about what supplies to purchase between each mini-game. The game grows increasingly complex in each round, but separating play into mini-games means you can start and stop whenever it's convenient.

Games for Children

I'm a mother, and I've been known to pass my tablet to one of my children to keep them entertained during a long car ride; however, I don't recommend most children's games.

Android tablets weren't designed with children in mind. Unlike iPads, Android tablets don't make it easy to lock away features like in-app purchases and web browsing. Some games attempt to compensate for this by locking you into an app until you perform some unlocking action; unfortunately, that often makes the device crash or ends up locking out the adult. If you allow your child to use a tablet and don't want her to accidentally delete your apps or find inappropriate Internet content, the best solution is still direct supervision.

One of the better "games" for kids is the app **Kid Mode** by Zoodles. This app lets you create a customized list of apps for your kids; it also includes a lock-out mode. Like most lock-outs, however, this one can be overridden by a child capable of reading the screen and following the directions.

My other beef with children's games is that many of them try so hard to be educational with letters or numbers or shapes that they're just not fun. You're better off letting children play fun games designed for players of all ages, such as **Angry Birds**.

One game that ends up being both a brain teaser and surprisingly fun for many ages is **Slice It!** by Com2us (see Figure 22–8). This game won't work well for pre-readers, but my nine-year old would play all day if I were to let her.

Figure 22–8. *Slice It! by Com2Us*

The mechanics of this game are simple. You're given a shape, and you use your finger to draw a virtual cut through the shape. The instructions tell you how many pieces you need at the end and how many slices you can make. The graphics are whimsical, and the challenges start easy, but get increasingly difficult. This game is also addictive for adults.

Chapter 23

The Clock, Calculator, and Other Utilities

This chapter will explore those little utilities that can end up being very handy in a pinch. As you might expect, we'll look at the **Clock** and **Calculator** apps; but we'll also look at a few other utilities you can download to get more out of your tablet.

The Clock

Android tablets come with a useful, albeit plain **Clock** app. You don't really need it for telling time because you can always glance down at the bottom-right corner of the screen to see that. However, the **Clock** app does come with an alarm. If you place your tablet in a charging cradle at night, this app can serve as a great alarm clock.

Follow these steps to start using the **Clock** app's alarm function:

1. Launch the **Clock** app either through the widget or by tapping its app icon.

2. Tap the **Set alarm** link below the time (see Figure 23–1).

Figure 23–1. *Setting an alarm*

3. If you have existing alarms, you can simply tap them to turn them on (see Figure 23–2). Otherwise, tap **+ Add alarm.**

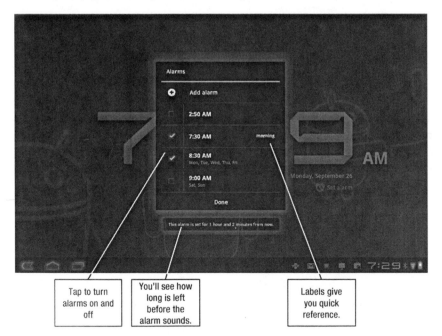

Tap to turn alarms on and off

You'll see how long is left before the alarm sounds.

Labels give you quick reference.

Figure 23–2. *Turning alarms on or off*

1. Set the time by tapping the **Up Arrow** or **Down Arrow**, and then tap **Set** (see Figure 23–3).

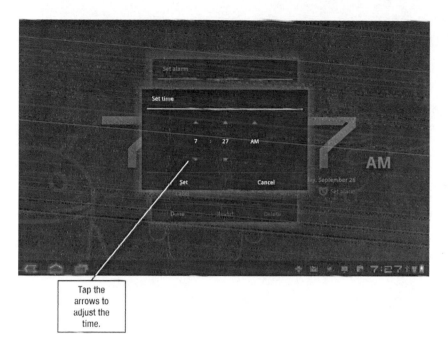

Tap the arrows to adjust the time.

Figure 23–3. *Adjusting the time*

4. Adjust any other settings (see Figure 23–4).

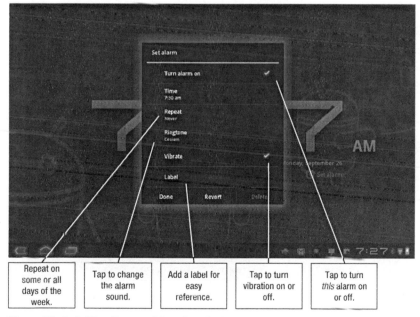

Repeat on some or all days of the week.

Tap to change the alarm sound.

Add a label for easy reference.

Tap to turn vibration on or off.

Tap to turn *this* alarm on or off.

Figure 23–4. *Setting the remaining alarm features*

Repeating Alarms

Each alarm turns off after it rings, unless you set it as a repeating event.

If you want to have an alarm that wakes you up only on weekdays, you can set the **Repeat for Monday–Friday** option. Each alarm can only ring once every 24 hours because it can only be set to one time; however, you can set each alarm for multiple days. You can also add as many alarms as you like; so, if you need to get to work earlier on Thursdays than you do the rest of the week, you can simply set two alarms.

> **TIP:** Since you can change the ringtone on a per-alarm basis, you can set one tone for the time you want to wake up and another for the time you want to leave for work.

Snoozing and Dismissing an Alarm

So it's morning and the alarm is ringing. How do you shut it off? You've got two choices: tap **Snooze** or tap **Dismiss.** But if you're as groggy as I am in the morning, you may hit the wrong option and realize you've hit **Snooze** when you meant to hit **Dismiss.** If that happens to you, just tap the notification alert on the bottom of the screen, as shown in Figure 23–5.

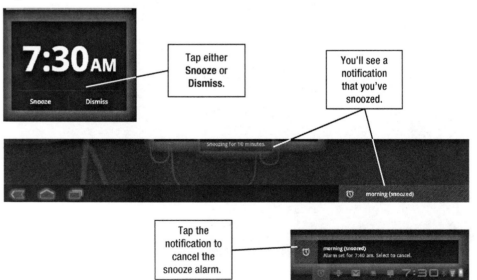

Figure 23–5. *Snoozing an alarm*

Extending the Clock

You may have noticed that your tablet's **Clock** app came with a rather boring digital **Clock** widget. In some cases, you may have a different widget that shipped with your tablet. In others, it's just the glowing blue digital clock. Fear not: there are tons of clock widgets in the Android Market available in both free and premium versions. Most combine weather forecasts with the time display, which is really useful when trying to figure out what you're going to wear in the morning. Figure 23–6 shows a few widgets you can download.

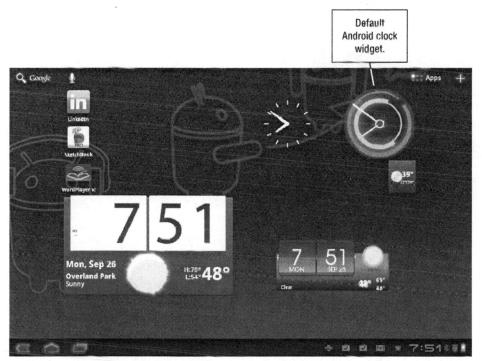

Figure 23–6. *Downloadable clock widgets*

Alternate Alarms

The app store has much more than widgets; it also has many alternative alarms. **Alarm Clock Plus** and **Alarm Clock Extreme** offer features beyond the basics. For example, **Alarm Clock Extreme** has a gigantic **Snooze** button, and it makes you solve math problems to prove you're awake. **Alarm Clock Plus** offers to speak the weather and time when the alarm goes off.

Before you commit to paying for an alternative alarm, however, you should verify that it will look good on a tablet.

The Calculator

It may seem like a minor detail, but you have a **Calculator** app built into your tablet with buttons big enough for your fingers. This calculator is capable of doing more than adding and subtracting, as shown in Figure 23–7.

Figure 23–7. *The Calculator app*

The features in this app are sufficient for solving most common math problems; however, it's not the fanciest calculator out there. If you need the capabilities of a true scientific calculator, you'll need to download another calculator app. You can find scientific calendars, tip calculators, interest calculators, BMI calculators, and more by searching the Android Market, as shown in Figure 23–8.

Figure 23–8. *A sampling of available calculator apps*

ES File Explorer

You can explore your SD card or internal storage contents by connecting your tablet to your computer using the USB cord and mounting it as a drive. However, this requires that you have a cable and computer nearby anytime you want to explore your files. I also recommend using an app like **ES File Explorer** from Estrongs, Inc. (see Figure 23–9).

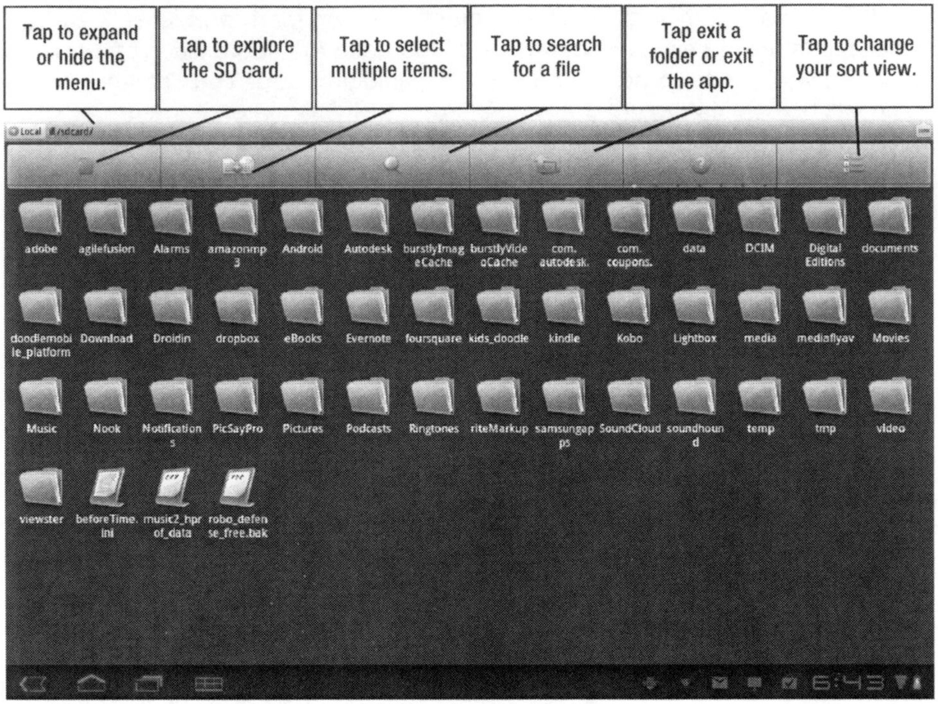

Figure 23–9. *The ES File Explorer app from Estrongs, Inc.*

ES File Explorer does exactly what its name implies: it lets you see and explore the files stored on your tablet. It also lets you copy and paste them. That's handy if you need to move an eBook onto your reading app, for example.

The interface for moving and copying files takes a little getting used to. You can either long-press an item; or you can tap to select it, and then press the **Operations** menu button in the lower-left corner, as shown in Figure 23–10.

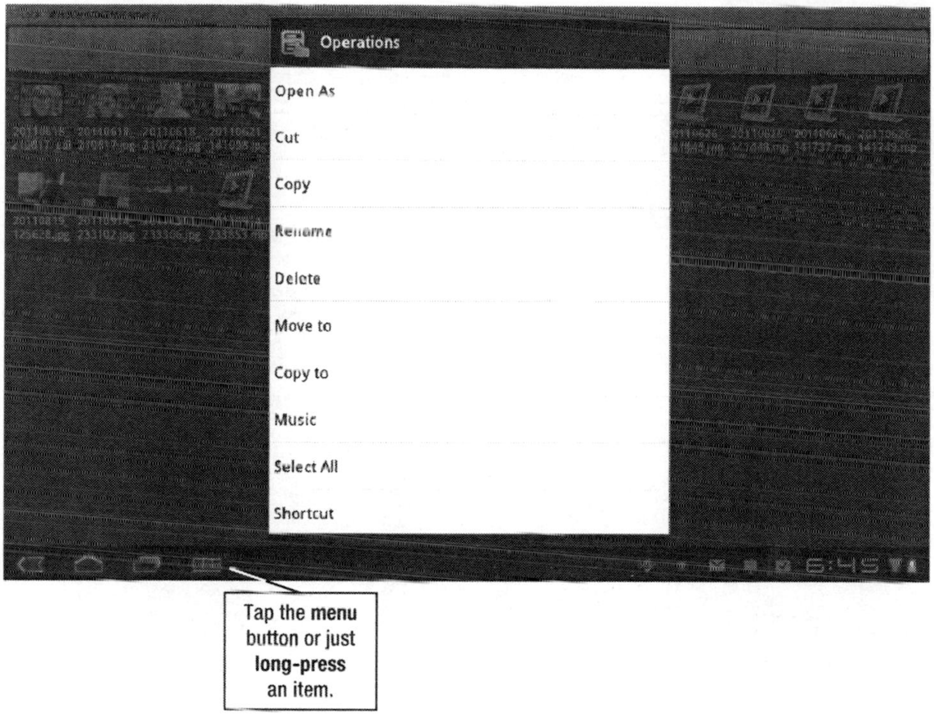

Tap the **menu**
button or just
long-press
an item.

Figure 23–10. *The Operations menu in ES File Explorer*

The Grocery List

There are many apps for shopping online, and we've explored a few of them in earlier chapters. Here's another one worth looking at: the **Grocery IQ** app lets you create a grocery list for shopping in the store. Although you can use this app on phones, the large display makes it appealing for tablets (see Figure 23–11).

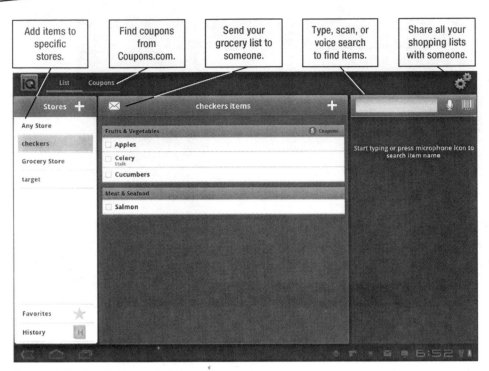

Figure 23-11. *The Grocery IQ app*

Grocery IQ comes from Coupons.com, so it emphasizes coupons and commercial products; however, it also allows you to share your grocery list with others, such as a spouse or a team. You can create different lists for different stores, and you can enter your list by typing, voice, history, or even a scanned barcode.

Speaking of barcodes: Any good Android tablet with a camera should have a barcode scanner. There are many that work well, from the basic **Barcode Scanner** to **Google Goggles**, which attempts to identify non-barcode objects as well.

Chapter 24

Using Bluetooth for Keyboards and More

Bluetooth is a short-range radio designed to serve as a wire-replacement technology. With Bluetooth, you can do many things that would otherwise have required you to plug something in, such as connecting devices to keyboards, mice, headphones, and printers. You can also use Bluetooth to transfer files between devices without using a USB cable. Thanks to improved Bluetooth technology, you can even listen to your music in stereo.

The name *Bluetooth* came from a Danish Viking credited with uniting Scandinavians: King Harald Blåtand. His name is roughly translated as "blue tooth." The idea is that, just as King Blåtand united Denmark, Bluetooth technology unites all your devices.

There are a lot of technical terms associated with Bluetooth technology, but it's not my intent to bog you down with jargon. This chapter will explore extending your tablet with Bluetooth to take advantage of devices like keyboards and headphones. You will also learn how to use this technology to transfer files to your laptop.

> **NOTE:** You must have a compatible Bluetooth adapter or device in order to stream music or use keyboards on your tablet. Not all devices are compatible with each other; for example, some keyboards are designed for specific tablets.

Turning on Bluetooth

If you're going to use Bluetooth on your device, you need to make sure it's enabled. Follow these steps to do so (see Figure 24–1):

1. Tap the bottom-right corner of your tablet.

2. Tap **Settings**.

3. Tap **Wireless & networks**.

4. Tap the **Checkbox** icon next to **Bluetooth** if it's not already checked.

Figure 24–1. *Going to Bluetooth in the Settings menu*

Bluetooth Profiles

Bluetooth profiles determine how devices interact with each other and control things like printing, transferring files, playing sounds, and using devices like joysticks. In order to be compatible, both items have to understand the same profile. That means you'll have to check your tablet and your device to make sure they're compatible.

Most current tablets support the following technologies:

- **A2DP (Advanced Audio Distribution Profile):** Stream audio to headphones.

- **AVRCP (Audio Video Remote Control Profile):** Use remote controls to control your tablet.

- **OPP (Object Push Profile):** Transfer files from one device to another.

- **PBAP (Phone Book Access Profile):** Access or transfer your contact list.

- **HID (Human Interface Design):** Use this for keyboard support.

These technologies are supported by most tablets, but more profiles may be available for some devices. Ice Cream Sandwich also adds more profile support.

Bluetooth and Pairing

Bluetooth can communicate with other devices up to 30 feet away; however, it has to know which device to communicate with. You can't just have random devices controlling each other and sending data. The process of connecting two Bluetooth devices with each other is called *pairing*. Not all devices are compatible with each other, so not all devices can be paired with each other.

To begin pairing a device with your tablet, go to the **Wireless & networks** area of the **Settings** menu, as shown in Figure 24–2.

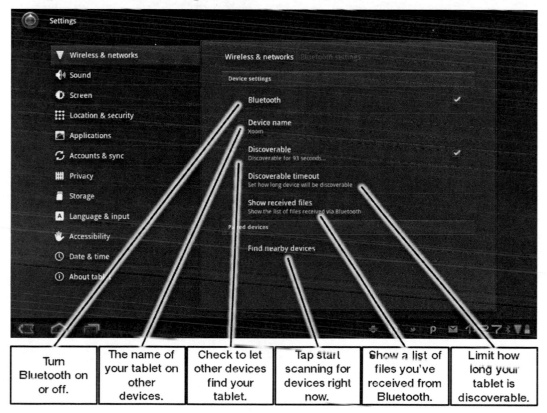

| Turn Bluetooth on or off. | The name of your tablet on other devices. | Check to let other devices find your tablet. | Tap start scanning for devices right now. | Show a list of files you've received from Bluetooth. | Limit how long your tablet is discoverable. |

Figure 24–2. *Getting to know the Bluetooth options in the Settings app*

Next, tap the **Find nearby devices** button, as shown in Figure 24–3.

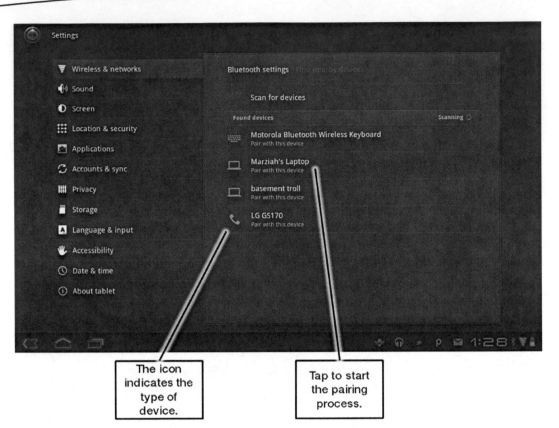

The icon indicates the type of device.

Tap to start the pairing process.

Figure 24–3. *Locating nearby devices*

You'll see how different devices have different symbols. Let's go ahead and tackle one of the more complicated pairings first. Follow these steps to pair your tablet with a computer:

1. Tap under the name where it says **Pair with this device.**

2. Confirm the pairing on both devices. This means you'll check to make sure the numbers match between your computer and your tablet; you'll also need to verify that you want to pair both devices (see Figure 24–4).

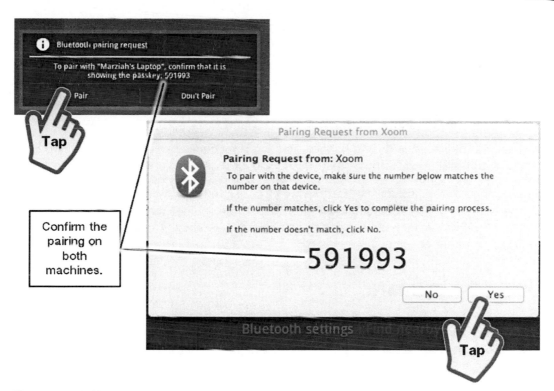

Figure 24-4. *Pairing your tablet with a computer*

Once you confirm the pairing on both ends, you'll see the device listed under the **Paired devices** section (see Figure 24–5).

Figure 24-5. *Paired devices on a tablet*

> **NOTE:** The laptop in Figure 24–5 is listed as "Paired but not connected." Devices like laptops and phones are *connected* when they're actively sharing data.

You use the same process to pair your tablet with a phone; however, there's one key detail you don't want to forget: both devices need to be discoverable.

Both your tablet and your phone are generally not discoverable, so you'll want to tap the **Discoverable** checkbox (see Figure 24–2). Once you have one device discovering the other, you can start the pairing process and confirm it on both ends, just as you would for a computer pairing.

Pairing with Keyboards and Headsets

Accessories like keyboards and headphones use a much simpler and easier pairing process. You will need to check the user manual for a given device, but most devices have some sort of button to press or hold down that will cause the accessory to go into

Discovery mode. Once you see the device (as shown in Figure 24–3), you'll just need to tap it to pair it with your tablet. There's no confirmation required on either end.

Using a Keyboard

Once you've paired a keyboard with your tablet, your tablet assumes you want to use the physical keyboard for text entry anytime it's powered on. Anytime you'd normally see the software keyboard pop up, nothing will happen. That's because you need to start typing on your keyboard.

If you want to temporarily turn it off, tap the **Keyboard** symbol on the bottom of the screen and toggle the **Use physical keyboard** setting (see Figure 24–6).

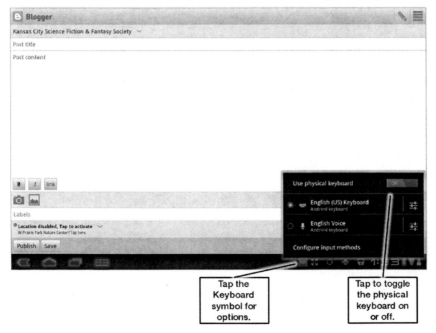

Figure 24–6. *Using a physical keyboard*

Remote Control

Remember that one of the supported Bluetooth profiles, AVRCP, is used for remote controlling other devices. Many keyboards offer options to play media and music, launch apps, start instant messaging, or browse the Web.

> **NOTE:** If your tablet starts acting erratically while paired with a keyboard, check to see that nothing is pressing a key. This happens to me sometimes when I carry my keyboard in my purse.

You can also use remote control features to control playback on many Bluetooth headsets and headphones.

Transferring Files

Earlier we paired a tablet with a laptop. Now it's time to send the laptop a photo.

Rather than using the USB cable, tap the **Share** button in the **Gallery** app. You'll see all the ways you can share this photo with different apps and services. Next, tap **Bluetooth**.

You'll be asked to confirm the transfer on your connected device (see Figure 24–7); however, you can also give permission for multiple file transfers at once.

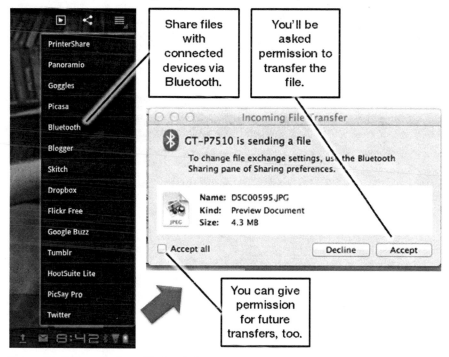

Figure 24–7. *Transferring a file to a laptop*

Unpairing Bluetooth Devices

At some point, you may want to disconnect a Bluetooth device; follow these steps to do so (see Figure 24–8):

1. Go to the **Bluetooth Settings** in the **Wireless & networks** area of the **Settings** menu. You'll see all paired devices.

2. Tap the **Wrench** icon.

3. Tap **Unpair.**

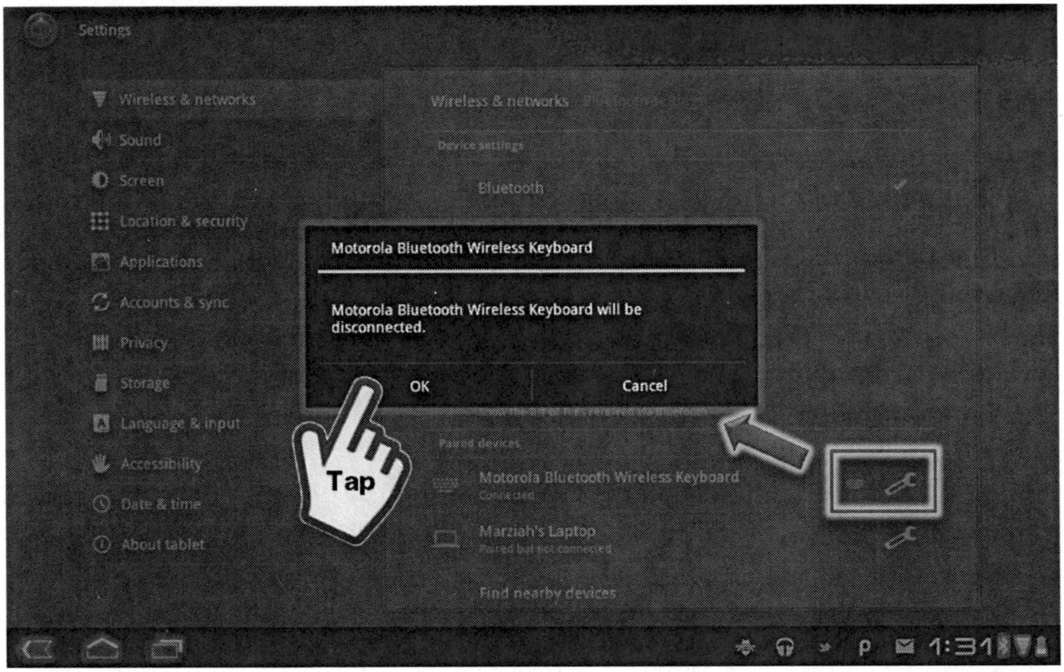

Figure 24–8. *Unpairing a device from your tablet*

Advanced Troubleshooting

I'd love to say that you and your tablet will have a trouble-free relationship, but that's not always the case. Sometimes things go wrong, and this chapter will show you a few things to try when they do. On top of that, I'll point you to a few resources you can turn to if you're feeling especially adventurous and want to get into extra trouble. For example, I'll cover some places to find information on hacking and extending your tablet.

Steps for Troubleshooting

If your tablet starts misbehaving in a really odd way—perhaps the sound no longer plays through headphones, apps repeatedly crash, or the screen keeps freezing—the first thing you should try is restarting it. Sometimes a good reboot is all your tablet needs to start working as well as possible. Power it all the way down, rather than just turning the screen on and off. The second step is a soft reset. As a last resort, you may consider a factory reset.

Soft Resets

If your tablet refuses to power down or stops responding to your touch, then you'll need to perform a *soft reset*. On a phone, you'd just yank the batteries; however, tablets are generally made with non-removable batteries. Reset maneuvers depend on the tablet. On many models, it may be as simple as holding down the **Power** button until it powers off. On the Xoom, you need to hold the **Power** and **Volume Up** buttons at the same time. Refer to your user manual to find the specific procedure for your device.

Factory Data Resets

If you ever sell your tablet or send it in for repairs or upgrades, you'll need to perform a *factory reset* or a *hard reset* to wipe all your personal information off the machine. This is also a last resort for troubleshooting problems with your device. Note that you won't lose information you've stored in the cloud, such as your Gmail messages, your app purchases, or any photos you've published to Picasa. Follow these steps to perform a factory reset:

1. Tap your finger on the bottom-right corner of the screen to open the **Settings** menu.

2. Tap the **Settings** icon. You should see the **Settings** menu.

3. Tap **Privacy** from the **Settings** menu. It should be on your left.

4. Look at the choices on the right. Under **Personal Data**, you'll see the **Factory data reset** choice.

5. Pressing this button will erase all your data and restore the factory default settings. You'll be asked for confirmation; and once you confirm, your data will be wiped from the table (see Figure A–1).

Figure A–1. *Performing a factory data reset*

Rooting Your Tablet

You may have a tablet that is capable of running a more advanced version of Android, but is locked into an older version. It's also possible you may have a tablet locked out of the Android Market, and you wish you weren't forced to buy apps from a more expensive app store. Alternatively, you may want a pure Android experience instead of the modified version of Android packaged with your tablet. It could just be that you do not like some of the core features of your device and want to try something more advanced. Or, perhaps you just want to test different versions of Android as a developer. If any of these cases describe you, you can hack your own tablet and install a different version of Android.

> **CAUTION:** *Rooting* your device—modifying the core, or *root*, files on the device so you can run a different OS on it—can cause your tablet to break and not ever boot up again. This is called *bricking* a tablet, since it will be as useful as a brick if that happens. With that in mind, there's a large community of hackers who take their tablet OS into their own hands and install a different version of Android onto their tablet.

The Barnes & Noble Nook Color has been a traditionally rooted device, since it is a low-cost device and does not allow apps to be installed out of the box. The Kindle Fire is scheduled to ship just as this book goes to press, but I feel confident that a rooting community will also develop around the Fire to enable it to install apps outside of the Amazon Market. Other tablets can also be rooted, although there's less incentive to try this technique on a more expensive device.

The methods for rooting depend on the device and may change as software is updated. For instructions and discussions on rooting Android tablets, visit the following sites:

- **Nook Devs** (http://nookdevs.com/): This site is dedicated to hacking the Nook.

- **Android Central** (http://www.androidcentral.com/root): This site is a root-specific section of Android Central. (Android Central's chief editor is Phil Nickinson, the technical reviewer for this book.)

- XDA Developers (http://forum.xdA-developers.com/forumdisplay.php?f=259 XDA Developers): This site is a group for Windows and Android enthusiasts.

Tablet Development

If you'd like to start developing for Android tablets, the best place to start is the official site for Android development at http://developer.android.com/. Here, you can download the Android software development kit and register as a developer. You can also find some terrific Android development books in the Apress library. Other resources include the following:

- **App Inventor for Android** (www.appinventorbeta.com/): This project was originally developed by Google and is now open-sourced and hosted by the Massachusetts Institute of Technology (MIT). It allows you to program apps on the Web using an easier to master interface based on the MIT Scratch project.

- **PhoneGap** (www.phonegap.com): This project uses CSS and JavaScript to create apps for multiple platforms.

- **Stack Overflow** (http://stackoverflow.com/): This site is a free question and answer forum for developers.

App Guide for Developers

Here's a guide to some of the must-have apps for Android tablets that were mentioned in this book. I've also included some extra apps that may not have been mentioned, but are worth checking out all the same. Not every app is free, and not every app is available for every device. I've grouped apps by the chapters by where they were either mentioned or are most relevant.

Typing, Copy, and Search

- **Swype**
  http://www.swype.com/category/get-swype/

- **Swiftkey**
  http://market.android.com/details?id=com.touchtype.swiftkey.tablet.trial

- **Thumb Keyboard**
  http://market.android.com/details?id=com.beansoft.keyboardplus

Syncing Your Tablet With Google

- **Blogger**
  http://market.android.com/details?id=com.google.android.apps.blogger

- **Finance**
  http://market.android.com/details?id=com.google.android.apps.finance

- **Gmail**
  http://market.android.com/details?id=com.google.android.gm

- **Google Books**
  http://market.android.com/details?id=com.google.android.apps.books

- **Google Maps**
  http://market.android.com/details?id=com.google.android.apps.maps

- **Google Reader**
  http://market.android.com/details?id=com.google.android.apps.reader

- **Google Search**
  http://market.android.com/details?id=com.google.android.googlequicksearch
  box

- **Google Voice**
  http://market.android.com/details?id=com.google.android.apps.googlevoice

- **YouTube** http://market.android.com/details?id=com.google.android.youtube

Understanding Connection

- **5 VPN**
  http://market.android.com/details?id=com.doenter.android.vpn.fivevpn

- **Android VNC Viewer**
  http://market.android.com/details?id=android.androidVNC

- **Jump Desktop**
  http://market.android.com/details?id=com.p5sys.android.jump

- **PocketCloud RDP VNC**
  http://market.android.com/details?id=com.wyse.pocketcloudfree

Icons and Widgets, and Tabs

- **3D Fireflies Live Wallpaper**
  http://market.android.com/details?id=com.AOI.hqq.LiveWallpaper_FireFliesl
  ite

- **Androidify**
  http://market.android.com/details?id=com.google.android.apps.androidify

- **Beautiful Widgets**
  http://market.android.com/details?id=com.levelup.beautifulwidgets

- **Fancy Widgets**
  http://market.android.com/details?id=com.anddoes.fancywidgets

- **HD Widgets** http://market.android.com/details?id=cloudtv.hdwidgets

- **Pure Calendar Widget**
  http://market.android.com/details?id=org.koxx.pure_calendar

Email and Instant Messaging

- **TouchDown HD for Tabets**
  http://market.android.com/details?id=com.nitrodesk.honey.nitroid

Working With Calendars

- **Astrid ToDo**
  http://market.android.com/details?id=com.timsu.astrid

- **GTasks**
  http://market.android.com/details?id=org.dayup.gtask

Using Maps

- **CoPilot Live**
  https://market.android.com/details?id=com.alk.copilot.market.usa

- **Foursquare**
  http://market.android.com/details?id=com.joelapenna.foursquared

- **Google Maps**
  http://market.android.com/details?id=com.google.android.apps.maps

- **Gowalla**
  http://market.android.com/details?id=com.gowalla

- **NAVIGON Select**
  http://market.android.com/details?id=com.navigon.navigator_select

- **Yelp**
  http://market.android.com/details?id=com.yelp.android

Browsing the Web

- **Adobe Flash**
  http://market.android.com/details?id=com.adobe.flashplayer

- **Dolphin Browser HD**
  http://market.android.com/details?id=mobi.mgeek.TunnyBrowser

- **Firefox**
  http://market.android.com/details?id=org.mozilla.firefox

- **Opera**
  http://market.android.com/details?id=com.opera.browser

Social Media

- **Blogger**
  http://market.android.com/details?id=com.google.android.apps.blogger

- **DroidIn**
  http://market.android.com/details?id=bostone.android.droidin

- **Facebook**
  http://market.android.com/details?id=com.facebook.katana

- **Friendcaster**
  http://market.android.com/details?id=uk.co.senab.blueNotifyFree

- **Google+**
  http://market.android.com/details?id=com.google.android.apps.plus

- **Hootsuite**
  http://market.android.com/details?id=com.hootsuite.droid.full

- **LinkedIn**
  http://market.android.com/details?id=com.linkedin.android

- **Plume for Twitter** (formerly Touiteur)
  http://market.android.com/details?id=com.levelup.touiteur

- **Seesmic**
  http://market.android.com/details?id=com.seesmic

- **Tweetcaster**
  http://market.android.com/details?id=com.handmark.tweetcaster

- **Tweetdeck**
  http://market.android.com/details?id=com.thedeck.android.app

- **Twicca**
  http://market.android.com/details?id=jp.r246.twicca

- **Twitter**
  http://market.android.com/details?id=com.twitter.android

- **Tumblr**
  http://market.android.com/details?id=com.tumblr

- **Uber Social** (formerly Twidroyd)
  http://market.android.com/details?id=com.twidroid

- **WordPress**
  http://market.android.com/details?id=org.wordpress.android

- **Yammer**
  http://market.android.com/details?id=com.yammer.v1

Video Conferencing

- **Fring**
  http://market.android.com/details?id=com.fring

- **Oovoo**
  http://market.android.com/details?id=com.oovoo

- **Qik Video**
  http://market.android.com/details?id=com.qik.android

■ **Skype**
http://market.android.com/details?id=com.skype.raider

■ **Tango**
http://market.android.com/details?id=com.sgiggle.production

Reading E-books, Newspapers, and Magazines

■ **Adobe Reader**
http://market.android.com/details?id=com.adobe.reader

■ **Aldiko**
http://market.android.com/details?id=com.aldiko.android

■ **Books WordPlayer**
http://market.android.com/details?id=v00032.com.wordplayer

■ **CNN App for Android Tablets**
http://market.android.com/details?id=com.cnn.mobile.android.tablet

■ **DC Comics**
http://market.android.com/details?id=com.dccomics.comics

■ **Droid Comic Viewer**
http://market.android.com/details?id=net.androidcomics.acv

■ **Goodreads**
http://market.android.com/details?id=com.google.android.gm

■ **Google Books**
http://market.android.com/details?id=com.google.android.apps.books

■ **Kindle**
http://market.android.com/details?id=com.amazon.kindle

■ **Kobo**
http://market.android.com/details?id=com.kobobooks.android

■ **Libris Lite**
http://market.android.com/details?id=com.hillbillyinteractive.librislite

■ **Moon Reader**
http://market.android.com/details?id=com.flyersoft.moonreader

■ **NPR News**
http://market.android.com/details?id=org.npr.android.news

■ **Nook for Android**
http://market.android.com/details?id=bn.ereader

■ **NYT App for Tablets**
http://market.android.com/details?id=com.nytimes.android.tablet

■ **Pulse News**
http://market.android.com/details?id=com.alphonso.pulse

- **Time Mobile**
  http://market.android.com/details?id=com.Time

- **USA Today for Phone**
  http://market.android.com/details?id=com.usatoday.android.news

- **Wordoholic Reader**
  http://market.android.com/details?id=com.wordoholic.reader

Taking Notes and Working With Documents

- **ColorNote**
  http://market.android.com/details?id=com.socialnmobile.dictapps.notepad.color.note

- **Documents to Go**
  http://market.android.com/details?id=com.dataviz.docstogo

- **DropBox**
  http://market.android.com/details?id=com.dropbox.android

- **EverNote**
  http://market.android.com/details?id=com.evernote

- **Google Docs**
  http://market.android.com/details?id=com.google.android.apps.docs

- **Skitch**
  http://market.android.com/details?id=com.evernote.skitch

Viewing Videos and Movies

- **Blockbuster**
  http://market.android.com/details?id=com.motorola.Blockbuster

- **GoogleTV Remote**
  http://market.android.com/details?id=com.google.android.apps.tvremote

- **Movies by Flixter**
  http://market.android.com/details?id=net.flixster.android

- **Netflix**
  http://market.android.com/details?id=com.netflix.mediaclient

- **PlayOn Mobile**   http://market.android.com/details?id=com.playon.playonapp

- **Smithsonian Channel**
  http://market.android.com/details?id=com.smithsonian.android

- **Syfy for Android Tablets**
  http://market.android.com/details?id=com.nbcuni.syfy.syfyforandroidtablet

- **TV.com**
  http://market.android.com/details?id=com.rhythmnewmedia.tvdotcom

- **TV Listings for Android**
  http://market.android.com/details?id=usa.jersey.tvlistings

- **TWiT TV**
  http://market.android.com/details?id=com.mediafly.android.video.twit

- **Google Videos**
  http://market.android.com/details?id=com.google.android.videos

- **WatchESPN**
  http://market.android.com/details?id=air.WatchESPN

Creating Photos, Videos, and Art on Android

- **Adobe Photoshop Express**
  http://market.android.com/details?id=com.adobe.psmobile

- **Eye-Fi**
  http://market.android.com/details?id=fi.eye.android

- **FX Camera**
  http://market.android.com/details?id=ymst.android.fxcamera

- **Google Earth**
  http://market.android.com/details?id=com.google.earth

- **HDR Camera**
  http://market.android.com/details?id=com.almalence.hdr

- **Lightbox Camera and Effects**
  http://market.android.com/details?id=com.lightbox.android.photos

- **Panaramio Uploader**
  http://market.android.com/details?id=com.google.android.apps.panoramio

- **PicSay Photo Editor**
  http://market.android.com/details?id=com.shinycore.picsayfree

- **PicSay Pro**   http://market.android.com/details?id=com.shinycore.picsaypro

- **PrinterShare Mobile Print**
  http://market.android.com/details?id=com.dynamixsoftware.printershare

- **SketchBook Express**
  http://market.android.com/details?id=com.adsk.sketchbookhdexpress

- **SketchBook Pro**
  http://market.android.com/details?id=com.adsk.sketchbookhd

- **Snapbucket**
  http://market.android.com/details?id=com.photobucket.android.snapbucket

Listening to Music

- **Amazon MP3**
  http://market.android.com/details?id=com.amazon.mp3

- **Google Music**
  http://market.android.com/details?id=com.google.android.music

- **Last.fm**
  http://market.android.com/details?id=fm.last.android

- **My Piano**
  http://market.android.com/details?id=com.bti.myPiano

- **Pandora Internet Radio**
  http://market.android.com/details?id=com.pandora.android

- **Perfect Ear**   http://market.android.com/details?id=ru.exaybachay.pearfree

- **RockOut Guitar**
  http://market.android.com/details?id=com.activefrequency.android.rockout

- **Shazam**
  http://market.android.com/details?id=com.shazam.android

- **SoundCloud**
  http://market.android.com/details?id=com.soundcloud.android

- **SoundHound**
  http://market.android.com/details?id=com.melodis.midomiMusicIdentifier

- **Spotify**
  http://market.android.com/details?id=com.spotify.mobile.android.ui

Games on Tablets

- **3D Bowling**
  http://market.android.com/details?id=com.threed.bowling

- **Angry Birds**
  http://market.android.com/details?id=com.rovio.angrybirds

- **Bejeweled**
  http://market.android.com/details?id=com.eamobile.bejeweled2_na_wf_vzw

- **Cordy**
  http://market.android.com/details?id=com.silvertree.cordy

- **Drag Racing**
  http://market.android.com/details?id=com.creativemobile.DragRacing

- **Dungeon Defenders**
  http://market.android.com/details?id=com.trendy.ddapp

- **Jewels**
  http://market.android.com/details?id=org.mhgames.jewels

- **Kid Paint Free**
  http://market.android.com/details?id=virtualgs.kidspaint

- **Kid Mode**
  http://market.android.com/details?id=com.zoodles.kidmode

- **Labyrinth Lite**
  http://market.android.com/details?id=se.illusionlabs.labyrinth.lite

- **Mrs PAC-MAN**
  http://market.android.com/details?id=com.NamcoNetworks.MsPacMan

- **Mystery of the Crystal Portal**
  http://market.android.com/details?id=com.g5e.crystalportal

- **PAC-MAN**
  http://market.android.com/details?id=com.NamcoNetworks.international.PacMan

- **Pocket Legends**   http://market.android.com/details?id=sts.pl

- **Pocket Soccer**
  http://market.android.com/details?id=com.rastergrid.game.pocketsoccer

- **Raging Thunder Lite**
  http://market.android.com/details?id=com.polarbit.rthunderlite

- **Robo Defense Free**
  http://market.android.com/details?id=com.magicwach.rdefense_free

- **SCRABBLE Free**
  http://market.android.com/details?id=ca.jamdat.flight.scrabblefree

- **Slice It**
  http://market.android.com/details?id=com.com2us.sliceit

- **Stand O'Food**
  http://market.android.com/details?id=com.g5e.standofood

- **TETRIS free**
  http://market.android.com/details?id=com.ea.tetrisfree_na

The Clock, Calculator, and Other Utilities

- **3D Flip Clock & World Weather**
  http://market.android.com/details?id=com.droid27.d3flipclockweather

- **Accuweather for Honeycomb**
  http://market.android.com/details?id=com.accuweather.android.tablet

- **Astro File Manager**
  http://market.android.com/details?id=com.metago.astro

- ▦ **AutoCAD WS**
  http://market.android.com/details?id=com.autodesk.autocadws

- ▦ **Barcode Scanner**
  http://market.android.com/details?id=com.google.zxing.client.android

- ▦ **Calorie Counter**
  http://market.android.com/details?id=com.fatsecret.android

- ▦ **Connect Bot**   http://market.android.com/details?id=org.connectbot

- ▦ **ES File Explorer**
  http://market.android.com/details?id=com.estrongs.android.pop

- ▦ **Google Goggles**
  http://market.android.com/details?id=com.google.android.apps.unveil

- ▦ **Google Body**
  http://market.android.com/details?id=com.google.android.apps.body

- ▦ **Google Shopper**
  http://market.android.com/details?id=com.google.android.apps.shopper

- ▦ **Google Sky Map**
  http://market.android.com/details?id=com.google.android.stardroid

- ▦ **Google Translate**
  http://market.android.com/details?id=com.google.android.apps.translate

- ▦ **Grocery IQ**
  http://market.android.com/details?id=com.coupons.GroceryIQ.Tablet

- ▦ **I Just Forgot**
  http://market.android.com/details?id=com.oceanhouse_media.booklcijustforg
  ot_app

- ▦ **Layar**
  http://market.android.com/details?id=com.layar

- ▦ **Mighty Meeting**
  http://market.android.com/details?id=mm.android.core

- ▦ **Mint**
  http://market.android.com/details?id=com.mint

- ▦ **Nasa App**
  http://market.android.com/details?id=gov.nasa

- ▦ **Oration Sensation**
  http://market.android.com/details?id=com.epicache.orationsensation

- ▦ **ShopSavvy QR and Barcode Scanner**
  http://market.android.com/details?id=com.biggu.shopsavvy

Index

A

Account syncing, 49
  apps, 57
  conformation message, 53
  corporate email account, 51
  data settings, 55
  exchange Email accounts, 51
  Internet service provider, 53
  manage accounts, 55, 56
  remove email account, 54, 56
  security warnings, 52
  steps, adding an account, 49, 50
Adobe Flash, 245
Airplane mode, 69
Alternative app markets, 163
  Barnes & Noble Nook apps, 169
  GetJar, 170–171
  handmark, 169–170
  Samsung app store, 168
  third-party apps enabling, 164
  uninstalling apps, 171
  unknown sources installation,
    163–165
  web apps installation, 167
Amazon appstore, 165
  browsing, 166
  downloading, 166
  My Apps, 167
  steps to install, 165
Amazon MP3s and Cloud Player, 283
  automatic downloads, 287
  downloading files, 285
  music hub app, 287
  pre-installed music players, 287
  previewing music, 286
  purchasing music, 285–286
  service, 284
  store and play music, 283
Amazon Videos, 251
Android, 1
  accessories, 12
  action and system bars, 19
  activation sequence, 16
  Android-powered microwave, 5
  ASTEROID, 5
  cameras, 10–11
  copy, cut, and paste, 32–33
  data plan activation, 17
  e-book readers, 3
  finger gestures, 22
  Google Account, 16
  Google search, 37
  Google TV, 5
  HDMI, 12
  high-end digital photo frames, 5
  history, 1–2
  home screen, 17, 18, 22–23
  Honeycomb, 2, 6
  HTC and Sense, 3
  input settings, 34
  internal storage, 11
  market, 151
    apps installation, 152–154
    apps uninstallation, 156
    apps updation, 158–159
    automatic updating, 159
    payment option, 151, 154–155,
     157–158
    websites, 160–161
  memory, 11
  movie rentals, 246
    Amazon videos, 251–252

downloading/pinning, 248–249
iPlayer, 251
Netflix, 251
rental period, 247–248
Syfy channel app, 249–250
TV show, 249
TWiT, 250, 251
website, 253
multimedia players, 4
navigation controls, 18
netbooks, 3, 4
NIM1000, 5
notification panel, 20–22
ODM, 5
pixel resolution, 8–9
readers, 4
Recent Apps button, 19
rooting process, 13
screen
    contrast, 10
    size, 7–8
    unlocking, 15
standard keyboard layout
    character combinations and
      long-presses, 27–28
    displaying capital letters,
      numbers, and symbols, 26–27
    Honeycomb, 26
swype typing, 29–30
touch revolution, 5–6
touchscreen sensitivity, 9
USB, 12
user dictionary, 31
virtual keyboard, 25
voice actions, 35–36
word suggestions, 30
Angry Birds, 293
App guide development
email and instant messaging, 330
clock, calculator, and other utilities,
    337, 338
games, 336–337
icons and widgets, and tabs, 330
listening to music, 336
maps, 331
photos, videos, and art creation, 335

reading e-books, newspapers, and
    magazines, 333–334
social media, 331–332
syncing your tablet,Google, 329
taking notes and working, 334
typing, copy, and search, 329
understanding connection, 330
video conferencing, 332–333
videos and movies viewing, 334–335
web browsing, 331
working with calendars, 331

B

Barnes & Noble Nook, 216
apps, 169
details page, 220
lendme books, 220–221
Nook app, 216–217
reading, 218
review your note, 219
saving bookmarks and notes, 219
sideloading, 221
Barns and Noble Nook Color e-reader,
    13
Bejeweled, 292
Blogger, 46
Bluetooth, 65
Board games, 296

C

Calculator, 312
app, 312
samples, 313
CDMA and GSM, 60
Cell phone towers, 123
Channel apps, 249–250
Clock
    alarm function, steps
      launch, 307
      remaining alarm features, 309
      set alarm, 307, 308
      time adjustment, 309
      turning alarms on/off, 308
    alternate alarms, 312
    downloadable widgets, 311
    extending, 311
    repeating alarms, 310

snoozing and dismissing alarm, 310
Cloud computing, 39
Contacts managing
    adding another field, 105
    adding custom fields, 105
    adding picture, 104
    adding/editing, 103–104
    contacts apps, 103
    email and gmail apps, 102
    filtering, 105–106
    importing and exporting, 109
    joining, 107
    layout,contacts app, 102
    sharing, 108
    tablets *vs.* phones, 101
    widgets, 109

D

3D Bowling, 297
Digital rights management (DRM), 276
Dolphin HD browser, 149–150
Drag Racing game, 298
Dungeon Defenders, 302

E

Email
    app, 96
    exchange account, 97
    and Gmail action bar, 97–98
    and Gmail widgets, 98–99
ES File explorer, 313–315
EVO View 4G, 6

F

Fantasy Football, 297
Fring, 197
Fun and games, 291
    Adobe Flash playback, 291
    arcade classics, 294
    board games, 296
    children games, 304, 305
    Drag Racing, 298
    Dungeon Defenders, 302
    Labyrinth Lite game, 297, 298
    match-three puzzle, 292
    MMOORGs
        downloading data, 300

pocket legends, 301
Mystery Adventure games, 299
sports games, 297
Tetris, 294
tower defense games, 295
virtual simulations, 303

G

G5 Entertainment, 299
GetJar, 170–171
Global positioning satellites, 123
Gmail, 45
    adding accounts, 88–89
    apps, 90–91
    attachments message, 94, 95
    automatic filters, 86–87
    checkbox icon, 82
    composing message, 94
    creating and deleting labels, 86
    forwarding and POP/IMAP, 89
    Google apps, 81
    labs and themes, 90
    mail settings, 87
    message reading, 91
    message sending, 94
    message viewing, 92
    navigating labels, 92, 93
    priority inbox, 84
    settings, 95–96
    stars and labels, 85–86
    trash and spam, 82
    web Gmail, 90
    web interface, 83
Google account, 39
    activation, 40–42
    cloud computing, 39
    data syncing, 47
    email, 39
    Gmail accounts, shortcut steps, 44
    Google account adding steps, 42
    Honeycomb tablets, 42
    services, 45–46
    tablet syncing, 48
    two step verification, 44
Google Book, 46, 201
    adjusting,reading options, 203
    Apple's iBook format, 201

buying/downloading, 204
  Android Market app, 204
  buy button, 206
  categories section, 205
  details page, 206
  shopping, 205
interface for reading, 202
navigation, library, 202
reading options, adjustments, 203
reading books offline, 204
scanned books, 201
Google browsing, 141
  account syncing, 145, 146
  android
    browser navigation, 141–142
    definition, 141
  bookmarking pages, 143
  bookmarks and history, 144
  browsing and history page, 145
  chrome, definition, 141
  desktop and mobile versions, 148
  flash, 147
  labs and quick controls, 148
  search engine setting, 147
  website finding, 143
Google Calendars, 45
  adding, 113
  apps, 115, 116
  events adding, 117
  general preferences, 119
  guests adding, 118
  Honeycomb event, 117
  importing and exporting, 114
  privacy levels, 112
  settings, 114, 118–120
  syncing, 114
  tablets, 115
  tasks, 121
  TouchDown, 115
  web based, 111–112
  widgets, 120
Google checkout service, 45, 151
Google docs, 229
  Android tablet browser, 229
  documents sharing, 229
  download apps, 229

downloading, 234–235
editing presentations, 232–233
  Microsoft PowerPoint, 233
  new documents, 232
  PPT/PDF file, 233
editing spreadsheets, 231
list view, 230
steps to edit document, 230–231
themes, 234
Google Maps, 45, 123
  cell phone towers, 123
  email and text directions, 137
  Foursquare, 138
  getting directions, 126
  Gowalla, 139
  GPS, 123
  handy finger gestures navigation,
    125
  labs layers, 130–131
  latitude, 131
    to add friends, steps, 132
    automatic detection, 131
    feature, 131
    hide your location, 131
    set your location, 131
    tapping sharing options, 132–133
    turn Latitude off, 131
  layer, 129
  location/compass button, 126
  location and security options, 124
  location-sensing social media and
    games, 137
  own maps making, 137
  places apps, 134
  places pages, 133
  satellite, 130
  starring locations, 135
  step-by-step directions, 127
  street view, 135–136
  tablet's Browser app, 124
  third-party navigation, 137
  traffics, 129
Google Music, 275
  adding song to playlist, 280–281
  controls, 279, 280
  different views, 278, 279

getting to music, 275
  music account, 275
  music manager, 276, 277
  steps to import, 276
instant playlists, 281, 282
listening offline, 282
new and recent view,app, 277, 278
perfect ear app, 290
playing songs, 279, 280
shopping for music, 283
soundhound app, 289
storing music, 275
your tablet app, 277
Google Talk, 189
  colors and status list, 190
  icon shape and information, 190
  launch, chatting, 189
  status messages, 190, 191
  video calling, 192
  video chat app, 189
Google Voice, 45
Google's Navigation feature
  definition, 128
  map information, 128
Grocery IQ app, 315–316
3G technologies, 60
4G technologies, 60

H

*High Definition Multimedia Interface
    (HDMI)*, 12
Home screen personalizing, 71
  app icons, 77
  elements, 72
  more menu, 78
  screen interface review, 71, 72
  wallpapers, 78–79
    gallery, 79
    live wallpapers, 79
    steps to pick, 80
  widgets
    adding, 73–74
    customization interface, 74
    drag and drop screen, 74
    exploration, 72
    honeycomb widgets, 73

moving and resizing, 76
removing, 75
HTC Flyer, 6
Hulu+, 253
  error message, 254
  PlayOn, 254
  streaming service, 253
  subscription, 254
  TV listings app, 255
  YouTube remote app, 255

I, J

Internet service providers (ISPs), 88
iPlayer, 251

K

Kindle Books
  adjustment, reading options, 211
  Amazons Kindle Store, 212
  buying magazines/newspapers, 213
  looking up words, 209
  purchasing items, 211–212
  reading, 208
  saving bookmarks and taking notes,
      209
Kindle Reader
  Amazon, reader, 207
  bookshelf view, 207, 208
  buying magazines/newspapers, 213
  dictionary downloading, 209
  Kindle edition, Kansas City Star, 214
  Shelfari, 214–215
  sideloading, 215
  whispersync, 207
Kobo, 221
  bookshelf, 222
  convertion, 226–227
  highlighting text and adding notes,
      224
  importing books, 225, 226
  online e-Book store, 221
  reading life
    adjustment, 224
    badges, 223
    book tapping, 223
    social and gaming aspects, 222
  reading PDF books, 226

L

Labyrinth Lite game, 297, 298
Long Term Evolution, 61

M

Managing syncing, 68
Match-three puzzle games, 292
Microsoft Live, 235
    definition, 235
    Documents to Go, 236
        account tapping, 236
        editing, 236, 237
        syncing, 237
Mobile hotspot, 65–67
Mozilla Firefox, 150

N

Netflix, 251

O

OoVoo, 198
Opera browser, 150
Original design manufacturer (ODM), 5

P

Pandora, 288
Photos, videos and art creation
    autodesk sketchbook, 273–274
    camera app
        front-facing camera, 259
        Galaxy Tab, 259
        steps to snap, 260
        video conferencing, 257
        xoom, 258
    camera difference, 272, 273
    deleting photos, 262
    gallery app, 264
        album view, 265
        sorting, 266
    GPS, 261
    panorama shooting, 260
    printing photos, 274
    reviewing pictures, 261, 262
    sharing, 267
    tablet difference, 257
    third-party photo apps, 267

Adobe Photoshop Express, 267, 268
        PicSay Pro, 269
        Snapbucket/photobucket, 268
    time lapse vs. timers, 264
    video editing
        adding titles, 272
        long-press options, 271
        movie studio, 269
        transitions, 271
        video effects and adjustments, 271
        YouTube uploads, 272
    video shooting, 263
Photos, videos, and art creation, 257
Picasa, 46
Picnik, 46
Pocket Soccer, 297

Q

Qik, 198
QuickOffice
    cloud syncing, 238
    dropbox, 238
    editing documents, 239
    evernote, 241
        adding note, 242
        calendar view, 241
        premium, 243
        storing, 241
    Internet browsing files, 239
    printing documents, 240
    pro (paid) version, 238
    sticky notes, 240, 241

R

Research trap, angry birds, 293
Roaming, 67, 68

S

Samsung app store, 168
Samsung Galaxy Player, 6
Skype, 193
    account creation, 193
    adding contacts, 194
    adding to your computer, 197
    chatting, 196

log in, steps, 194
making calls with, 195
monthly subscription, 196
phone calls, 193
receiving calls with, 196
Social media, 173
blogger, 186
droidIn, 185
Facebook, 173
apps, 175, 176
concept, 173
contact syncing, 175
fan pages creation, 174
Google+, 182
app, 184
+1 button, 183
circles, 183
hangouts, 183
huddles, 184
photos, 184
sparks, 183
stream, 183
hashtags, 178
linkedIn, 185
salesforce, 182
Seesmic apps, 180
tumblr, 187
Tweetdeck, 181
Twitter and Microblogs
Android tablets, 179
concept, 176
direct messages, 177
hashtags, 178
HootSuite apps, 181, 182
lists, 178
mechanics and culture, 177
picture services, 178
@Replies, 177
retweets and modified, 177
Seesmic apps, 180
Tweetdeck apps, 181
URL shorteners, 178
wHootSuite, 182
wordpress, 186

Yammer, 182
Spotify, 289
Swype typing, 29

T, U

Tango, 198, 199
Tetris, 294
This Week in Tech (TWiT), 250, 251
T-Mobile–branded Sidekick phones, 1
Tower defense game, 295
Troubleshooting, 325
connections, 67
steps, 325
factory data resets, 326
soft resets, 325
tablet development, 327, 328
tablet rooting, 327
TWiT. *See* This Week in Tech
Twitter accounts, 106

V

Virtual keyboard, 25
VNC, 69
Voice over Internet Protocol (VoIP), 101, 189
Virtual Private Network, 69

W, X

Wi-Fi, 62
concepts, 123
definition, 62
private setting, 63
Samsung Galaxy, 123
secure network, 64
security, 64–65
WiMAX, 61Words With Friends games, 296

Y

YouTube, 46, 245

Z

Zynga game, 296

CPSIA information can be obtained at www.ICGtesting.com
Printed in the USA
LVOW130419220212

269849LV00004B/1/P